The Politics of Inequality

The Politics of Inequality

Carsten Jensen

Kees van Kersbergen

First published 2017 by
PALGRAVE

Palgrave in the UK is an imprint of Macmillan Publishers Limited, registered in England, company number 785998, of 4 Crinan Street, London, N1 9XW.

Palgrave Macmillan in the US is a division of St Martin's Press LLC, 175 Fifth Avenue, New York, NY 10010.

Palgrave is a global imprint of the above companies and is represented throughout the world.

Palgrave® and Macmillan® are registered trademarks in the United States, the United Kingdom, Europe and other countries.

ISBN 978–1–137–42701–4 hardback
ISBN 978–1–137–42700–7 paperback

This book is printed on paper suitable for recycling and made from fully managed and sustained forest sources. Logging, pulping and manufacturing processes are expected to conform to the environmental regulations of the country of origin.

A catalogue record for this book is available from the British Library.

A catalog record for this book is available from the Library of Congress.

Printed and bound by CPI Group UK Ltd, Croydon, CR0 4YY

'Inequality is the root of social evil'

Pope Francis

'It is not inequality which is the real misfortune, it is the dependence'

Voltaire

'The disposition to admire, and almost to worship, the rich and
the powerful, and to despise, or, at least, to neglect persons of poor
and mean condition, though necessary both to establish and to
maintain the distinction of ranks and the order of society, is, at
the same time, the great and most universal cause of the
corruption of our moral sentiments'

Adam Smith

'Everyone but an idiot knows that the lower classes must be
kept poor, or they will never be industrious ...'

Arthur Young

Contents

11 What future for the politics of inequality?   155

List of Tables and Figures

Tables

Figures

Acknowledgements

We have accumulated a lot of intellectual debt writing this book. For helping out in various ways, we would like to thank (in the random order we prefer): Johannes Lindvall, Patrick Emmenegger, Paul Marx, Jonas Pontusson, Jason Beckfield, David Rueda, Silja Häusermann, Jochen Clasen, Daniel Clegg, Marius Busemeyer, Maurizio Ferrera, Martin Seeleib-Kaiser, Hanspeter Kriesi, Gøsta Esping-Andersen, Philipp Rehm, Barbara Vis, Daniele Caramani, Lasse Nielsen, Mikkel Schmidt Jensen, Jonas Kraft, Magnus Rasmussen and Dan Nguyen. We also want to thank the people at Palgrave, not least Stephen and Lloyd, who have been extremely encouraging and helpful from the beginning. Finally, we would like to thank each other for being such a good friend and co-author.

We have received generous support from Aarhus University Research Foundation's AU IDEAS programme and from the Danish Research Council for Independent Research (grant no. 1327-00074).

Chapter 1

What is the politics of inequality?

Inequality is a fundamental feature of all human societies. Without some degree of economic inequality, it is difficult to imagine how modern democracies could function. In pre-historic communities, kinship ties and moral norms might have been enough for everybody to make an effort, but in today's world, monetary rewards are necessary. Yet, while some inequality is unavoidable, too much inequality can have consequences that many will find unacceptable. High inequality is associated with deteriorating health outcomes, reduced social mobility and lack of democratic participation.

Most people would probably agree that neither perfect equality, where all have exactly the same, nor perfect inequality, where one person owns everything, is desirable. But because neither of these options is on the table anyway, such a consensus is not very telling. The question is not *whether* there should be economic inequality, but *how much* there should be. Deciding how much inequality is appropriate, however, takes us from the domain of common agreement to the realm of contested politics. Few topics can cause as much debate as the proper level of inequality. Often, the discussion turns nasty, because moral condemnation quickly kicks in. Those in favour of less inequality frequently end up suggesting that their opponents are greedy and mean-spirited, while they themselves get portrayed as envious and lazy.

The topic of inequality is a hot-button one because it combines these strong normative feelings with a core of material self-interest. Creating a more equal society entails that the well-off need to give up some of their money so that others can have more than they originally had. Underpinning the normative arguments often heard in public debate, then, are less lofty motives. Those who benefit materially from low inequality also tend to believe that equality is morally just, whereas those who have to pay for the implied redistribution take the opposite view. This is not to negate the sincerity of people's beliefs, but to underscore just how politically sensitive and potentially divisive the topic is. Writing a book about the politics of inequality, therefore, means sailing into waters filled with – well, politics.

The core argument of the book is that the question of how much inequality there should be in a country is fundamentally a political one. There is no way to deduce the correct answer from theoretical principles. Many have tried, though. Philosophers have speculated for centuries about what the just society should look like. What is the appropriate balance between equality and freedom? Economists, too, have come up with suggestions. Based on theories of human behaviour, countless policy recommendations have been formulated about how to maximize society's efficiency and what level of inequality is required to do so. A lot of insights have been gained from such work, but at the end of the day, it is politics that determines what paths will be chosen. This is why understanding the politics of inequality is so important.

Politics is everywhere when thinking about inequality. Simply being interested in the topic is sometimes in and of itself considered to be a political act, with the assumption that an interest in inequality implies that one wants to fight it. But given that inequality is one of the most important issues today, we would argue that everyone with an interest in society, no matter what their ideological orientation is, ought to pay attention to it. As we will show in this book, economic inequality is a multifaceted phenomenon. It affects, and is affected by, everything from the growth of the economy, to the structure of the welfare state, to the involvement of citizens in the democratic process. If you care about any of these things, you should care about inequality too.

To study the politics of inequality is not to take a political stand-point. Indeed, it is to become aware that there are many standpoints out there and that several are tenable positions. Different countries have opted for divergent levels of inequality for all sorts of reasons. Rather than passing judgment, we want to know *why* countries ended up a certain way and *how* they did so. This requires us to investigate how the economies of different countries work, how welfare states are organized, what ordinary citizens want in terms of inequality, and how all of this is transformed into political decisions about redistribution. Hence, in this book on the politics of inequality we need to cover a lot of ground just to answer seemingly simple questions such as why and how countries foster different levels of income inequality.

The book focuses on the democracies of North America, Europe and Asia-Pacific. This is a widely diverse group of countries, but they share the basic feature that their citizens have the right to vote and, conse-quently, influence who gets to rule. Democracy as a form of government entails that both rich and poor individuals have a single vote with equal weight. To the extent that people care about their own material posi-tion, democracy is certain to create conflicts between those who stand to win and those who are likely to lose from redistribution. In authoritar-ian systems, such redistributive conflicts are normally subdued, but in democracies they can take centre stage.

Given that in all democracies there are people with both the incen-tives and the means to push for equality, it is striking just how much countries differ in the levels of inequality they tolerate. In some places, such as the United States and the United Kingdom, inequality is high and rising. In the United States, the share of all labour market income going to the richest 1 per cent has increased from 8 per cent in 1975 to 17.9 per cent in 2014, while it rose from 6.1 to 12.7 per cent in the United Kingdom over the same period. In other places, such as the Nordic countries, inequality is low and relatively stable. In Sweden, for instance, the top 1 per cent's share only rose from 5.3 to 7.2 per cent, while the share in Denmark even fell slightly, from 6.8 to 6.4 per cent (Alvaredo et al. 2015; see also Chapter 5). It is a true puzzle, worthy of a book-length treatment, why democracies perform so differently.

We continue this introductory chapter by discussing inequality as a solution and as a problem. Chapters 2 and 3 devote much more space to this, but it is important to understand up front why inequality matters enough for us to write a whole book about it – and for you to read it. Next, we present an explanation of what more precisely is meant by the politics of inequality: how we define politics and how it is related to the economy, the welfare state and so on. The final section outlines the structure of the book.

Inequality as a Solution and a Problem

Economic inequality means that some have a greater income or wealth than others. In capitalist societies, where earnings and wealth are not fixed by law, the position an individual has in the economic hierarchy can change over time. The drive to become economically successful is, indeed, the very engine of market economies. Without it, there would be little incentive to set up new businesses, put in extra effort at work or simply avoid shirking responsibilities. As noted before, it is not that other motives do not exist, such as feelings of commitment and loyalty to the success of a group, but it is unlikely that such motives would be enough on their own in societies where most people do not know each other. If inequality did not exist, it would have to be invented.

Some would add to this that inequality is also fair. If you have worked harder than we have, or simply are smarter, then it is right for you to get more than we do. Others would take the opposite position and argue that inequality, certainly above a given level, is unfair. In Chapter 2, we go into details about the normative issue and consider the various and exciting arguments. Although it might be disappointing to some egalitarians, in our view it is not possible to argue that inequality is a bad thing per se. There is nothing morally wrong with inequality in and of itself. If inequality is a cause for concern, it is because of the negative consequences it has for other outcomes, including people's health and social mobility.

A large and growing literature documents beyond any reasonable doubt that inequality creates health problems (Daniels et al. 1999; Marmot

2005; Wilkinson and Pickett 2009; McKnight and Cowell 2014). Poor people systematically have worse health and shorter lives than rich people, and in unequal countries this health gradient is amplified. Being poor in the United States or the United Kingdom is worse for your health than being poor in Sweden or Norway. Few would argue that poor people *ought* to die 10 years earlier than their affluent fellow citizens, but that is often what happens, and inequality is to blame. But what is more, in unequal societies almost everyone's health suffers, so that even the better-off stand to gain from lower income inequality. A similar point can be made regarding social mobility (Corak 2013). Children from well-educated or rich families get a head start everywhere, but the likelihood of breaking away from the bottom is substantially lower in unequal countries than in equal ones. As with health, few people would argue that there *ought* to be such immobility, since it means that children are not rewarded in life according to their own talents, but according to who their parents happened to be. Those who believe social mobility is desirable must therefore also agree that economic inequality is a problem, given that it is one of the main causes of social immobility.

Inequality, in sum, is important to know about because it matters for things that almost everybody agrees are vital. Whether the ills that come with inequality are worth the good it also brings, however, is a question that cannot be settled in an objective manner. It depends on each individual's own norms and worldview, which once again brings us back to inequality as a fundamentally political, not scientific, question.

The Politics of Inequality

Politics is about who gets what, when, how (Lasswell 1936). In other words, politics is about determining the distribution – and *redistribution* – of resources. In modern democracies, voters choose their representatives, who then call the shots until the next election. In this sense, politics is simple. Yet, clearly, such a naïve vision of politics is not helpful when trying to understand the large cross-country differences in inequality. Countries do not emerge into the world as either equal or unequal; it is something they become with time. Much, in fact, suggests that the major differences between Western democracies only arose after World War II (Huber and Stephens 2001; Korpi 2002; 2006; Piketty 2014). Knowing that a country is democratic is not enough for us to understand the politics of inequality.

First, all current-day democracies are market economies, but not all market economies are of the same sort. *Liberal market economies* (mostly found in the Anglo-Saxon and Asia-Pacific countries) combine predominantly private human capital formation with individualized wage-setting and a very business-friendly environment. *Statist market economies* (mostly in continental and southern Europe) combine limited public human capital formation with collective wage-setting and a lot of red tape that complicates running a business. *Social market economies* (in the Nordic countries), finally, combine extensive public human capital formation with collective wage-setting and a business-friendly environment. The varying organization of the economy has a huge effect on inequality directly, but also on the way politics operates.

Second, the effect of the different types of market economies is amplified by the fact that each comes with a special welfare state model too. A country's market economy is intricately linked to its welfare state. For example, in the Nordic countries, heavily subsidized childcare services mean that women are able to combine motherhood and employment. Because of this, female employment rates are high, providing employers with an important pool of labour that otherwise would have been denied to them. By spending public money, the state helps both women and companies make ends meet. The examples of how the welfare state interacts with the market economy are almost endless, but mostly relate to either the quantity or the quality of the workforce, i.e., how many people are willing to take on jobs and how qualified they are.

Together, these country-specific factors exert a powerful influence on the distribution of earnings and wealth in societies. This, in turn, affects the political process itself. Poor people, on average, vote less frequently than richer people, but a high level of inequality enhances this effect. Since the poor and the rich do not agree about the proper amount of redistribution, the fact that the poor vote much less than the rich has serious consequences for policy-making. In some countries, most notably the United States, high levels of inequality have become virtually self-reinforcing, in the sense that the well-off become more and more powerful compared with the poor and even the middle class (Bartels 2008; Hacker and Pierson 2010; Gilens 2012). Elsewhere, and most prominently in the Nordic countries, the comparatively low levels of inequality are maintained by strong public support for generous welfare state programmes and a normative belief in the value of equality (Rothstein 1998; Larsen 2008; Jensen 2010; 2014).

Structure of the Book

Chapter 2, as stated, asks whether we should care about inequality as such. We go through the main positions in the normative literature on equality, clarifying why we, on balance, believe that it is not possible to argue that inequality is either good or bad per se. In Chapter 3, we turn to the consequences that inequality has for health and social mobility, arguing that it is because of these unjust consequences that we ought to be bothered about disparities in earnings and wealth.

Chapter 4 takes a step back. In public debates on inequality, a vast number of figures are routinely tossed around. Terms such as the Gini coefficient, income distribution, disposable income, income ratios, etc. are used by politicians and commentators constantly, but are seldom well defined or properly understood. In this chapter, we go through the main concepts one by one. What is the difference between earnings and wealth inequality? What actually is this Gini coefficient, which has become a synonym for inequality? What other, and perhaps much better, measures of inequality exist? These sorts of questions are answered in Chapter 4. Based on this, Chapter 5 presents the major empirical patterns both across countries and over time. It is essentially these patterns that the book is interested in exploring.

Chapters 6 and 7 discuss the relationship between inequality and economic growth. There are many hypotheses about how the two relate. An optimistic account suggests that economic growth will eventually lead to lower inequality. This means that the main task for politicians is to facilitate private enterprise by cutting taxes and bureaucracy, so that businesses can create profits, which eventually will trickle down to ordinary folks. An alternative, pessimistic account argues that growth is hindered by too much equality. There is, in this view, an efficiency–equality trade-off, entailing that when you get more of one thing you will automatically get less of the other. As it is, there is not much to indicate that either of the two accounts is valid, because the different types of market economies presented previously entail distinct trade-offs.

Chapter 8 moves to the welfare state's role vis-à-vis inequality. Contrary to the popular understanding of what welfare states do, there is no necessary relationship between spending a lot on welfare and having low inequality. We explain in detail why that is the case, and also show just how non-egalitarian some welfare states actually are. We end by elaborating the links between the welfare state regime of a country and its type of market economy.

Chapters 9 and 10 investigate more directly the political processes around the issues of inequality and redistribution. In Chapter 9, we look at the input into the political system and ask what citizens' preferences are regarding redistribution and how well they are articulated. There are quite substantial differences in the public's preferences. The well-off, as a general rule, do not support redistribution, and think that a society does not need to be equal in order to be fair. The rich do not support unemployment protection very much either, and tend to believe that social benefits make people lazy and put a strain on the economy. Among the economically insecure, preferences are, to a large extent, the exact opposite. With these differences in preferences, it is particularly noteworthy that there is also huge variation in the degree to which the poor and the rich are interested in politics and participate in elections.

Chapter 10 studies how the public's input is transformed into policy. Many different theories exist about this transformation, but at the most basic level, there is a distinction between bottom-up and top-down theories. The former posit that policy, at least to a degree, reflects the preferences of the voters, while the latter claims that elites, rather than voters, are the real power holders. In the chapter, we argue that the theories may be less at odds with each other than might appear at first glance. Whether the politics of a country is characterized by elite dominance can be explained to a large extent by how strong the bottom-up mechanisms are. The more the poor are active in politics and the better their preferences are represented, the more elites are constrained in pursuing policies with potentially inegalitarian consequences.

Chapter 11 wraps up. The chapter contains a summary of our argument as well as an assessment of recent trends following the Great Recession. The distinctive political-institutional features of the different kinds of democratic capitalist systems and their matching welfare states go a long way towards explaining why there is such a huge cross-national variation in the level of inequality and why such differences are so persistent. It is unlikely that we will witness spectacular path-diverging developments in the liberal and statist market economies that will reverse inequality trends. In fact, there are huge challenges – fiscal problems, changing family structures, new social risks, mass migration and globalization – that reinforce, rather than moderate, inequality, even in the social market economies. Hence, we expect increasing conflicts and struggle over the distributional issues. The politics of inequality is here to stay.

Chapter 2

Is there something morally wrong with inequality?

The main purpose of this chapter is to spell out the primary argument or controversy that lies at the heart of the politics of inequality. It can be portrayed as follows. For some, a certain degree of inequality is a natural phenomenon, and not much can (and therefore should) be done about it. Moreover, some level of inequality is to be valued positively, because it is associated with good things: it is an incentive for people to work hard and it stimulates economic growth. Redistributive policies are bad to the extent that they are necessarily ineffective, slow down economic growth and hence harm total societal prosperity. Therefore, everybody (including the poor) will ultimately be better off, at least in an economic sense, if politics allows an appropriate level of inequality (however defined). Still, even those who view inequality as a natural phenomenon recognize that too much of it may have harmful consequences that demand political action, among them rising crime, political unrest and disorder.

For others, the very causes of inequality are deeply political, and much can (and therefore should) be done about it. Moreover, a high level of inequality is to be valued negatively because it is associated with bad things: more unequal societies are, on average, unhealthier, less trustful and unhappier than more equal societies. Redistributive policies are good because they are potentially effective, stimulate social, cultural, political and economic participation, and hence advance societal well-being. Therefore, everybody (including the rich) will ultimately be better off, in more ways than just an economic one, if politics intervenes to create more equality. Still, even those who view inequality as largely politically created recognize that too much equality may have harmful consequences, for instance on work ethic and effort, which calls for caution in terms of political interventions for redistributive purposes because they may harm prosperity.

It is not our ambition in this chapter to develop a moral argument in favour of those who abhor large differences in wealth and income or those who adore them – or to formulate an alternative normative position. Ours is not an exercise in normative political theory as such. And yet, writing about the politics of inequality means that we cannot possibly avoid discussing the moral issue too, at least to some degree, simply because it is an intrinsic part of the contemporary political controversies over inequality and redistribution. Why should we care about inequality at all? Is inequality intrinsically good, bad or irrelevant? Should we morally care about inequality at all?

The chapter is structured as follows. In the next section, we shortly describe how, in the period since World War II, the *Zeitgeist* has shifted from one in which striving for more income equality seemed part of a widely shared political goal (the 1960s and 1970s) to one in which policies with an (intended or unintended) inegalitarian impact became dominant (the neoliberal era from the late 1970s until at least the financial crisis of 2008). In the most recent decade, the issue of income inequality has gradually begun to occupy centre stage on the political agenda in most, if not all, advanced democratic states. In the next sections, we pose the problem of the moral evaluation of inequality, and map and discuss what arguments people use to applaud or condemn inequality. We show that political theorists have not provided a straightforward answer to whether inequality is bad in and of itself, or, at least, there is no agreement on an answer to this question.

Zeitgeist

The 20th century, roughly until the late 1970s, was the century of redistribution, in which – after the spread of universal suffrage – inequality was spectacularly reduced. Labour protection laws, progression in taxation, extensive coverage of the population by social insurance against the risks of modern capitalist society (Rosanvallon 2013: 165) and wage compression in the wake of World War II all contributed to this. It seemed that the idea of equality became firmly instituted as a keystone of public policy in democratic societies, although more so in north-western Europe, and particularly the Nordics (e.g. Castles 1978), than elsewhere (see Therborn 1995: 354ff). Faith in equality as a political project was at its height in the mid-1970s, as, for instance, in the Netherlands, where the centre-left ruled with a programme that promised to *eradicate* deprivation and inequality of income, wealth, power and knowledge (Van Kersbergen 1998).

But the idea of equality turned out to be much more superficially rooted than was perhaps imagined at the time. In the 1980s and 1990s, the *Zeitgeist* became, rather, characterized by a 'culture of inequality' (Lewis 1993) that elbowed out any remnant of the earlier ideal and promise of economic equality. 'We are learning that the way to prosperity', said Ronald Reagan at a welcoming ceremony for Margaret Thatcher (Reagan 1988), 'is not more bureaucracy and redistribution of wealth but less government and more freedom for the entrepreneur and for the creativity of the individual.' Gradually, national governments and international organizations alike committed to public policies inspired by neoliberalism, which – in all likelihood – were bound to have inegalitarian consequences: the deregulation of labour and financial markets, the privatization of public companies and services, the import of market-like techniques in the public sector (e.g. New Public Management), less progression in taxation, and the retrenchment of the welfare state (see Campbell and Pedersen 2001; Harvey 2005). The resonance that Thomas Piketty's *Capital in the Twenty-First Century* has enjoyed in the public debate on inequality all over the world since its publication in 2014 would have been unimaginable in the neoliberal 1990s and 2000s.

Although the financial crisis of 2008 did not cause the immediate death of neoliberalism, as some perhaps expected or hoped (Crouch 2011), the Great Recession, for some, signals severe structural short-comings of contemporary global capitalism (Kotz 2015). It is in this con-text that an increasing number of voices – in academia, journalism and politics – articulate their anxiety about, and discomfort with, the large and still rising income disparities that the neoliberal era has produced. Even the Organisation for Economic Co-operation and Development (OECD) – a major advocate of neoliberalism that promoted the free market, flexible labour markets and limited government – has become very critical of inequality and is currently advising governments to take action against it (OECD 2011). Similarly, the International Monetary Fund (IMF) (2014; 2015) has published studies showing that there is no trade-off between redistribution and growth, but that inequality, in fact, may be harmful for economic growth. The IMF, thus, exposes two of the neoliberal articles of faith as myth, namely, that higher inequality leads to higher economic growth and that gains at the top of the income distribution will gradually 'trickle down' (see also Chapter 6).

Are we, then, witnessing the birth of a new era of equality? Not quite, as there are still powerful groups and individuals – perhaps more so in the United States and the United Kingdom than elsewhere – who express their persuasion that rising inequality is not something to worry about or to reject on moral grounds. On the contrary, they argue that redistribution is morally and economically bad. The Republicans in the United States, for instance, described President Barack Obama's proposal for a millionaire tax as 'class war'. Paul Ryan, then chair of the House of Representatives' budget committee, wrote: 'The president says that only the richest people in America would be affected by his plan. Class warfare may or may not be clever politics, but it is terrible economics. Redistributing wealth never creates more of it, and sowing class envy makes America weaker, not stronger' (*Chicago Tribune*, 16 May 2011). Some years before, Warren Buffett, chief executive of Berkshire Hathaway (and the man who inspired Obama's tax proposition), said: 'There's class warfare, all right, but it's my class, the rich class, that's making war, and we're winning' (quoted in *The New York Times*, 26 November 2006). As journalist Andrew Anthony expressed it recently, 'Like feminism and beards, class has made a dramatic comeback' (*The Observer*, 30 November 2014).

Income inequality has been on the rise for more than 30 years now, though more in some countries than others. This empirical fact (Atkinson

2003; see also Chapter 5), typified as the Great U-turn (Harrison and Bluestone 1988) or the Great Reversal (Rosanvallon 2013), is not disputed by anyone, at least not on any serious grounds. How to evaluate this truth normatively is a whole different issue, however, and a constant source of political controversy. In the last few years, the problem of income inequality has (again) become a central issue in politics and a hotly debated topic. It arouses strong feelings on both the left and the right of the political spectrum. Surely, distributional issues always occupy centre stage in politics, but now increasingly so, not only because they are fundamentally a matter of power, but also because there is an important moral issue at stake. Is income inequality morally bad, or can it be justified on normative grounds?

The Problem of the Moral Evaluation of Inequality

It seems that in normative political theory there are basically four ways of evaluating inequality. The first is evaluating inequality *intrinsically* by asking whether inequality is bad in and of itself. Do we have a moral obligation or duty – based on our conception of justice or fairness – that demands equality? Second, we can assess inequality *extrinsically* by looking at its effects relative to some other value. This is the instrumental or outcomes-oriented view that would reject inequality as (instrumentally) bad or embrace it as (instrumentally) good because it has bad or good consequences. Third, seen from a *virtue-ethical* point of view, and particularly the capability approach – mainly associated with Amartya Sen (e.g. 1989) and Martha Nussbaum (e.g. 1993, 2001, 2006; but see 2011) – inequality is bad if it hinders human beings from using their powers (virtues) to flourish in a truly human way. Finally, one can look at inequality in a functional, *pragmatic* and evolutionary way, and hold that the right norm as to which level of inequality is acceptable in a society will be the norm that actually emerges and persists in that society (see Gosepath 2011).

In our view, both the virtue ethics approach and the pragmatic view essentially embrace an instrumentalist position; the virtue ethics approach because it traces the effect of inequality on human flourishing, and the pragmatic view because it is exclusively concerned with the process outcome. Hence – and in spite of the undoubtedly many important nuances that normative political theorists would wish to subjoin here – we argue that to all intents and purposes there are basically two ways to evaluate inequality: 1) as morally either good or bad and 2) as having good or bad consequences.

Whether inequality has good or bad consequences obviously depends on the criterion one uses to evaluate the outcomes. If economic growth is highly valued and inequality hinders it, then inequality is to be qualified as bad. Whether inequality in fact hampers economic growth is strictly an empirical matter, however.

But is inequality good or bad in and of itself? This question is sur-prisingly more difficult to answer than one would perhaps intuitively think. Politicians, especially of the left, often suggest that we should care about inequality as such, but almost always fail to provide the necessary argumentation to support that position. In December 2013, for instance, President Obama (Obama 2013) gave a speech on inequality and social mobility. He said: 'The combined trends of increased inequality and decreasing mobility pose a fundamental threat to the American Dream, our way of life, and what we stand for around the globe. And it is not simply a moral claim that I'm making here.' It is the final sentence, said almost in passing, which is intriguing, because it reveals that – apart from all sorts of possible negative consequences they might have – increased inequality and decreasing mobility *as such* are apparently considered to be immoral. This implies that the president was indeed making the moral claim that inequality in itself is bad – ostensibly against those who see no moral problem here. However, he offered no argument to support the moral claim, perhaps leaving it to our normative intuition or innate aversion to inequality to provide it?

Empirical researchers of inequality – for instance, when they try to jus-tify why they study the topic – also struggle with the moral evaluation of inequality. They find it particularly difficult to provide convincing argu-ments as to why we should be concerned about inequality in and of itself. One of the world's leading economists of inequality, Anthony Atkinson (2015a: 12), for instance, argues that there are also intrinsic reasons for believing that the current degree of inequality is excessive. But his short trip along theories of justice does not culminate in a clear statement on why (the current degree of) inequality is *intrinsically* unacceptable. In an interview, Atkinson (2015b) said: 'It does matter that some people can buy tickets for space travel when others are queuing for food banks.' This again seems to appeal to our normative intuition or innate aversion to inequality to argue that we should care about inequality in and of itself. But, taken as such, Atkinson does not defend the position that we should *always* care about the fact that there are some people queuing for food banks *regardless* of whether there is anyone who can buy tickets for space travel (see the sufficientarian view below; Frankfurt 2015).

Lane Kenworthy (2008), a prominent student of inequality, has struggled with the issue too, and argued that we should mainly care about poverty, but that low inequality also matters in and of itself. His approach was as follows. He compared four hypothetical societies that vary in income level and level of inequality (see Table 2.1) to see which distributional situation is to be preferred, to make a case for why equal-ity matters in and of itself. What are his arguments?

Contrasting countries A and B, he writes (2008: 22): 'Inequality is greater in B than in A, but perhaps the difference is not large enough for concern about inequality to trump concern about the income level

Table 2.1   *Income distributions in four hypothetical societies*

	Household Income			Average Income	Gini Coefficient
	Poor Household	Middle Household	Rich Household		
Society A	20,000	40,000	75,000	45,000	0.27
Society B	15,000	40,000	100,000	51,667	0.37
Society C	25,000	40,000	200,000	888,333	0.44
Society D	30,000	40,000	10,000,000	3,356,667	0.66

Source: Adopted, with permission, from Kenworthy (2008: 22, table 2.1).

of the poor or about the average income level.' Perhaps, but even if one intuitively agrees, the question remains why only *large* differences would matter. And how large would the difference in income have to be to make us worry about inequality? Comparing countries A and B with C, he concludes (ibid.) with the following rhetorical question: 'Inequality is considerably greater in C than in A. But is the difference large enough that a "sensible egalitarian" would object?' We do not know; is it? And what is a sensible egalitarian? Finally, Kenworthy argues that one might prefer the situation in country D over all others because the poor households are clearly better off, while the middle and rich households are not worse off. The level of inequality, which – caused by the extremely high income of the rich – is clearly highest in country D, is morally irrelevant. But if the highest incomes are for the most part the result of sheer luck, Kenworthy (2008: 23) asks, '[s]hould we prefer society D on normative grounds?' He concludes: 'Though I am not certain how many readers will agree, I do not think we should.' However, the question of why exactly we should not prefer country D on normative grounds remains unanswered. Kenworthy (ibid.) expresses the feeling that 'there is reason to be concerned about both poverty and inequality, rather than only about poverty', but in the absence of a strong argumentation we cannot conclude that we should care much about inequality in and of itself.

Normative political theorists and others have, of course, focused on the issue and are engaged in an ongoing debate on questions such as whether equality or inequality is desirable, what kind of inequality should be avoided or promoted, and how we can decide when one situation is worse or better than another with respect to inequality (see e.g. Temkin 1993; Hausman and Waldren 2011). We now first discuss the arguments philosophers offer in favour of the claim that there is nothing intrinsically wrong with equality, and then move to the question on what grounds, if any, we could argue that inequality is wrong in and of itself.

There Is Nothing Wrong with Inequality as Such

Those who dislike the political attention that the problem of inequality is receiving fear the increasing redistribution that may come in its wake, or see no moral reason to reject inequality use a number of arguments to support their view that *as such* there is nothing wrong with inequality.

The first argument is that even though all men are created equal in a formal sense, they become unequal in their pursuit of happiness because of differences in (natural) endowments (say mental and physical abilities, talents) that translate into unequal social endowments, primarily as the result of individual *effort*. An unequal distribution of wealth and income that is the result of this is just. Even if one considers the initial unequal distribution of endowments to be unfair, the income differences that result from differences in commitment, perseverance and hard work are still to be judged as fair. Selectively invoking Sen (1992), the argument, then, is that nobody can be against inequality as such, because it simply reflects human diversities. And, ending up close to the position that Nozick (1974) has defended, it would be an unacceptable interference with individual freedom and a breach of (property) rights to undo such inequality. If an unequal distribution of income came about legitimately, then that distribution is legitimate (Nozick 1974: 232).

Note that it is incorrect to infer from this that Nozick preferred inequality. Although he went up against egalitarianism, he would also argue that if an equal distribution of income came about legitimately, no political interference is justifiable that would impose more inequality. As Wolff (1991: 123) in his critical book on Nozick argued, 'It is likely – some would say certain – that in a libertarian society massive inequalities would develop, but if equality of wealth came about by chance or voluntary co-operation this would be remarkable but unobjectionable. It would, however, be objectionable, to bring about equality by "social planning", via some central redistributional scheme, for this would violate people's entitlements to their property.'

The second argument is similar to, yet distinct from, the first, and refers to the working of the free market, which produces unequal outcomes simply because the market values and rewards hard work, good ideas and risk-taking, while it punishes indolence, bad ideas and playing it safe. Confronted with an Oxfam (2014) calculation that the richest 85 people on the planet owned as much as the poorest half of humanity (approximately 3.5 billion people), Kevin O'Leary, a Canadian entrepreneur, said: 'It's fantastic. And this is a great thing because it inspires everybody, gets them motivation to look up to the one percent [sic] and say "I want to become one of those people, I'm going to fight hard to get up to the top." This is fantastic news and of course I applaud it. What can be wrong with this?' The interviewer responded with a long pause and then: '... Really? ... So somebody living on a dollar a day in Africa is getting up in the morning and saying, "I'm going to be Bill Gates"?' O'Leary replied: 'That's the motivation everybody needs' (*Huffington Post* 2014).

Although this looks like an instrumentalist argument, it is an – admittedly rather extreme – example of the kind of reasoning that refers to an intrinsic quality of inequality, namely, that it stimulates people to become better. Those who think inequality is bad are just envious. 'The envious person', says Nozick (1974: 239), 'if he cannot (also) possess a thing (talent, and so on) that someone else has, prefers that the other person not have it either.' But resentment is not an acceptable foundation for moral judgement. Differences in remuneration generated by the market appeal to another innate feature of human nature, namely, greed, and hence give people incentives to work hard, take risks (invest), and produce goods and services. Those who *contribute* the most receive the most.

The third argument is that those who worry about economic inequality are misguided because they do not realize that inequality is entirely irrelevant; it is neither good nor bad. What should matter is 'welfare' or overall economic well-being, not inequality. The illustration of this position is similar to Kenworthy's exercise, but with the purpose of showing that inequality is irrelevant. Usually two income distributions are compared, one in which inequality but also the income of the worst off is low, and one in which inequality is high, but the bottom group is better off than in the first scenario. Hence, if one cares about the worst off and the poor, one should not lose sleep over inequality, but be concerned about their income. And if – re-invoking the second argument – the collective *efficient* outcome of greed is a rising tide that lifts all boats, then greed is good, as is the resulting inequality.

A fourth argument is one of *futility*, as aptly summarized by Roemer (2011: 7): 'even if the degree of inequality that comes with laissez-faire is not socially necessary in the sense that the incentive argument claims, attempts by the state to reduce it will come to naught, because the government is grossly incompetent, inefficient, or corrupt. Thus, better to let the rich keep their wealth and invest it profitably, than to hope that the state can manage it more fruitfully'.

The final argument is a distinct political-philosophical position ('sufficientarianism') that claims that equality in itself is morally irrelevant (e.g. Raz 1988: chapter 9; Frankfurt 1988, 2015), too demanding, or the wrong expression of what are genuine political goals: to eliminate suffering, deprivation, discrimination, etc. Crisp (2003: 762, our emphasis), for one, formulated the sufficiency principle: 'compassion for any being B is appropriate up to the point at which B has a level of welfare such that B can live a life which is *sufficiently* good'. Apart from the question when enough is enough, this position clearly rejects the idea that equality as such is good and argues that beyond a certain level of welfare inequality is morally irrelevant. Similarly, Sher's (2014) moral position is that each individual should be able to live his or her life *effectively*, which can only be done if all have access to a sufficient share of social goods. If the consequence is inequality, with individuals suffering from their own choices, that is morally irrelevant compared with the goal of living a life effectively. Finally, Axelsen and Nielsen (2014) argue that justice does not require equality; above a certain threshold, when people have enough, inequalities are morally irrelevant. What should matter is sufficiency as 'freedom from duress', where duress is understood as 'a situation in which one is under significant pressure in central areas of human life, pressure that would impede any normal human being's ability to *succeed* in a similar situation' (Axelsen and Nielsen 2014: 3, original emphasis). When people are morally offended by inequality they are usually upset by the fact that some people do not have enough and not by the observation that some people have more than others (Frankfurt 2015).

In summary, there is nothing intrinsically wrong with inequality, because it is the result of individual *effort* and *contribution* and an *efficient* end result that benefits all, or even if it was not all this, we still should not care about inequality because it is *irrelevant*, and other goals, such as welfare, matter more. Inequality is *morally irrelevant* beyond a point where certain conditions are guaranteed for living a sufficiently good and effective life or a life free of duress. Also, doing something about inequality would be *futile*. It is redistribution for egalitarian reasons, which is illegitimate and inherently wrong, because it implies a violation of the higher value of liberty and the fundamental right of property and because it will produce a social outcome that is even worse.

Something Is Wrong with Inequality as Such

The opposite answer to the question whether inequality is bad in and of itself, namely 'yes', comes from those who take one of the various egalitarian positions. Shortly put, inequality is bad if those who are worse off are so because of bad luck for which they cannot be held responsible (Cohen 2008). This bad luck should be 'brute luck' and not 'option luck': 'Option luck is a matter of how deliberate and calculated gambles turn out – whether someone gains or loses through accepting an isolated risk he or she should have anticipated and might have declined. Brute luck is a matter of how risks fall out that are not in that sense deliberate gambles' (Dworkin 1981: 293).

It would be incorrect to conclude that luck egalitarians are against inequality as such. Only to the extent that inequality is a result of bad luck is it to be considered unjust. That some people are better off than others because of good luck, is in itself not unacceptable (see for an elaborate defence: Lippert-Rasmussen 2015, chapter 3).

Rawls (1985 [1971]: 73–4) famously argued that a liberal conception of justice that 'permits the distribution of wealth and income to be determined by the natural distribution of abilities and talents' is flawed, because 'distributive shares are decided by the outcome of the natural lottery; and this outcome is arbitrary from a moral perspective'. The same holds for the social lottery that decides one's starting position in life. 'No one deserves his greater natural capacity nor merits a more favorable starting place in society [...]' (Rawls 1985 [1971]: 102).

Rawls considered the natural distribution of talents and abilities as well as the social distribution of fortune as neither just nor unjust in and of itself. 'What is just and unjust is the way that institutions deal with these facts' (idem). Redistribution from the lucky to the unlucky would be morally acceptable when institutions are so organized that the brute luck of some is to the benefit of all. Assuming no violation of the morally prior liberties, that distribution that maximizes the income of the worst off is the just one. Hence Rawls' difference principle, the final statement of which reads: 'social and economic inequalities are to be arranged so that they are both (a) to the greatest benefit of the least advantaged, consistent with the just savings principle, and (b) attached to offices and positions open to all under conditions of fair equality of opportunity' (Rawls 1985 [1971]: 302). Expressed in the terms of speech we use here, the argument is that inequality is not wrong in and of itself unless it violates the second principle. In fact, Kenworthy's most unequal society D (see Table 2.1) would be the preferred Rawlsian society because that distribution maximizes the income of the worst off.

Most, if not all, moral judgements that do declare inequality as such wrong, employ some strong variant of the bad luck and lottery argument. Or as Arneson (2008: 80) put it: 'The concern of distributive justice is to compensate individuals for misfortune. Some people are blessed with good luck, some are cursed with bad luck, and it is the responsibility of society – all of us regarded collectively – to alter the distribution of goods and evils that arises from the jumble of lotteries that constitutes human life as we know it ... Distributive justice stipulates that the lucky should transfer some or all of their gains due to luck to the unlucky'.

Luck egalitarianism, as it has been labelled, is the normative political theory that defends the view that inequality as such is morally wrong. But the theory has encountered powerful counterarguments that seem difficult to defy (Kauppinen 2012; but see Lippert-Rasmussen 2012 and 2015 for a recent restatement and defence). First, the luck egalitarian position crucially depends on the distinction between choice and circumstances. If bad luck is a result of choice, then tough luck, so to speak. But is it really possible to make the distinction between choice and circumstances? It does not seem possible to calculate in any precise or even approximate manner how much of a person's situation must be attributed to choice and how much to fortune. All choice involves risk and uncertainty, some choices turn out to be good and others bad, and the consequences of past choices enter the circumstances of further choices. Given this, it becomes impossible to determine what responsible choices are. Even if this to some extent would be possible, then who is to decide on that? Moreover, is it morally acceptable that we remain indifferent to the human suffering that is the consequence of bad choice?

Second, it is not only difficult to put into operation the luck egalitarian distinction between luck and choice, but it is potentially offensive and stigmatizing to do so because it implies that we dig deep into people's lives to establish who is deserving (those who lack talent, ability, intelligence etc.) and undeserving (those who made no effort or made the wrong choice). 'Would you rather say', asks Kauppinen (2012: 21), 'that you haven't bothered to look for work (so not entitled) or that you're too slow and dumb to meet the demands of the modern workplace?'

In a famous paper, Elizabeth M. Anderson (1999) has further argued that luck egalitarians have employed bad arguments in favour of their position because their reasoning is founded on a flawed understanding of what the point of equality is and because it tends to prove the inegalitarians right: egalitarians are motivated by envy, are willing to support irresponsibility and sloth, and require the state to violate privacy and to tax so as to subsidize private wasteful practices (Anderson 1999: 287–8). In sum, luck egalitarianism's vision reflects a 'mean-spirited, contemptuous, parochial vision of a society that represents human diversity hierarchically, moralistically contrasting the responsible and irresponsible, the innately superior and the innately inferior, the independent and the dependent. It offers no aid to those it labels irresponsible, and humiliating aid to those it labels innately inferior. It gives us the cramped vision of the Poor Laws, where unfortunates breathe words of supplication and submit to the humiliating moral judgments of the state' (Anderson 1999: 308). Luck egalitarianism cannot provide a foundation for the moral claim that inequality in and of itself is wrong.

The point of equality, Anderson argues, is not to compensate for the underserved outcomes of bad luck: 'The proper negative aim of egalitarian justice is not to eliminate the impact of brute luck from human affairs, but to end oppression, which by definition is socially imposed. Its proper positive aim is not to ensure that everyone gets what they morally deserve, but to create a community in which people stand in relations of equality to others' (Anderson 1999: 288–9). Equality, in other words, is social and political – labelled democratic equality – and refers to a situation in which there is no domination, exploitation and marginalization (see Scheffler 2003). There is nothing wrong with income inequality in and of itself, unless it comes at the cost of democratic equality. 'Once all citizens enjoy a decent set of freedoms, sufficient for functioning as an equal in society,' says Anderson (1999: 326), 'income inequalities beyond that point do not seem so troubling in themselves. The degree of acceptable income inequality would depend in part on how easy it was to convert income into status inequality ....'

To sum up, it does not seem that political theory as yet has been able (or willing) to make a strong and convincing case that inequality as such must be viewed as intrinsically bad. Luck egalitarians, for instance, hold that it is unjust if a person is worse off than others as a result of bad luck for which he or she cannot be held responsible. Yet, they are silent or indifferent to income inequality resulting from good luck. Similarly, those who endorse social and political equality as a moral yardstick reason that income inequality as such is only unjust to the extent that it thwarts democratic equality.

Conclusion

We have argued that in the post-World War II period the *Zeitgeist* profoundly changed. In the 1960s and 1970s there was a widely shared endorsement of the idea that reducing the level of income inequality was a good thing. It even seemed to be the politically correct normative position to take. During the neoliberal era that succeeded this period (roughly until the 2000s) income inequality lost its status as a social and political problem and the moral outlook became predominantly one of indifference towards inequality or one that endorsed and even celebrated large income differentials. Most recently, consistently high and rising income inequality has caught the attention of public opinion makers (academics, journalists and pundits) and politicians and hence has reappeared on the political agenda.

We have shown that even the best academic empirical analysts of income inequality (e.g. Kenworthy and Atkinson) have found it difficult to provide a solid answer to the question why we should worry about income inequality as such from a normative point of view. Posing the question what, if anything, is morally wrong with inequality in and of itself, we turned to political theorists. Some have argued straightforwardly that inequality is not bad in and of itself. Income inequality results from the fact that some people simply work harder than others, happen to be more talented than others and hence contribute more to society than others. In this perspective, redistribution of income is unjust, because it violates higher values such as liberty and the right to own property. Redistribution is also uneconomical (because it takes away the incentive to work hard and contribute) and ineffective (since governments always do a worse economic job than markets). In addition, to define income inequality as a moral problem is beside the point, because welfare is what really matters. Finally, inequality becomes morally a non-issue beyond the point where people have enough to live a decent life. Even those political theorists who adopt an egalitarian normative position and reject that type of income inequality that stems from bad luck do not argue against inequality as such.

So, if the intrinsic moral argument against inequality breaks down, what other justification, if any, is there then for rejecting inequality morally? Following Sher (2014), Axelsen and Nielsen (2014) and O'Neill (2008: 121–3), one could accept non-intrinsic egalitarianism, which offers a plurality of reasons for reducing inequality. Inequality is morally unacceptable because it causes suffering and deprivation, is stigmatizing and promotes status differences, fosters unacceptable forms of power and domination, weakens self-respect, and produces servility and less than healthy fraternal social relations and attitudes.

Similarly and with obvious overlap, Hausman and Waldron (2011: 576–8) produce a list of ends that equality may serve and to which it is intrinsically linked: '1) Inequalities in opportunities or in the distribution of benefits and burdens may be unfair ... 2) Inequalities in wealth and political power may undermine the integrity and impartiality of social institutions and practices ... 3) Inequalities in valued possessions, life prospects, political influence, and social status threaten self-respect ... 4) Inequalities in life prospects, opportunity, political influence, and social status may fail to show equal respect ... 5) Inequalities in crucial resources, in status, and in socially valued possessions may create barriers to friendship, community, and love ... 6) Inequalities in political power, crucial resources, or life prospects, may subjugate some people to others.'

Their point is that these are considerations that matter for egalitarians, although they do not necessarily have to accept all of them. Whether these considerations provide a firmer foundation for the egalitarian position as such continues to be a controversial issue in normative political theory, no doubt, and no list of ends that equality may serve is likely to settle it any time soon.

We ourselves are agnostic on this issue: we do not know whether inequality as such is good or bad from a moral point of view. We rather adopt an instrumentalist position: inequality is bad because it has bad consequences in areas that are crucial to people's lives and well-being, including income anxiety, health problems, low life satisfaction and faltering social mobility (poor life chances for children). We should, thus, care about inequality because it greatly affects people. In Chapter 3 we elaborate on this position: inequality is to be evaluated as bad because we can show that it has bad objective and subjective outcomes for individuals and society as a whole.

Why should we care about inequality?

Our discussion in Chapter 2 suggests that it is difficult, if not impossible, to find a convincing answer to the question of why inequality should be considered to be bad in and of itself. Maybe it is, maybe it is not. It will probably be equally difficult to defend the position that equality is intrinsically good because it avoids unfairness, protects impartiality, sustains self-respect, shows equal respect, nurtures fraternity and prevents domination (Hausman and Waldron 2011). Maybe it does, maybe it does not. As argued, we are agnostic about the issue.

But, even if we were to come to the conclusion that we should not care about inequality as such, we still could have good reasons to care about inequality because of its bad consequences. 'The surprising persistence of a very vague, unfocused discourse about "inequality" in standards of living as bad may stem from inadequate attention to the absolute value of social states for persons. A consequentialist perspective may help here, as it obliges one to focus on what really matters for individuals about inequality' (Picavet 2013: 496). It is this line of reasoning that we follow. We care about inequality because it greatly matters to people. We are able to reject some forms or degrees of inequality as bad because we can show that they have bad outcomes, not least in the eyes of the people most directly affected by inequality.

In this chapter, we present and discuss some of the evidence on the negative effects of economic inequality. The empirical evidence is voluminous, and it is not our ambition to make a complete survey of the research, because this would take us too far away from the topic of the book. We begin the next section by displaying two very simple figures showing the correlation between individuals' position in the income distribution and their well-being. There is a negative correlation in all countries that we know of, and the two figures exemplify that. But there is also a tendency for the correlation to be more negative in more unequal countries. The subsequent two sections focus on health and social mobility more specifically, reviewing some of the most important insights from recent research.

Some Initial Empirics

Figure 3.1 summarizes data from the European Social Survey on how people in different income groups (organized into deciles, with the poorest 10 per cent in the first decile, and so on, until the richest 10 per cent in the 10th decile; see Chapter 4) feel about their economic position. On the vertical axis, the percentage of citizens saying that they find it either 'difficult' or 'very difficult' to cope on present income is reported. The figure clearly shows a strong income gradient in how people evaluate their household's income situation. The richer people are, the less they report that they are living through economic hardship. In the poorest first decile, no fewer than two thirds (66.2 per cent) of the people feel that it is difficult or very difficult to cope on present income. This subjective feeling of income deprivation rapidly declines if we climb up the income ladder, up to the point where only 13.7 per cent of the richest decile feels that their household's income position is a major cause for concern.

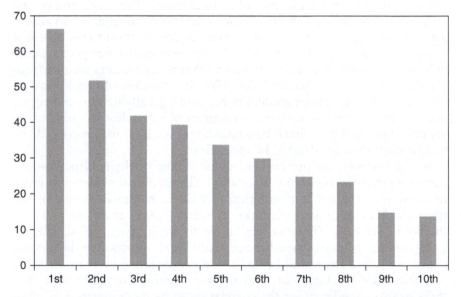

Figure 3.1   *Objective inequality and subjective feeling of economic hardship*

Note: Respondents were asked how they feel about their household's income nowadays. The reported percentages on the vertical axis are those within each income decile who say that it is either difficult or very difficult to cope on present income. Post-stratification and population size weights have been applied to correct for sample bias, as recommended by the European Social Survey.

Source: European Social Survey Round 6 (2012).

In a sense, it is, of course, to be expected that more people in lower than in higher income groups will experience economic hardship. Still, the data clearly tell us that differences in income have a substantial negative effect on how people evaluate the economic situation in their household. Perhaps money does not always bring happiness, but it certainly does make people a lot less anxious about making ends meet (we return to this issue in more detail in Chapter 6).

More importantly, however, the feeling of economic hardship strongly affects other aspects of well-being, most strikingly health and satisfaction with life in general and, as we show below, social mobility. Figure 3.2 also shows a strong income gradient: very few people who live comfortably on present income report that they have bad health (4 per cent) or are dissatisfied with life (2.4 per cent). The more people find it difficult to cope on present income, the more they report health problems and unhappiness. In fact, no fewer than 27.5 per cent of the people who find it difficult to make ends meet on present income report that they are in bad health, a 23.5 percentage point difference from the well-to-do group. The contrast between the two groups is even more marked if we look at life satisfaction: there is almost a 37 percentage

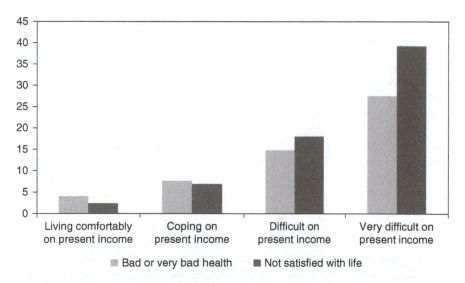

Figure 3.2 *Economic hardship and misery*

Note: The light grey bars represent the percentage of respondents reporting that their health is either bad or very bad. The dark grey bars represent the percentage of respondents reporting a low degree of satisfaction with life as a whole (defined as the bottom four categories on an 11-point scale). Post-stratification and population size weights have been applied to correct for sample bias, as recommended by the European Social Survey.

Source: European Social Survey, Round 6 (2012).

point difference in life satisfaction between the well-off and those who experience economic hardship. Apparently, differences in income have huge consequences for life satisfaction and health (and, as we show below, this effect is bigger in more unequal countries).

Inequality Gets under Our Skin

There is a strong positive correlation between income and health outcomes: the higher their income, the healthier people are. Why, precisely, is there a strong social gradient in health? And what is the direction of causality? It could, in principle, be that the healthier people are, the easier it is to earn a high income.

In a paper tellingly titled 'Sick of Poverty', Sapolsky (2005) does away with what seem obvious answers to these questions. One of these answers is that the poorer people are, the less access to good health care they have. This negatively affects their physical well-being. However, several cleverly designed studies among people with the same access to medical care have shown that the social gradient in health outcomes remains strong. Also, poorer people more often have diseases for which access to healthcare does not matter. Another answer that can be discarded (for the most part) is that poorer people tend to have unhealthier lifestyles. There is some truth in this, but it explains only a small part of the social gradient. Moreover, if it is lifestyle that matters most, one would expect the poor in wealthy countries to be healthier than the poor in less affluent societies. This, however, is not the case (see Babones 2008; Kondo et al. 2009).

Sapolsky, therefore, proposes an alternative explanation for why health risks increase with lower income or lower socio-economic status more generally ('status' refers to income, but also looks at occupation, education and housing conditions). Shortly put, the lower one stands on the socio-economic ladder, the higher the level of chronic psychosocial stress tends to become. There are a large number of biomedical studies that identify under which conditions individuals become chronically stressed and hence have a higher risk of developing stress-related diseases. Such conditions, such as little control over what causes stress and no prospect of when it will end, are more common and frequent among individuals with a low socio-economic status. 'Psychosocial stressors', writes Sapolsky (2005: 94), 'are not evenly distributed across society.' It is worth quoting him at some length (ibid.):

> Just as the poor have a disproportionate share of physical stressors (hunger, manual labor, chronic sleep deprivation with a second job, the bad mattress that can't be replaced), they have a disproportionate share of psychosocial ones. Numbing assembly-line work and an

occupational lifetime spent taking orders erode workers' sense of control. Unreliable cars that may not start in the morning and paychecks that may not last the month inflict unpredictability. Poverty rarely allows stress-relieving options such as health club memberships, costly but relaxing hobbies, or sabbaticals for rethinking one's priorities. And despite the heartwarming stereotype of the "poor but loving community," the working poor typically have less social support than the middle and upper classes, thanks to the extra jobs, the long commutes on public transit, and other burdens. (Sapolsky 2005: 94)

The association between inequality and health (and other social problems) – although a complicated causal one – has been established and confirmed in a large number of studies (McKnight and Cowell 2014). Famously, Wilkinson and Pickett, in their much-debated *The Spirit Level* (2009), created an index of health and social problems (including data on life expectancy, infant mortality, homicides, imprisonment, teenage births, societal distrust, obesity, mental illness, educational attainment and social mobility) and related this to inequality among rich countries. Their findings are shown in Figure 3.3 and clearly illustrate that the higher the level of inequality, the worse health and social problems tend to be (see also Daniels et al. 1999; Marmot 2005).

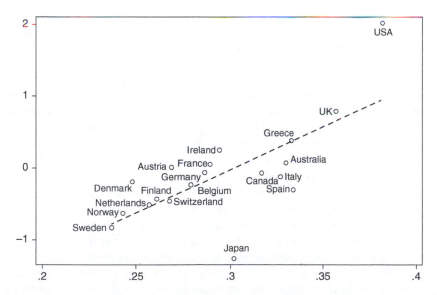

Figure 3.3 *Inequality and the Health and Social Problems Index*

Note: Inequality is measured as the Gini coefficient on the horizontal axis, while the Health and Social Problem Index is on the vertical axis.

Source: The Equality Trust (2016) and LIS (2015).

Wilkinson and Pickett's crucial contribution, however, is that they have shown that this is not just because the poor have more problems in more unequal societies. The important finding is that the negative consequences of inequality hold for the population as a whole. Wilkinson and Pickett stress that

> health disparities are not simply a contrast between the ill-health of the poor and the better health of everybody else. Instead, they run right across society so that even the reasonably well-off have shorter lives than the very rich. Likewise, the benefits of greater equality spread right across society, improving health for everyone – not just those at the bottom. (Wilkinson and Pickett 2009: 84)

Because of lack of data on the health of the very rich, we cannot say that in the most unequal societies *everybody* is worse off, but Wilkinson and Pickett's analysis definitely suggests that most people would benefit from less inequality. In a recent comprehensive review of all major studies of the health consequences of inequality, Pickett and Wilkinson (2015) found overwhelming evidence that inequality strongly and negatively affects overall population health and well-being.

These findings imply that Sapolsky's explanation of why poor health is correlated with low income in terms of psychosocial stressors only goes so far, because it does not explain why in more unequal societies everybody's health suffers. The Wilkinson and Pickett explanation holds that income differences increase social distances. Increasing social distance, in turn, accentuates social class and status differences. Such differences increase status competition, feelings of disrespect and social evaluation anxiety; they lower self-esteem and status; they negatively affect friendships, and increase feelings of shame. And this holds for people in all layers in society, all of whom experience a rise in chronic stress that damages health. This biology of chronic stress ensures that inequality gets under the skin and explains 'why unequal societies are almost always unhealthy societies' (Wilkinson and Pickett 2009: 87). Income inequality is positively associated with status anxiety, and status anxiety increases among all individuals in all income groups if inequality increases, albeit more among the poor than among the rich (Paskov et al. 2013). In addition, neuroscience studies, which document the concrete physical (brain) responses to psychosocial factors, report that social pain (social exclusion) and physical pain activate the same parts of the brain.

In sum, inequality is a social stressor, and the psychosocial stressors caused by inequality negatively influence health for all social groups in society. One implication is that bringing income inequality down will have huge positive consequences for public health, with a potentially equally huge positive financial knock-on effect. The Equality Trust (2014) has estimated that if the United Kingdom were to reduce its level of inequality to the OECD average, it would improve the physical and mental health of its population to such an extent that it would also save £39 billion per year.

Inequality Is Bad for Social Mobility

Recall (see Chapter 2) Kevin O'Leary's warm welcoming of (extreme) income and wealth inequality as something people need to get stimulated to work hard and to climb the income ladder. Essentially, this describes the idea that inequality stimulates social mobility, and hence that inequality is a good thing, because it rewards industrious people and punishes the indolent. Indeed, if inequality does not imply class closure, but increases opportunities and life chances, then inequality is not necessarily a bad thing. The relationship between inequality and social mobility should, then, be a positive one: the higher inequality is, the higher the level of social (income) mobility should be, both over the life course and between generations.

There are different ways of looking at social mobility. A first one focuses on wage inequality and wage mobility (Bachmann et al. 2012). Wage mobility measures the extent to which and how often people's earnings change (going up or down the wage ladder) over the life course. Here, the incentive argument seems most relevant. On the one hand, high wage mobility indicates that people have a good chance of increasing their earnings, although, on the other hand, it also implies higher uncertainty about future income. Cross-national 'snapshots' of the level of earnings inequality at a single point in time do not inform us about income inequality over the life course (see also the discussion in Chapter 4).

Wage mobility turns out to have a small equalizing effect on wage inequality if one looks at people's average earnings over a few years, and a somewhat bigger positive effect on wage equality if one studies (simulates) individuals' wage history over the whole life course. This is because in a certain year there will always be a number of workers or employees who have a higher or lower income than normal because of temporary factors and incidents such as unpaid leave, a short period of unemployment or a one-time bonus (De Beer 2014). In other words, a snapshot of the income distribution might (slightly) overestimate inequality, and hence averaging over several years or the whole life course will dampen the impact of these highs and lows. Most important in this context is that the cross-national empirical evidence suggests that there is only a very weak positive relationship between the level of wage inequality and wage mobility (Bachmann et al. 2012: 12). High wage inequality might incite people to make a greater effort to climb the income ladder, but only a few actually manage to do so.

Another approach to social mobility focuses on intergenerational mobility. To what extent can children from poor families rise above or fall below their parents' educational level and income? In other words, what degree of equality of opportunity do societies have? Do more unequal societies have higher levels of education and income mobility? Empirical studies of the 1970s and early 1980s tended to report that social mobility in developed countries was very high, and somewhat lower in less developed ones. Becker and Tomes (1986: 32) concluded their survey and research as follows: 'Almost all earnings advantages and disadvantages of ancestors are wiped out in three generations. Poverty would not seem to be a "culture" that persists over several generations', implying that most likely 'both the inheritability of endowments and the capital constraints on investments in children are not large. Presumably, these constraints became less important as fertility declined over time and as incomes and subsidies to education grew over time.'

The picture, however, has changed fundamentally. Most importantly, it is by now well established that social mobility did not increase as Becker and Tomes expected, that there are still large differences between countries, and that a very high level of inequality is harmful for social mobility. An OECD (2010: chapter 5) study of western European countries reports that intergenerational education and earnings mobility is much lower in the most unequal countries. In all these countries, children who grow up in a well-educated family will in later life earn more than the less lucky ones, in some countries up to 20 per cent more. There is also a strong correlation between the educational level of parents and the achievements of their children. Children with the lowest-educated parents are the least likely to attain an education beyond upper secondary education.

Other studies document, too, that there is, in fact, a distinct *negative* relationship between inequality and social (education and income) mobility (Hout and Beller 2006; Björklund and Jäntti 2009; Esping-Andersen 2009; OECD 2010; Corak 2013; Chetty et al. 2014). Miles Corak refers to this as the *Great Gatsby Curve* ('The American dream gone wrong'), which shows that there is a strong positive relationship between income inequality and intergenerational earnings elasticity (how much a son's earnings depend on parental earnings). The OECD reports similar results with recent data for European countries: the more unequal societies have lower intergenerational social mobility. Figure 3.4 shows the correlation between inequality (Gini coefficient for disposable household income) and wage persistence, which measures 'the gap between the estimated wage of an individual whose father had achieved tertiary education and the wage of an individual whose father had achieved below upper secondary education' (OECD 2010: 197). The larger this gap, the stronger is wage persistence, and, hence,

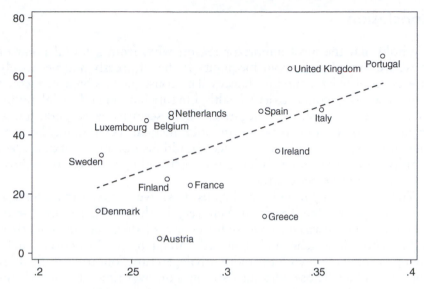

Figure 3.4 *Inequality and intergenerational wage persistence in the 2000s*

Note: The data on wage persistence relates to men 35–44 years old.

Source: OECD (2010: 197) and LIS (2015).

the lower intergenerational social mobility is. The correlation is 0.56 and significant at the 5 per cent level.

Does this association mean that high inequality causes low social mobility? This is a complicated issue. The extent to which children of poorer families can move up the education and income ladder depends on their personal characteristics, the circumstances in which they grow up and the personal choices they make. So, there are various factors at play. The evidence that it is really inequality that drives the lack of social mobility comes from studies that focus on what happens early on in childhood. Empirical research (see Currie and Almond 2011; Heckman and Mosso 2014; Esping-Andersen 2015) demonstrates that life chances are to a disproportionally large extent determined already in early childhood, i.e. the period before children enter school, when cognitive abilities are developed, and hence long before something like 'personal choice' is at all possible. Moreover, even in very democratic educational systems, early child deprivation is difficult, if not impossible, to remedy. Children with a low socio-economic status always start their education less well prepared than those with a high one. Even though money and education are the most important instrumental goods in terms of moderating inequalities of opportunity (Fishkin 2014), the gap between the two never closes as children grow older (Smeeding 2013: 14).

Conclusion

We hold that the most important reason why, from a moral point of view, we should care about inequality is that it greatly and negatively affects people's lives and life chances. The consequences of large income differences for income anxiety, health, life satisfaction and social mobility are clearly and strongly negative. There seem to be no good moral arguments to defend why people in more unequal societies, just because they are economically in dire straits, should also be more anxious, less healthy, less happy and with fewer prospects of improvement than those who happen to be better off.

The injustice is particularly obvious when we consider that children born into poorer families from their very birth (and hence because of no fault of their own) have worse life chances (education, income) than children born into richer and higher-educated families. Moreover, catching up via education with the more privileged turns out to be difficult, if not impossible: 'Those who start strong will, over time, distance themselves from the rest; those who have a poor start will fall ever more behind' (Esping-Andersen 2015: 127; see Jerrim and Macmillan 2015).

We know that the advanced capitalist democracies vary enormously in the levels of inequality they tolerate (see Chapter 5) and hence foster widely diverging social consequences. We claim in this book that institutions and public policies make a huge difference and to a large extent explain the cross-national variation in inequality. Our message is, therefore, that talking about inequality inevitably implies talking about the *politics* of inequality.

Moreover, opinion polls (e.g. PEW 2014) show that people consider inequality a very or moderately big problem. Even in the United States and the United Kingdom, where tolerance of inequality is traditionally comparatively high, around 80 per cent of the people agree that inequality is a big problem in their country, while in crisis-ridden Greece virtually everybody (97 per cent) thinks so. From a political science perspective, then, we also care about inequality because it matters in politics. As we show in Chapter 9, a large part of the population in European countries believe that income inequality is an important issue and that their governments should redistribute income.

Income inequality must be considered morally wrong because, if it gets out of hand, it has demonstrably bad consequences for people's lives and life chances. In addition, the causes and consequences of inequality are shaped by politics (institutions and public policies), and people (voters) consider inequality a political problem. Hence, we care both morally and as political scientists about inequality.

Chapter 4

How to measure inequality?

A necessary prerequisite for talking about economic inequality in any serious way is to know how to measure it. If we do not know that, we cannot begin to understand whether or not inequality is rising, let alone what causes such change. As will become apparent later, this is not an issue with marginal consequences, but can have real implications for the conclusions drawn. In this chapter, we therefore go into detail about how economic inequality is measured, and the advantages and disadvantages of different measurement choices. We do so by first asking what economic phenomena we could and should study. Is it inequality before or after governments have clawed in taxes and handed out social benefits? Is it inequality in the yearly earnings of citizens or, rather, in their accumulated wealth? Is it inequality of individuals or entire households?

We next ask how economic inequality can be summarized into relevant metrics. The most famous summary statistic by far is the Gini coefficient. Though widely used, the Gini coefficient has some drawbacks, which means that it is often helpful to supplement it with other summary statistics, such as ratios between income groups. After that, we briefly go through the main data sources available for empirical analysis and outline their respective strengths and weaknesses. The main trade-off is between an extensive coverage of countries and years and the high quality and degree of detail of the data. Chapter 5 then explores the empirical trends, and there it will become apparent that how inequality is measured really matters.

What to Measure?

The first thing to decide in an analysis of economic inequality is whether to study earnings or wealth. Earnings refer to the income that people make every year, or whatever other time period one is interested in, from having a job, self-employment, public transfers, or getting rent from various capital assets such as stocks, savings and houses. Leaving aside for the moment government redistribution, the vast majority of earnings come in the form of wages and salaries from having a job and profits from self-employment, i.e. income from the labour market. When we talk about earnings inequality, we therefore mainly refer to inequality in labour income. It is only for the rich that capital income is a really

31

important source of earnings. Yet, even for this select group, capital income is not the main thing. In the United States, for example, the average person in the top 1 per cent made 1,264,065 US dollars (USD) in 2012, but less than 20 per cent came from capital income. In Sweden, among the advanced democracies in many ways the polar opposite to the United States, almost the exact same portion, 21.6 per cent, came from capital income (Alvaredo et al. 2015).

To emphasize the significance of labour income is not to imply that capital income is irrelevant. Especially during economic booms, such as those in the late 1990s and mid-2000s, capital income constitutes a handsome additional gain that to a large extent benefits the rich only. In 2007, just before the Great Recession commenced in earnest, the proportion of top 1 per cent Americans' income coming from capital peaked at 30 per cent. One reason why mostly the rich have an income from capital is that they have accumulated a lot of wealth. This is a trivial but important point. While the rich, on average, have a higher labour income than the less well-off, they have comparably even more wealth. Indeed, whereas by definition no one can have a negative labour income, millions across the Western world are burdened by negative wealth, i.e. they owe more than they own. Frequently, such negative wealth originates from the purchase of the family's home or other necessities that people in affluent societies expect. As a result, inequalities in wealth are much bigger than inequalities in earnings (Davies 2009: 127). By one estimate, the top 1 per cent own 41.8 per cent of all wealth in the United States (Saez and Zucman 2014: 47), whereas they more modestly get 17.9 per cent of all earnings, excluding capital gains (Alvaredo et al. 2015).

One problem with studying wealth inequalities, however, is the lack of data that allow comparison between countries and over time. Good comparative information about people's wealth is hard to come by. One reason is that wealth is comparably easy to place in tax havens, out of reach of the taxman. Zucman (2013) estimates that as much as 8 per cent of all wealth is placed in tax havens. No matter what the reason, wealth is notoriously difficult to study, which is why the majority of scholars interested in cross-country patterns focus on earnings inequality instead. This they can do with good reason. Differences in how much people earn are big enough to matter on their own, without taking differences in wealth into account too. Moreover, if anything, most empirical associations are likely to be underestimated when relying on earnings, exactly because this form of inequality is less pronounced. For instance, several scholars have shown that inequality depresses electoral turnout, suggesting that inequality reduces the resources of the poor and enhances those of the rich (Goodin and Dryzek 1980; Anderson and Beramendi 2008; Solt 2008; 2010; see also Chapter 9). These findings are based on earnings inequality only, and we may plausibly expect that the resource disparity between the poor and the rich, and hence differences in turnout, would increase if the empirical analyses included wealth.

Given that inequality nearly always is measured as inequality in earnings, a central question becomes whether attention should be on earnings before or after redistribution, i.e. after taxes have been paid and social benefits received. Scholars normally study post-redistribution earnings because this captures people's disposable income, i.e. what is available for housing and other everyday living expenses. Disposable incomes tell us something about the ability of people to maintain a certain standard of living. What neighbourhood do they live in? What school can they afford for their children? Do they have the means to buy private health insurance? When talking about inequality, it is differences in such standards of living, opportunities and lifestyles we are concerned with, and here disposable income is the relevant thing to look at. This does not mean that earnings inequality before redistribution is irrelevant. Someone having a high income before redistribution will still tend to have a high income afterwards. So it remains relevant to look at the causes of pre-redistribution, or market inequality, but mainly because it matters for post-redistribution inequality. It can, in a similar way, be valuable to study the amount of redistribution itself, because it indicates the ability and willingness of a society to reallocate money from richer to poorer citizens. But, again, the implicit reason why this is interesting in the first place is that a lot of redistribution makes people's disposable incomes more equal than they were before.

Redistribution is, in principle, easy to measure. Just subtract the taxes paid from the gross income and add the social benefits received. This yields the post-redistribution income. The only problem is that social benefits come in two forms – transfers and in-kind services – and the former are much easier to account for than the latter. Transfers consist of money paid by the government to recipients, directly boosting the income of those getting the transfer. Some well-known transfer schemes are old-age pensions, unemployment insurance and social assistance. In-kind services are goods provided by the government to the public, such as hospitals, nursing homes and kindergartens. The value of such goods for the users is obvious. Getting treatment for an ailment has value in itself, for instance, and paying for it out of pocket can be ruinous. Unfortunately, the monetary value of in-kind services at the individual level is hard to measure empirically. Asking people themselves via household surveys, a common technique, as explained below, will hardly do the trick, because most people have no clue about the monetary value of whatever medical treatment or care they have received during the past year. As a result, no proper cross-country data exist that take in-kind services into account. Post-redistribution consequently usually means post-tax and transfer. All else being equal, this implies that redistribution is underestimated, since the provision of in-kind services is paid for by taxes that disproportionally hit the well-off, but is made available to everybody, and sometimes even only to the less well-to-do. For example, the post-redistribution Gini coefficient in Denmark, a country that collects particularly good data and therefore can produce a valid estimate, drops from 0.244 to 0.192 when in-kind services are included in the calculation (Ministry for Economic Affairs and the Interior 2013: 7).

If all countries provided the same amount of in-kind services, this lack of data would not be a big concern. In such a scenario, we would be underestimating the level of redistribution, but it would not affect the cross-country patterns we are interested in. The ranking of countries from most to least unequal would remain the same even though the level would be lower. The problem is that the provision of in-kind services varies greatly across countries. The Nordic countries host the largest public in-kind service sector. Denmark, Finland, Norway and Sweden on average spend USD 4333 per capita on in-kind services, versus USD 2787 across the OECD. This sums up to 13.9 per cent of the gross domestic product (GDP) compared with the OECD average of 9.1 per cent (OECD 2013a). Some scholars even label the Nordic countries *social services states* to emphasize the central role of in-kind services in the make-up of their social systems (Huber and Stephens 2001; see Chapter 8). The Nordic countries, as we will see later, also boast exceptionally low levels of inequality compared with virtually all other countries. This entails that in all likelihood they are even more outstanding than they appear with the available data. Put another way, not being able to account for the redistributive effect of in-kind services entails that the cross-country diversity we observe is subdued.

Another issue to consider is what the relevant social unit is (Jenkins and van Kerm 2009: 44–5). Should it be individuals or households? The problem from a methodological perspective is that although it is individuals who make an income, they normally pool this with that of other members of the household. The traditional scenario is that the husband earns more than the wife, who again earns more than the children. If the husband spent all his money on himself without regard to the needs of his wife and children, it would make sense to study individuals as the relevant social unit. In reality, of course, most breadwinners do not behave that way – at least not if they want the marriage to last. A woman with a small income who is married to a wealthy man is not a poor woman, exactly because the man shares his money with her. Sharing material resources is everywhere a defining characteristic of marriage, and in some countries it is even a legal requirement. This is why the household is the relevant social unit for most analyses of inequality.

Relying on households as the unit of analysis means that the researcher must handle the fact that not all households are of similar size. This is important, because the average member of a big household costs less money than one in a small household. Singles need to purchase many commodities and pay many taxes and fees that couples can share between them. In a technical formulation, we say that the marginal cost of an additional household member is decreasing. To deal with this, most studies of inequality use equivalized income, which factors in decreasing marginal cost. In the Luxembourg Income Study (LIS), the standard approach is to divide the disposable income of the household by the square root of the number of household members. Imagine a situation with two households, one with a single person and another with a couple. The single household has a disposable income of USD 50,000, and the household with the couple USD 100,000. If we did not take the marginal costs of living together into account, the conclusion would be that the average disposable income of both the single and the couple would be identical (USD 50,000, since the couple have to divide their 100,000 by two). Using the equivalized income formulae of LIS, however, the average disposable income of the couple is in fact USD 70,710. If the couple have a child, the average equivalized income drops to USD 57,735. So, even though the third family member does not earn an income to the household, by the formula of equivalization, the average disposable income is still higher than for the single. For each additional child, the equivalized disposable income drops further, so it quickly becomes more profitable to be single. Other data sources use other equivalence scales, but with the same intention and roughly the same result. Eurostat, for instance, counts the first household member aged 14 or more as 1 person, each additional household member 14 or above as 0.5, and each household member aged 13 or below as 0.3.

A final thing to be aware of is the timeframe (Jenkins and van Kerm 2009: 43–4). The standard approach is to measure the level of inequality in a given year. Individual A made so-and-so in a particular year, individual B so-and-so, etc., leading to an overall distribution of income that then can be used to calculate the amount of inequality, as explained in the next section. This can be called a snapshot approach because it conveys a static picture of inequality here and now. Snapshots are valid for many purposes, but have the downside that they fail to capture the mobility of individuals over time. A student may be relatively poor when attending university, but eventually end up making a solid income. In contrast, a long-term unemployed person is also relatively poor, but has much dimmer prospects of becoming better off at some future point. A snapshot of inequality cannot separate those who only temporarily suffer from few resources from those who permanently do so. When making a study of inequality today, it is impossible to know who is only temporarily stuck and who is stuck for good. Getting information on that would require researchers to follow the same individuals over many decades. Fortunately, data on people's occupation, including whether they are students, are collected regularly as part of the snapshot approach, making it possible to look at inequality of particular groups, such as working-age adults excluding students.

Summing up, in comparative research something rather specific is usually meant when talking about inequality: disparities in the post-tax-and-transfer disposable income of equivalized households in a given year. The definition stems in part from lack of alternative measures, which is something future data-collection efforts hopefully will amend. Yet, it still captures some crucial aspects of inequality at the heart of both public debate and scholarly research. Inequality is about the ability of households to maintain economically a certain standard of living and lifestyle. If most families are able to make identical choices of how to live their lives, we intuitively think of them as living in an equal society. In contrast, where families have very different options presented, we intuitively consider them as living in an unequal society. In short, focusing on households' disposable income – as the majority of comparative researchers, in fact, do – is, in our view, frequently the best way to explore inequality.

How to Measure?

Knowing what to measure is only the first step in an analysis of inequality. We also have to figure out how to summarize the empirics into statistical measures that facilitate comparisons across time and place. To begin with, it is necessary to understand the concept of the income distribution. This is the most basic concept to get hold of, because it is inequality in this distribution that traditionally defines what is meant by inequality. Note that the distribution could also be a distribution of wealth, but since earnings inequality is what can be studied in practice, at least in a cross-country comparison, we stick to the common term of income distribution.

Imagine that all the people in a country are lined up according to their income, with the poorest first. The first person in that line would make very little, and perhaps nothing at all. The next person in the line would earn a tiny bit more, and the person after that just a tiny bit more still, and so on. As you pass along the line, incomes will gradually begin to pick up, and towards the end the rich will be standing. Figure 4.1 visualizes the logic. On the horizontal axis, people are lined up with the poorest person first. In this example, it is assumed that there are 99 citizens in the country, so the richest is person number 99. On the vertical axis, the income of each individual is recorded. Here, we assume that the poorest earns 500 and the richest earns 50,000. It is a fundamental feature of all real-world income distributions that they are curvilinear, i.e. flat at the beginning and then getting steeper. After a certain point on the

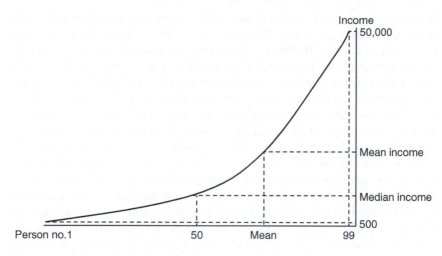

Figure 4.1   *The income distribution*

Source: Created by the authors.

income distribution, incomes do not increase at a steady pace anymore, but accelerate at an ever-higher speed. The very top, as a consequence, is always in a league of its own, even compared with those just before it in the distribution.

Another fundamental feature is that the median income is lower than the mean income. Median income is defined as the income of the person who occupies the middle space in the line of people. In Figure 4.1, that is person number 50, because there are 49 persons to the left and right, respectively, but the same logic applies when the population is counted in millions. In 2013, the median equivalized (i.e. per capita, taking account of household size) disposable income in the United States was USD 31,955, and the mean equivalized disposable income was USD 39,647, a difference of USD 7692, or 24 per cent. In France in 2010, median and mean incomes were EUR 21,021 and EUR 23,882, a difference of 13.6 per cent. In Denmark at the same time, median and mean incomes were DKK 230,668 and 247,152, a 7.1 per cent difference (LIS 2015). As these examples show, mean income is higher than median income even in egalitarian Denmark, but it is also apparent that the difference varies between countries. The methodological challenge is to summarize all this information about the income distribution into one or a few summary statistics, so that comparison becomes easy.

The first summary statistic, the ratio, is in many ways the most straightforward measure both to calculate and to understand (for a general introduction to this and other summary statistics of inequality, see Jenkins and van Kerm 2009: 46–62; Cowell 2011: 17–76). One begins by separating the income distribution into segments, each consisting of 1 per cent of the population. The first 1 per cent encompasses the poorest 1 per cent in society; the next 1 per cent comprises the second poorest 1 per cent, and so on. By convention, the first 1 per cent is called the 1st percentile, the next 1 per cent the 2nd percentile, and the last 1 per cent, unsurprisingly, the 100th percentile. So, when we talk about the 100th percentile, we talk about the richest 1 per cent, and when we talk about the 1st percentile, we talk about the poorest 1 per cent. Naturally, deciles or quintiles can be used instead of percentiles, meaning that rather than separating the income distribution into 100 parts, it is separated into ten or five. The principle is exactly the same, and decile/quintile and percentile ratios can be used in identical ways, assuming that the data are fine-grained enough to allow disaggregation into percentiles. If this is not the case, then deciles and quintiles are employed in empirical research.

The percentile/decile/quintile ratio approach involves comparing how many times richer higher percentiles/deciles/quintiles are compared with lower ones. One commonly used ratio is 90:10, which compares the income of persons in the 90th percentile with the income of persons in the 10th percentile. For example, if the latter group earns USD 10,000 and the former USD 60,000, the 90:10 ratio is 6 (60,000/10,000). Another widely applied ratio is the 90:50. Whereas the 90:10 can be said to compare the income of the rich with the poor, the 90:50 ratio arguably compares the rich with the middle class. Although the 90:10 and 90:50 ratios are the conventional ratio measures, it is possible to calculate any relevant ratio, e.g. the 50:10 comparing the middle class with the poor or the 80:20 comparing the well-off (but not rich) with the low-paid (but not poor). A great strength of the ratio approach, in other words, is that it is flexible to the needs of the researcher. On the other hand, there is no single ratio that sums up all information about the income distribution. They are always partial, focusing on just two groups and ignoring the rest.

The Gini coefficient solves this problem, at least to a point. It is by far the most prominent summary statistic of inequality, and has the undeniable quality that it expresses the degree of inequality in a single figure. Presumably, it is this feature that has made the Gini coefficient the star of the show when it comes to measuring inequality, because it makes it easy to communicate. The underlying logic is uncomplicated and is captured by the Lorentz curve displayed in Figure 4.2. The figure resembles the previous one. Again, the horizontal axis represents the line of people from the poorest to the richest. But this time the vertical axis measures accumulated income, i.e. the total income of all 99 citizens of the country. The Lorentz curve (marked with an A) indicates the distribution of accumulated income. In the example of Figure 4.2, the 50 per cent poorest only earn 15 per cent of all income, while the 80 per cent poorest earn 50 per cent of all income. Hence, the additional 30 per cent of the population bring home 35 per cent of all income – compared with the meagre

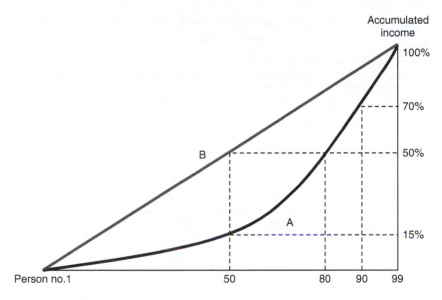

Figure 4.2   *The Lorentz curve*

Source: Created by the authors.

15 per cent the 50 per cent poorest had to share. The 90 poorest earn 70 per cent of all income, meaning that the additional 10 per cent of the population from 80 to 90 per cent get 20 per cent of all earnings. This leaves 30 per cent of all income for the richest 10 per cent.

Having been familiarized with the income distribution earlier, there is not much new about the Lorentz curve itself. Indeed, the Lorentz curve is just another, but slightly less intuitive, way of representing the income distribution visually. Now, consider the linear line labelled B. This is the distribution of accumulated earnings if perfect equality is achieved. Here, the 50 per cent poorest earn half of all income and the 50 per cent richest earn the other half – in which case, calling some rich or poor is obviously nonsense. The Gini coefficient measures how much income needs to be redistributed to get from line A to line B, or, more formally, how big the area between the two lines is relative to the entire area under line B. If everybody has the same income, the Gini coefficient is 0 (perfect equality), and it is 1 if all income belongs to one person alone (perfect inequality). These extremes are never approached. In modern societies, the Gini coefficient normally ranges between 0.2 and 0.5, and year-on-year changes rarely exceed 0.01.

Despite its popularity, the Gini coefficient has some shortcomings. The most important one is that there is little information about the shape of the income distribution contained in the Gini coefficient. The problem is that many different income distributions can generate the same coefficient. Table 4.1 provides an example of this. The five quintiles in

Table 4.1   *Three income distributions with associated Gini coefficients and 5:1 ratios*

Quintiles	Distribution I	Distribution II	Distribution III
1	1000	450	1000
2	1500	2000	1500
3	2000	2400	1600
4	2500	2400	2900
5	3000	2750	3000
Total income	10,000	10,000	10,000
Gini coefficient	0.20	0.20	0.22
5:1 ratio	3.00	6.11	3.00

Source: Created by the authors.

both Distributions I and II have an accumulated income of 10,000 and a Gini coefficient of 0.2. This means that to obtain perfect equality, the same amount of money needs to be reallocated in the two distributions. This is valuable knowledge, but looking more closely at the distributions, it becomes clear that they are very different from each other. In Distribution I, the poorest quintile makes 1000 and the richest 3000, leading to a 5:1 ratio of 3. In Distribution II, the poorest quintile earns 450, compared with 2750 for the richest. This implies a 5:1 ratio of 6.11, or twice the size of the one in Distribution I. In this example, then, the same Gini coefficient masks dramatically different ratios of top vs. bottom earners.

A related shortcoming is that the Gini coefficient is particularly sensitive to changes in the middle of the income distribution (Atkinson 1970: 256–7). Table 4.1 illustrates the problem. In Distribution III, quintile 3, i.e. the median income segment, only earns 1600 rather than 2000 as in Distribution I. The total income is still 10,000 and the 5:1 ratio remains 3, as in Distribution I. Yet, now the Gini coefficient increases to 0.22, whereas in Distribution II the much bigger 5:1 ratio did not translate into a higher Gini coefficient. The wider point of the illustration in Table 4.1 is that changes in the income of the median income segment are likely to have a relatively big effect on the Gini coefficient, while changes in the extremes of the income distribution tend to have a smaller effect. This is relevant, because those using the Gini coefficient often are concerned with how either the rich or the poor are doing, and less with the middle class. But if you want to know whether the well-off are running away from the rest, or whether the poor are being left behind, the Gini coefficient is not all that helpful.

With the publication of Thomas Piketty's *Capital in the Twenty-First Century* (2014) and the associated release of the World Top Incomes Database (Alvaredo et al. 2015), it has become popular to measure inequality as the share of all income going to the rich, e.g. the top 1 per cent or 0.01 per cent earners. For instance, in 2014, 17.9 per cent of all income in the United States went to the 1 per cent richest and 3.1 per cent went to the 0.01 per cent richest. This is interesting, but only tells something about this select segment of the public. There is no information about the shape of the income distribution outside the top, although by definition the great majority of citizens belong exactly there. Are the poor losing ground compared with the middle class? Is the middle class being distanced by the well-off? This kind of question cannot be answered with data on top income shares, at least not without supplementing them with other summary statistics such as the ratio or the Gini coefficient.

There are other measures than the ratio, the Gini coefficient and the share, but these three are the most widely used in comparative research and easy to understand at the same time. The other measures include the Theil and Atkinson indices, which may be suitable for specific types of analyses. The Atkinson index, for instance, is designed to explore which end of the distribution is contributing most to a given level of inequality. It is possible to add weights to the index so that rising inequality in one part of the distribution is considered more important than in other parts. Although a measure like the Atkinson index is more refined than traditional measures, in cross-country comparisons it is seldom likely to lead to substantially different conclusions. For the 30 countries this book draws on when providing empirical illustrations, the bivariate correlation between the Atkinson index and the Gini coefficient is between 0.98 and 0.99, depending on the exact weight of the Atkinson index. For all practical purposes, there is no difference.

Poverty

In debates about inequality, the issue of poverty often emerges. But what is the relationship between inequality and poverty? Poverty comes in two forms: absolute and relative. Absolute poverty is defined as the level of poverty below which people are unable to maintain minimal standards of nutrition, shelter, etc. The threshold of absolute poverty varies between countries because prices vary. The World Bank, for instance, uses USD 1.25 per day as the absolute poverty line for developing countries. In affluent nations the bar is set a little higher, but the measure is meant to capture the same thing. In the United States, the 2014 poverty line was USD 33.74 per day, which is supposed to cover all expenses from housing, through food and sanitation, to whatever other basic needs humans have (US Census Bureau 2014). The poverty line is meant to reflect what such a package of basic goods costs on average, so falling below the absolute poverty line implies that a person has to go without some or all of these basic requirements.

Relative poverty is defined as being poor relative to the normal way of living in a society. The famous free market economist Adam Smith (1776 [1991], Book V, Part II) claimed that poverty is the inability to purchase 'not only the commodities which are indispensably necessary for the support of life, but whatever the custom of the country renders it indecent for creditable people, even of the lowest order, to be without.' Arthur Okun (1975: 69), no unconditional fan of equality, as will become apparent in a subsequent chapter, observes: '[n]o self-respecting family in Boston can sleep in the streets, although that practice is quite acceptable in Bombay. Less dramatically, incomes that would have been regarded as reasonable and respectable a generation ago now leave a family outside the mainstream of middle-class life.' In a nutshell, you are poor not only if you cannot afford enough food and shelter, but also if you have to live in ways that are socially stigmatizing. Relative poverty is usually measured as the share of the population that has less than, say, 60 per cent or 40 per cent of the median income. Earning significantly less than the median income entails that people are denied the opportunity to have the same standard of living and lifestyle as people with a median income. This highlights that relative poverty measures are measures of inequality, nothing more and nothing less. If the median income rises and the bottom incomes stay where they are, relative poverty will increase because the total income of society becomes more unequally distributed.

Some politicians and commentators dislike the term *relative poverty* because to them it signals that people earning less than 60 per cent or 40 per cent of the median income are poor in an absolute sense. Following this line of argument, using the term *relative poverty* artificially inflates the number of poor people. In this way, it becomes impossible to differentiate between 'real' poverty and 'mere' inequality. In principle, we agree with this point of view. Relative poverty is all about inequality, and it would have been preferable if it originally had been baptized so as to make that clear. Inequality, however, is in itself no marginal phenomenon, but has profound consequences for political participation and influence, as we will explain in Chapter 9, but also for outcomes such as social mobility and health, as described in Chapter 3. What is more, earning 40 per cent or even 60 per cent of the median income is no walk in the park. According to the data on equivalized households collected by LIS, the daily 40 per cent threshold was USD 35.02 in the United States in 2013, while the 60 per cent threshold was USD 52.53. In places such as Austria, the Netherlands, Sweden, Germany and Denmark, 40 per cent of median income is no more than around EUR 20 per day, while 60 per cent of median income is around EUR 30 per day (Inequality

Watch 2012). So, although the relative poverty measure is about inequality, the living conditions for those below the relative poverty lines, especially the 40 per cent threshold, often approach absolute poverty.

Data Sources

How do we know what the income distribution looks like? Two different ways of obtaining such knowledge exist. The first is conducting household surveys in which a representative sample of households is asked about income and other relevant factors. Because the sample is representative of the whole population, it is possible to infer the income distribution of the whole country from the survey. The benefits of using a survey are that it is possible to tailor-make it to the study of inequality and to do so in a way that, at least in theory, is similar in all the countries surveyed. The alternative to surveys is the administrative records of national authorities, especially tax collectors. These have data with a much wider coverage, in principle all taxpaying residents, but may not be comparable across countries, because the definitions of what constitutes a certain type of income or tax can vary significantly. Decisions of how to register income and taxes have not been made to facilitate comparative research, so those wanting to use this type of data have to go through a laborious process of streamlining the data. Additionally, national tax records by their nature depend on people not placing their income in tax havens, an assumption that clearly is heroic (Atkinson et al. 2011: 19–29; Zucman 2013).

As mentioned, LIS is traditionally regarded as the golden yardstick of comparative inequality data. It is not that LIS is without its own flaws, but a sustained effort has been made to ensure harmonized data of high quality (Atkinson 2004). LIS is based on household surveys organized in waves that gradually have included more and more countries. Wave I was collected around 1980 and included 12 countries, while the latest waves include more than 30 high- and middle-income countries. In addition, LIS contains nine historical surveys from Canada, Germany, Sweden, the United Kingdom and the United States, covering the period from 1967 to the late 1970s. The individual surveys are typically conducted by agencies of national governments who also sponsor LIS, e.g. the American Census Bureau or the Office of National Statistics in the United Kingdom. In a few cases where administrative data are easily available, notably the Nordic countries, either the survey is not conducted as an interview with members of households, but compiled solely from official registers, or the interview is supplemented with data from such registers. Apart from the data quality, LIS is unique especially in the long time period (several decades) it covers. A downside is that the waves are only collected at 5-year intervals. This means that it can be tricky to isolate the specific causes of a change from one wave to the next, at least within individual countries, where several things might have changed since the last wave. For broader comparisons of country differences, however, the 5-year wave structure is not a major problem.

LIS was a pioneer in terms of comparative inequality data, but today other good data sources exist. The OECD collects data in much the same way as LIS. That is, the organization collects the best national household surveys and then harmonizes them into a common framework. Many of the surveys are, in fact, the same. The OECD dataset has the advantage over LIS in that since 2004 it has aimed at assembling yearly household surveys, which clearly is an improvement. The statistical agency of the European Union, Eurostat, launched its yearly household surveys in 2003, and today covers 32 European countries. Whereas the OECD and LIS data to a large extent come from the same underlying sources, Eurostat's data are collected exclusively for this agency. The member states manage the individual surveys, so the data still require harmonization after being collected, but for most countries this procedure should secure a fairly high quality. Across the three data sources there may, moreover, be slight differences in the exact definition of variables, such as the diverse equivalence scales mentioned above.

To get a sense of how much LIS, OECD and Eurostat diverge from each other, Figure 4.3 displays the Gini coefficient after taxes and

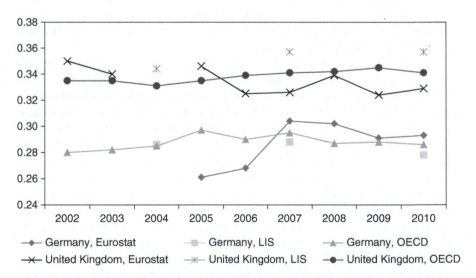

Figure 4.3   *Comparing the Gini coefficient in Germany and the United Kingdom from different data sources*

Note: There is a break in the Eurostat data in 2005 for the United Kingdom.

Source: Eurostat (2015), LIS (2015), OECD (2013b).

transfers in Germany and the United Kingdom. On the horizontal axis the years are listed, starting in 2002 and ending in 2010, and on the vertical axis the Gini coefficient is recorded. Several things are worth noting. First of all, according to all three data sources, the United Kingdom is more unequal than Germany. In 2007, the data series are closest together, but even here a fairly respectable 0.02 points separate them. Most of the time the distance between the two countries is a substantial 0.04 to 0.06 points. This speaks well of the ability of the various data sources to capture the same basic country variation. More worryingly, the reported Gini coefficients are not the same within each country. Most of the time they are quite close, but for Germany in 2005, OECD and Eurostat differ by 0.03, which is too much for comfort. In Germany, LIS and OECD are almost identical, but they rely on the same household survey, the German Social Economic Panel Study, so it is actually more notable that they differ by as much as 0.008 in 2010. Why this is the case is difficult to determine with the available information, but it must stem from the way the raw income data have been aggregated. At the end of the day, however, the main takeaway point from Figure 4.3 is that the different data sources, in fact, did agree on the most important issue, namely, what country is the most unequal. With the exception of Eurostat for Germany, they also agree that there has been no systematic increase in inequality during the, admittedly rather short, time period explored here – but more on this in the next chapter.

There are other data sources than those of LIS, OECD and Eurostat. The Standardized World Income Inequality Database (Solt 2014) collects a huge number of Gini coefficients from around the globe from a variety of data sources. The traditional problem with assembling Gini coefficients in this way is that the underlying data are not harmonized. Some are based on market income, some on post-tax-and-transfer income; some use household equivalence scales, others do not. Based on the large quantity of Gini coefficients, the Standardized World Income Inequality Database innovatively employs a statistical technique called multiple imputation to create new harmonized time series for a full 174 countries, many as far back as 1960. The benchmark used to standardize the array of coefficients is LIS, the methodologically finest data source for comparative research. The Standardized World Income Inequality Database is valuable for studies of inequality outside the Western world, because especially here a lack of good data has been a problem. It is also useful if one is dependent on a long unbroken data series for the analysis. It is important to note, though, that imputation techniques, no matter how sophisticated, essentially construct observations that have never actually been measured empirically. When actually observed data from LIS, OECD or Eurostat are available, the rule of thumb is to rely on these data instead.

The World Top Incomes Database (Alvaredo et al. 2015) is very different from the other data sources. It focuses on the very rich, the top 1 per cent, 0.1 per cent or even 0.01 per cent of the income distribution. In particular, the super-rich, say the top 0.01 per cent, are difficult to interview in household surveys because, by definition, they are so few in number. A survey with fewer than 10,000 interviews would typically not even contain a single respondent from that group, and to get a sufficient number of respondents to draw firm conclusions would require an enormous sample size. The World Top Incomes Database follows the alternative route of collecting tax statistics from governments' administrative records. The researchers behind the database have obtained data on top incomes far back in time, for some countries all the way back to the turn of the 19th century. Such longitudinal data are unmatched by other data sources and provide insights into some of the major transformations Western societies have undergone in the last 100 years.

That said, there are shortcomings with the World Top Incomes Database, which need to be appreciated. First, the incomes are before taxes, whereas transfers have been taken into account. The data, in other words, systematically tend to overestimate the amount of inequality, because richer individuals always pay more in taxes than they receive in social benefits, leading to lower post-redistribution inequality than market inequality (OECD 2011: 227–8). Second, as noted, the database only contains information about the share of all income going to the top. There is no information about the rest of the income distribution. Third, tax data are, as also touched upon before, vulnerable to misreporting by the tax filers, as well as the idiosyncrasies of national tax systems that can make cross-country comparisons hard (Atkinson et al. 2011: 19).

It should be clear from the above that there is rich data material for those wanting to study inequality. The list of data sources highlighted here is, furthermore, not exhaustive. There are, first, the national statistics produced in the individual countries. If the research question relates mostly to developments within a single country, such national statistics are often the best choice. Conversely, national statistics can cause major comparability problems for comparative research. It is exactly the demanding and time-consuming task of harmonizing the data into a common scheme that makes data sources like LIS and Eurostat so valuable. There also exist other multi-country data sources, including the Socio-Economic Database for Latin America, the World Bank's Eastern Europe and Central Asia Database, and the World Income Distribution. All these are worth knowing about for researchers interested in less developed countries. However, many of these datasets do not harmonize the data, so users need to be cautious. It makes a huge difference whether a Gini coefficient measures market or post-tax-and-transfer inequality, or whether it is based on individuals' or households' incomes, just to mention some of the most apparent pitfalls.

In this book we are concerned with developed democracies, and therefore mostly rely on LIS for the empirical illustrations that are provided throughout the book. LIS is used because this is perhaps the best and most reliable measure in existence, although today it is admittedly getting some tough competition for that title from other data sources. The fact that LIS only comes at roughly 5-year intervals, with a lot of variation in how many waves countries have participated in, is not a problem currently. Researchers wanting to estimate time series–cross section regression need to take the unbalanced nature of the LIS dataset into account, but we deliberately keep the statistical analyses simple. LIS also goes reasonably far back in time, beating at least Eurostat, so using LIS allows us to look at historical trends over the past decades. Even LIS data may, however, have shortcomings, and it is, therefore, always a good idea to read the documentation of this and the other data sources before use to make the most informed decision about not only what and how to measure, but also with what data.

Conclusion

Central to most debates about inequality are statements or assumptions about how much inequality there 'really' is in a country and how much it 'really' has grown or dropped. Such empirical facts are vital for understanding the societies we live in, and in Chapter 5 a host of different measures will be presented. Too often, however, people jump directly to such descriptions and forget to consider what the data reported show. How much do we, for example, learn from a rising Gini coefficient? If we want to know about the grand total of inequality in society, perhaps a lot, but if we want to know whether those in the bottom are getting left behind or those in the top are running away from the rest, not much at all. Here other metrics are needed. Measures such as the 90:10 or 90:50 ratios are simple, but frequently more informative than the famous Gini coefficient, and there are many other measures readily available.

Even more basic than the metrics used is the question of what sort of inequality to study. There are many good reasons why inequality in earnings is the main focal point in most research: earnings are hugely important for ordinary people; there are big disparities in earnings, with massive consequences for outcomes such as health and social mobility; and data on earnings inequality exist for many countries and for several decades. Still, earnings inequality is only part of the story. Inequalities in wealth – houses, stocks and all sorts of other assets – are, as far as the data allow us to conclude, even bigger than for earnings. It is worth bearing in mind that most of the data reported in news media and used by politicians and commentators in the public debate relate to earnings, and, as a result, significantly underestimate the true extent of inequalities.

Chapter 5

What are the empirical patterns?

This chapter outlines the main cross-country and temporal variation in economic inequality. It is the political causes and consequences of this variation that the rest of the book is concerned with, so we spend some time mapping the details. For starters, some countries are much more unequal than others, but, contrary to the impression one regularly gets from the public debate, it is not simply a matter of 'the United States versus the rest'. Many countries exhibit a high level of inequality, including some that are not traditionally associated with American-style capitalism. Other interesting observations relate to the trends in inequality over time. The first decades after World War II signalled a period of exceptionally low levels of inequality across all Western democracies, although cross-country difference still existed. Since then, dramatic changes have occurred. Some countries have witnessed large increases in inequality, while others have stayed more or less as they were. It is the combination of this cross-country and over-time variation that we need to account for if we wish to understand the politics of inequality.

Cross-Country Patterns of Inequality

This section looks at how countries vary in their levels of inequality. Figure 5.1 displays the Gini coefficients in a total of 30 developed democracies, employing the latest year with available data on equivalized disposable household incomes from LIS. For the majority of countries, the latest year is 2010. The Gini coefficient is the natural statistic to start with because it captures the overall amount of inequality in a society. On the horizontal axis the Gini coefficient is recorded, and on the vertical axis the countries are listed, with the most unequal at the top and the most equal at the bottom. The United States sits at the top. Its Gini coefficient weighs in at 0.382. It is followed by a mix of countries. One group exhibiting high levels of inequality comprises the Anglo-Saxon nations, including – apart from the United States – the United Kingdom (0.357), Australia (0.330), Canada (0.317) and Ireland (0.294). Another group is southern Europe, with Spain (0.334), Greece (0.333) and Italy (0.327), whereas a third group consists of a mixed bag with Israel (0.379), Taiwan (0.318) and South Korea (0.311). Towards the bottom one finds the Nordic countries, with Sweden (0.237), followed by Denmark

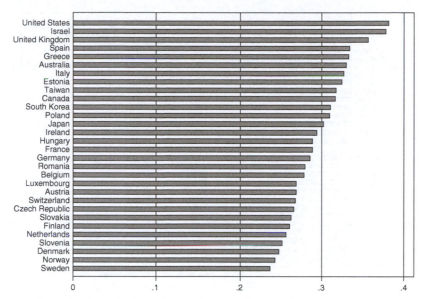

Figure 5.1 *Gini coefficients in 30 developed countries*

Note: Calculation based on equivalized disposable household incomes. Data for the latest available year is reported.

Source: LIS (2015).

(0.248), Norway (0.243) and Finland (0.261). Other small northern and continental European countries have similar levels. Slovenia (0.252) is the third most equal country, with the Netherlands (0.257) and Slovakia (0.263) coming in as fifth and seventh, respectively. In the middle of the scale, the big continental European countries of Germany (0.286) and France (0.289) reside.

The Gini coefficient is a fairly artificial measure, and the meaning of a given coefficient is not intuitive. Is the difference between Sweden and the United States, 0.150 points, big or small? Additionally, the Gini coefficient tells us nothing about the share of the different income groups in the distribution. Both of these issues can be helped by moving to ratios. Figure 5.2 shows the 90:10 ratios. The ratio is on the horizontal axis. Recall, a ratio of, say, 4 means that the income in the 90th percentile is four times bigger than the income in the 10th percentile – after taxes and transfers are accounted for, that is. This is a substantially more meaningful figure than the Gini coefficient. It transpires that the ranking of countries is by and large the same as before, even though Israel now takes the prize as the most unequal country, with a 90:10 ratio of 6.280. Someone in the 90th percentile of the income distribution in Israel will have over six times more to spend than someone in the 10th. At the other end of the scale we find Sweden, which has a 90:10 ratio of 2.821, i.e. around

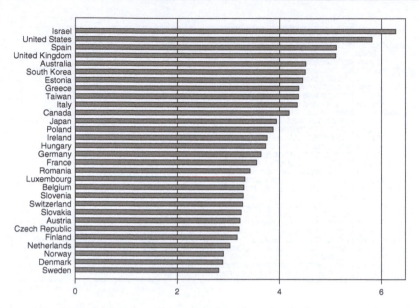

Figure 5.2   *90:10 ratios in 30 developed countries*

Source: LIS (2015).

half the size of Israel. It is worth underscoring that this does not make Sweden an equal society in any absolute sense. The well-off household in the 90th percentile still has almost three times the disposable income of the not so well-off household in the 10th percentile.

The 90:10 ratio gets at the difference between those at the top, the affluent, and those at the bottom, the poor. The 90:50 ratio, in contrast, measures the distance between the affluent and the median income. The median income segment is interesting because it reflects the situation of the middle class in society. As explained in later chapters, the median-income voter, or more broadly the middle class, is often crucial in political terms, so knowing about the ratio between the median income and the top is important. Figure 5.3 displays the 90:50 ratios for the 30 countries. The ranking of countries is roughly the same as before, with Israel as the most unequal, followed closely by the United States and the United Kingdom. At the bottom end Norway is located, in company with Denmark and Sweden. It is, moreover, not surprising that the ratios in general are smaller than before. Israel has a ratio of 2.302, indicating that households in the 90th percentile have a disposable income a little more than twice the size of the income of households in the 50th percentile. The smaller ratios follow mathematically from the fact that the median income is higher than the income of the 10th percentile.

However, it is surprising that the variation between countries is much smaller than for the 90:10 ratio, even allowing for the lower levels of

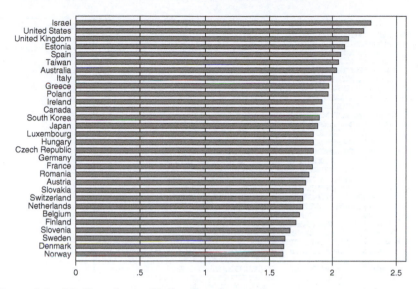

Figure 5.3 *90:50 ratios in 30 developed countries*

Source: LIS (2015).

the ratios. One way to gauge this is to calculate the coefficient of variation, which is done by dividing the standard deviation of a number by its
mean. The standard deviation of the 90:10 ratio is 0.867 and the mean
is 3.891, yielding a coefficient of variation of 0.222. For the 90:50 ratio,
the standard deviation is 0.177, the mean 1.885 and the coefficient of
variation as a result 0.094. In sum, cross-country variation is more than
double for the 90:10 ratio relative to the 90:50 ratio. The small cross-
country variation is an interesting phenomenon and mirrors Palma's
(2011: 101–4) finding that almost everywhere across the world, the 40th
to 90th percentiles earn 50 per cent of all income. The remaining 50 per
cent is then split between the top 10 per cent and the bottom 40 per cent
of the population in ways that vary dramatically between countries. It is
possible to speculate that this is a manifestation of the universal importance of the middle class in democratic politics, making it hard anywhere
to let this income group fall too far behind the affluent. The poor, as represented by the 10th percentile, are, on the other hand, less universally
important as a political force. We will return to this discussion later on.
For now, the thing to notice is how this basic fact points to the need for
exploring the shape of the income distribution with great care.

Another ratio worth studying is the 80:20. It supplements the other
ratios because, on the one hand, it disregards the extreme ends of the
income distribution, but, on the other, it still provides a measure of
the distance between top and bottom. By disregarding the extremes

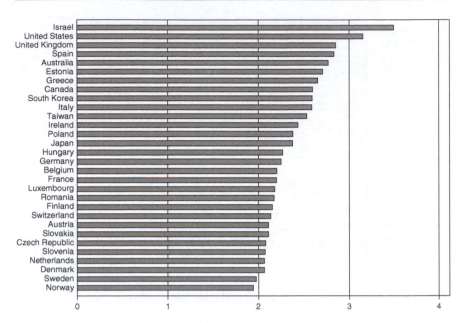

Figure 5.4   *80:20 ratios in 30 developed countries*

Source: LIS (2015).

of the distribution, the 80:20 can be argued to better capture the reality of people in the economic mainstream. The middle class is, in daily parlance, everybody who is not outright poor or rich. In this expansive sense, the 80:20 ratio informs us about the heterogeneity of the middle class. The 80th percentile can be said to constitute the upper middle class, while the 20th percentile constitutes the lower middle class. In Figure 5.4 the familiar ranking appears again, with Israel, the United States and the United Kingdom at the top and Norway, Sweden and Denmark at the bottom. Israel's ratio is 3.498 and in Norway it is 1.943, so even in egalitarian Norway someone from the upper middle class has twice the amount to spend as someone from the lower middle class. The coefficient of variation is 0.153, midway between those of the 90:10 and 90:50 ratios. This shows that the need or desire to ensure a homogeneous middle class differs quite a bit between countries.

Another helpful measure when evaluating the heterogeneity of the middle class is the median-to-mean distance. The income distribution is always right-skewed, meaning that the median income is lower than the mean income (see Figure 4.1 for an illustration). If the mean and median incomes were identical, the 'richest' half would have exactly as much as the 'poorest' half. The median-to-mean distance captures just how far away is the income of the person who, numerically speaking, cuts the population into two equally sized portions from the income that cuts

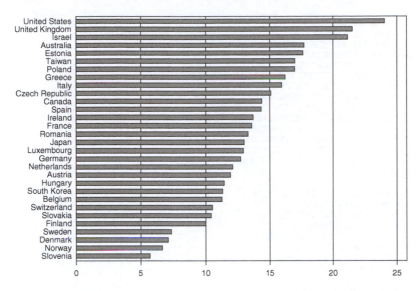

Figure 5.5 *Percentage difference between the median and the mean income*

Source: LIS (2015).

the total income of a society in half. It is calculated as the percentage by which the mean income is bigger than the median income. Whereas the 80:20 can be said to imply a broad definition of what constitutes the middle class in economic terms, the median-to-mean distance implies a narrow one. It focuses on inequalities within the core of the middle class, namely, those households earning at least the median income. Figure 5.5 summarizes the details. It is important to note that the figure displays percentages and not ratios, so the variation between countries automatically appears larger than in the previous figures. Because we want to look at a minor section of the income distribution, this is a valid method, but it means that it is not possible to compare the variation directly across measures. The mean income is more than 20 per cent bigger than the median income in the United States, the United Kingdom and Israel. At the bottom, in the Nordic countries and Slovenia, the distance is three to four times lower. Even within the middle class, in other words, there is inequality in some countries, but much less in others.

Figure 5.6 displays the proportion of a country's households that earn less than 40 per cent of the median income. This is the debated relative poverty measure, which some view with suspicion because it can give an inflated impression of the number of really poor people. As pointed out, relative poverty is a measure of inequality, not poverty, but we also stressed that those households making 40 per cent or less of the median income frequently border on being poor in an absolute sense as well;

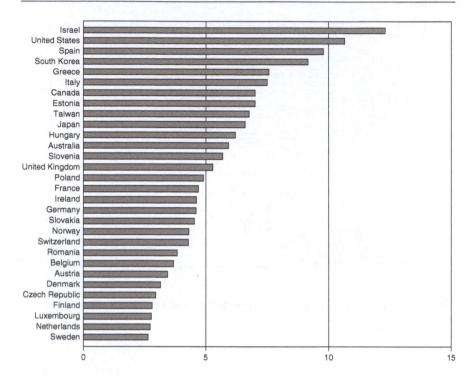

Figure 5.6   *Share of population earning 40 per cent or less of the median income*

Source: LIS (2015).

i.e. they have difficulty in paying for housing, food and other basic requirements. As a minimum, earning 40 per cent of the median income means that the standard of living one is able to enjoy is very different from that of the middle class, no matter how broadly this is defined. In the figure, the horizontal axis shows the percentage of the population living in households earning less than 40 per cent of the median income. There is big cross-country variation. Israel stands out as hosting the largest share, 12.3 per cent, followed by the United States with 10.7 per cent. It is noteworthy that the southern European and East Asian countries cluster more towards the top on this measure than on the previous ones, whereas a country like the United Kingdom is now placed in the middle. This probably reflects a more effective social assistance system in the United Kingdom compared with the other nations. At the bottom, a fairly large group of countries all have less than 5 per cent of their population living on less than 40 per cent of the median income. Sweden comes in as the least unequal with 2.6 per cent, but in a country with 10 million inhabitants, this still amounts to many thousands of households.

Several things are worth noting from these six figures. First, and most obviously, there is a huge cross-country variation in the degree of inequality. It may come as no surprise to most that the United States is at or near the top on all the measures displayed here. The egalitarian streak of the Nordics is probably also well known to many. Consistently, however, the southern European countries exhibit high levels of inequality too, as do South Korea, Taiwan and Israel. Israel is, in fact, by several counts more unequal than the United States. The eastern European countries, in particular Slovenia and Slovakia, are characterized by almost Nordic levels of equality. Second, there is more variation in some measures than in others. Taken together, the lesson is that cross-country variation in inequality above all reflects that the less well-off are lagging severely behind the rest in some countries but less so elsewhere. In contrast, at least when compared with the 90th percentile, the middle class appears to be treated in a similar fashion everywhere, although there is more heterogeneity in the middle class in those countries that in general are most unequal.

Trends in Inequality

To study the development in inequality, we focus on six countries that together represent distinct social models. The United Kingdom and the United States are characterized by low levels of government intervention in the economy. Both countries have comparably small welfare states (but see Chapter 8) and deregulated business environments. Germany and Italy are far away from this hands-off model. Germany is the arch-typical conservative welfare state, with occupational-based social insurance programmes and tight integration of unions and employer organizations into corporatist structures that facilitate negotiation and compromise in the labour market. Italy shares many traits with Germany, especially the occupational-based social insurances, but has a bigger divide between labour market insiders and outsiders, i.e. between those with a secure job and those who are either unemployed or on a temporary contract. Lastly, Sweden and Denmark represent the Nordic social model, with generous social benefits and a small pool of labour market outsiders (Esping-Andersen 1990; Pontusson 2005: 15–28; Häusermann and Schwander 2012; Van Kersbergen and Vis 2014: 53–77; for more details, see Chapters 7 and 8).

Figure 5.7 presents the trends of the six inequality statistics from the previous section in the United Kingdom and the United States. For both countries, the data series begin around 1970, and they end in 2010 for the United Kingdom and in 2013 for the United States. Starting in the top left corner, the Gini coefficient is reported. The open circles symbolize the United States and the filled circles the United Kingdom. In the

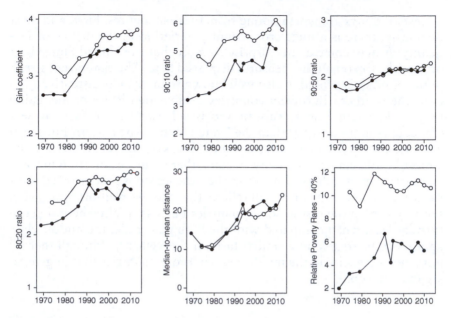

Figure 5.7   *Trends in inequality in the United Kingdom and the United States*

Note: Filled circles represent the United Kingdom; open circles represent the United States.

Source: LIS (2015).

early 1970s, the Gini coefficient was 0.268 in the United Kingdom and 0.316 in the United States, but in the early 1980s a dramatic increase sets in. In the United Kingdom, the Gini increases from 0.267 in 1979, the year Margaret Thatcher's Conservative Party enters government, to 0.303 in 1986, and continues to rise to 0.336 in 1991. The growth levels off a bit in the rest of the period, but the economic boom years of the mid-2000s witness an additional rise to 0.357. In the United States, the story is much the same, and coincides with Ronald Reagan's presidency. From an all-time low of 0.299 in 1979, the Gini coefficient increases rapidly throughout the 1980s until 1997, where it reaches a plateau at 0.372, which is more or less maintained for the rest of the period. The 90:10 ratio follows a similar pattern, with substantial increases in the first part of the 1980s that persist up till today. The rise is particularly significant in the United Kingdom, where household income in the 90th percentile was three times that in the 10th percentile in 1969, but five times in 2010. The 90:50 ratio also exhibits an increase, but much smaller than the one in the 90:10. It is also remarkable that the two countries throughout the four decades have virtually the same ratios.

Moving to the bottom row, the 80:20 informs us about how economically alike people belonging to the middle class are. In the United

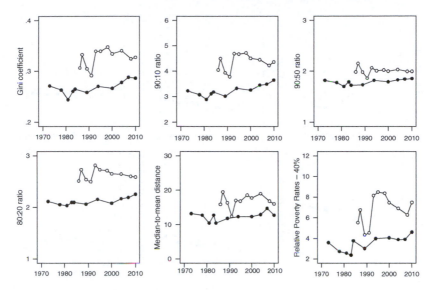

Figure 5.8   *Trends in inequality in Italy and Germany*

Note: Filled circles represent Germany; open circles represent Italy.
Source: LIS (2015).

Kingdom, someone from the upper middle class (the 80th percentile) in the 1970s earned a little more than twice the amount of someone in the lower middle class (the 20th percentile). During the 1980s, that gap expanded to a little less than three times. A similar, but less marked, trend can be seen in the United States. The next panel focuses on the median-to-mean distance. In the mid- to late 1970s, mean income is only 10 per cent higher than the income of the median, but again, the 1980s are a watershed, after which the distance doubles to 20 per cent by the early 1990s. The final measure is the relative poverty rate. The United States has mostly seen stability, although the 1980s saw increases. In the United Kingdom, the share of households living on less than 40 per cent of the median income tripled from 1969 to 1991. Tellingly, the United Kingdom and the United States have had very different levels of relative poverty. Whereas it is around 10 per cent in the United States, it used to be just 2 per cent in the United Kingdom, and still remains half of the American rate. This indicates, as mentioned above, that the United Kingdom has a social system that protects reasonably well against serious poverty, certainly compared with the United States.

Figure 5.8 presents the same six measures for Italy (open circles) and Germany (filled circles). The same scale is used on the individual panels of the figure as in Figure 3.10, to facilitate comparison. The contrast with the Anglo-Saxon experience is stark. There has only been a slight tendency towards more inequality when one looks at the Gini coefficient

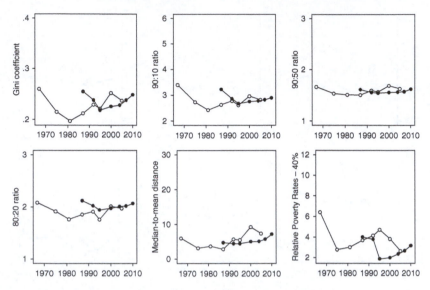

Figure 5.9   *Trends in inequality in Sweden and Denmark*

Note: Filled circles represent Denmark; open circles represent Sweden.

Source: LIS (2015).

and the 90:10 ratio. In Italy, the Gini increased from 0.306 in 1986 to 0.327, and the 90:10 ratio from 4.045 to 4.350. In Germany, where data are available for a longer period, the Gini coefficient increased from 0.271 to 0.286 and the 90:10 ratio from 3.221 to 3.638. In Germany, practically all the increase has occurred since 2000, when a string of reforms, including the iconic Hartz IV, changed the unemployment system. In Germany in the 2000s, there are also minor surges in the 80:20 ratio and the median-to-mean distance. In Italy, the movement is actually in the opposite direction, towards less inequality. To a large extent, the most dramatic change happened in Italy in the early 1990s, when an economic crisis reversed the decline in inequality that had been going on since the mid-1980s. The most pronounced manifestation of the Italian crisis of the early 1990s was in the 90:10 ratio and the relative poverty rate, demonstrating that the main victims of that event were the low-income groups.

Figure 5.9 shows the trends for Sweden (open circles) and Denmark (filled circles). The two countries resemble each other, but the Swedish data go back to 1967, whereas the Danish data begin in 1987. Throughout the observed period, the countries boast low levels of inequality compared with not just the United Kingdom and United States, but also Italy and Germany. The Gini coefficient and the 90:10 ratio declined in Sweden from the late 1960s to the 1980s. A crisis in the early 1990s

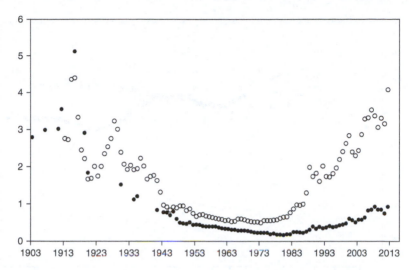

Figure 5.10 *Trends in top 0.01 per cent income share in Sweden and the United States*

Note: Filled circles represent Sweden; open circles represent the United States.

Source: Alvaredo et al. (2015).

can be spotted, especially in the relative poverty rate, which, however, dropped from the late 1990s back to its level in the 1970s. Denmark has seen an increasing Gini coefficient, 90:10 and 80:20 ratios, and relative poverty rate since the mid-1990s, but the order of magnitude is small relative to the changes in the United Kingdom and the United States. The overwhelming impression is one of stability and, at least until the 1990s, even reduction of inequality. Still, it is worth noting that those changes that do occur relate to the position of low-income groups, not the more well-to-do as represented by the 90:50 ratio. In this sense, the Nordic countries embody the same tendencies as the other four countries.

So far, the affluent of society have been measured with the 90th percentile. Someone in that income bracket is indeed well off by the standards of most people, but is not rich. To get at the truly rich – the millionaires and billionaires – it is necessary to select a much narrower group. As discussed in the previous chapter, that is not possible with household survey data. Instead, the tax-based data of the World Top Incomes Database can be used. These data allow us to look at the top 0.01 per cent of earners, a much more exclusive segment than the 90th percentile. It is also possible to trace developments for more than 100 years. Figure 5.10 displays the income of the top 0.01 per cent in the United States (open circles) and Sweden (filled circles), the two countries most vividly representing the polar opposites of equality. For these

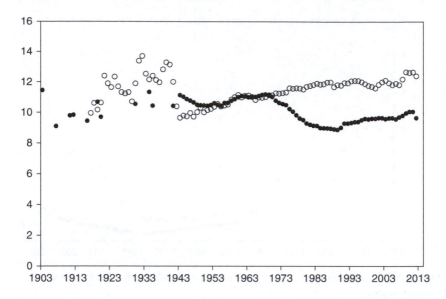

Figure 5.11   *Trends in top 10–5 per cent income share in Sweden and the United States*

Note: Filled circles represent Sweden; open circles represent the United States.

Source: Alvaredo et al. (2015).

countries, there are, furthermore, particularly good data series. The vertical axis lists the share of total income going to the top 0.01 per cent. In 1903, that share was 2.8 per cent in Sweden, or almost 300 times bigger than if there had been perfect equality. In 1916, that figure had doubled to 5.1 per cent. Much the same levels are observed in the United States. In 1913, the first year with data, the top 0.01 per cent's share is 2.8 per cent of all income, rising to 4.4 per cent in 1916. In both countries, these high levels collapse after World Wars I and II.

In the post-war decades, both countries exhibit comparably low shares. In Sweden in 1970, 0.3 per cent of all income went to the top 0.01 per cent, compared with 0.5 per cent in the United States. This means that the top 0.01 per cent got roughly 30 and 50 times, respectively, more than they would have had under perfect equality. In other words, even though inequalities are reduced, they are not eliminated. From the early 1980s onwards, the countries part ways. The United States begins a dramatic increase in the income share of the top 0.01 per cent, which is much less visible in Sweden. By 2012, the American share had reached 4.1 per cent compared with the Swedish share of 0.9 per cent. The rising shares in the United States, and to a lesser extent in Sweden, suggest that even though the 90th percentile may not have distanced itself from the median income, the rich are pulling away from everybody else. To show that this is what happens, Figure 5.11 displays the income share of the top 10–5 per cent, i.e. from the 90th to the 95th percentile. The difference in the top 0.01 per cent is revealing. In both Sweden and the United States, the income share of the affluent-but-not-rich has been more or less stable for three decades.

Summing up, several observations stand out. The most crucial is that inequality has grown more in the United Kingdom and the United States than in the Nordic and continental European countries. This is a consistent finding whether using data from LIS or from the World Top Incomes Database. The 1980s, the decade of Margaret Thatcher and Ronald Reagan, mark a turning point in these countries, setting in motion developments that, with varying speed, have continued until today. Another point is that inequality appears to have increased mostly because of what happens at the bottom and the very top. In the United Kingdom and the United States, the middle class is also stretched out a bit more than before. Yet here, too, the most substantial change has been that those at the bottom have been detached from the middle class, while the really rich, the top 0.01 per cent, have grown very wealthy, isolating them from the rest of society.

Conclusion

The chapter started by emphasizing that great care is needed when studying inequality empirically. The conclusions that can be made are in large part a function of the methodological decisions of the researcher, as we discussed in Chapter 4. In this chapter, we documented that it is by no means irrelevant which measures are chosen. Some, such as the 90:10 ratio and the relative poverty rate, exhibit great cross-country and temporal variation, while others, such as the 90:50 ratio, exhibit much less. Importantly, the measures capture different aspects of inequality and should never be used interchangeably. That the 90:50 ratio is less variable than the 90:10 does not mean that the former does not work for measuring inequality. It means, rather, that while people in the 90th percentile make more money than those in the 50th, the ratio between the two is broadly the same everywhere and has remained stable for decades. This information is just as valuable as knowing that the losers of the past couple of decades, and especially so in the United States and the United Kingdom, are the least well-off in society.

The data chosen ought to reflect the question at hand. Do we want to know about whether a group in society is being left at the bottom? Then a combination of the 90:10 and 50:10 ratios will probably be a good way to start. If we want to know whether the rich are getting isolated at the top, then the top income shares may be relevant. If we want to know about the middle class, probably the best place to begin is by looking at the 90:50 and 50:10 ratios. It is interesting to note that very few politically relevant questions actually are best answered using the Gini coefficient, because this particular measure captures the entire income distribution. Yet, normally, we want to know about how some groups are doing compared with others. Although we ourselves, for the sake of sticking to conventions, will use the Gini coefficient a lot in the rest of the book, it is a very imprecise measure for many purposes.

Chapter 6

Does inequality matter for growth?

There is no such thing as a free lunch, so if you want equality, you have to accept the damage that it does to the drive and energy of society. This is because people who live in unequal societies have more to fight for, and therefore make a greater effort to be successful in life, whereas people in more equal societies are sheltered from their own bad decisions and laziness. To ensure a vibrant and growing economy, it is, consequently, necessary to make sure that equality does not get out of hand or, if it has already done so, to scale it back. In a nutshell, this is the equality–efficiency trade-off. To many, this type of reasoning about the relationship between growth and inequality sounds intuitively correct. However, as we will explain in this chapter, the most balanced conclusion is that there is no correlation between the inequalities that are observed in rich democracies and economic growth. The reason is not that inequality and growth are unrelated, but that there is more than one road to economic development: one that entails high levels of inequality and another that involves low levels. These different paths are explored in Chapter 7.

We begin by sketching two classic perspectives on the relationship between inequality and growth. The first is optimistic and essentially says that attention should be on creating as much growth as possible, because equality will automatically follow. Among the optimistic accounts, the so-called Kuznets curve is prominent. The argument is that countries go through a sequence as they develop economically, with inequality first rising and then dropping as affluence spreads widely throughout society. The Kuznets curve implies that it has to get bad before it gets good, but that eventually both prosperity and equality will be achieved. Other related arguments are 'trickle-down' economics and the notion that a rising tide lifts all boats. 'Okun's leaky buckets' is the most famous formulation of the pessimistic perspective. The pessimists hold that creating equality inevitably implies a loss of efficiency, and the leaky bucket metaphor has become a symbol for those opposing extensive redistribution.

After having discussed the optimistic and pessimistic accounts below, we introduce a competing argument, which holds that too much inequality can hurt growth. High levels of inequality mean that the purchasing power of ordinary people gets reduced, and this, in turn, reduces demand for the goods and services of the private sector. This is particularly relevant because the share of GDP going to wages has declined substantially since the 1970s. The chapter ends by discussing alternative measures of prosperity to GDP, which has been criticized for being biased and imprecise. Rather than GDP, happiness has been proposed as an alternative, though still unconventional, measure, and we end by outlining how inequality affects happiness.

The Optimistic View

The Kuznets curve was originally presented, though not labelled, by Simon Kuznets. In his own words, '[o]ne might thus assume a long swing in the inequality characterizing the secular income structure: widening in the early phases of economic growth when the transition from the pre-industrial to the industrial civilization was most rapid; becoming stabilized for a while; and then narrowing in the later phases' (Kuznets 1955: 18). This means that economic growth in the long run will be beneficial not only for the rich, but also for the less well-off. This basic notion resembles, and has probably to a certain extent inspired, several other optimistic arguments about the effect of economic growth on inequality (Piketty 2014: 13–15).

One of these is the so-called *trickle-down economics*, a viewpoint embraced by fiscal conservatives since the 1980s, especially in the Anglo-Saxon countries (Jones and Williams 2008; Quiggin 2012: 136–73). The argument is that, although the immediate consequence of a tax cut may be to raise the earnings of the wealthy compared with the rest of society, the money will eventually flow downwards. In Quiggin's formulation,

> [t]he general idea is that, the greater the rewards given to owners of capital and highly skilled managers, the more productive they will be. This will lead both to the provision of goods and services at lower cost and to higher demand for the services of low-skilled workers who will therefore earn higher wages. (Quiggin 2012: 148)

Less starkly, another variant poetically claims that economic growth is a tide that lifts all boats, including those with poorer passengers. Policies to enhance growth may, in other words, increase inequality, but are not bad for the less well-off, at least not in the long run.

Kuznets' argument is, in all fairness, very different from the broad-ranging propositions of trickle-down economics and related allegories. Kuznets discusses a specific historical phenomenon, namely, the transition from agricultural to industrial production, and focuses on the experience of the United States and a few European countries in the late 19th and early 20th centuries (until roughly the 1950s). For this period in time, it seems to be correct that inequality first rose and then later dropped (see for a contemporary application Milanovic 2016). The last phase appears in Figure 5.10, where the collapse in the top 0.01 per cent's income share in the first half of the 20th century is clearly visible in both Sweden and the United States. That said, Figure 5.10 also documents that this is not a tendency that continues. In both Sweden and the United States, inequality later increases, and particularly so in the latter country. In Figures 5.7–5.9, similar trends were found for the period since the 1970s across a wider set of countries and measures. The United Kingdom and the United States have witnessed a tremendous growth in inequality, with Germany, Italy, Denmark and Sweden trailing behind at various distances. Including other countries would not change this impression, because they all have seen increases that fall between the lows of Denmark and Sweden and the highs of the United Kingdom and the United States.

The point is twofold. First, because all these countries have experienced real growth of the economy for almost all the time since the 1970s, there is nothing to indicate that growth automatically, or even as the general rule, leads to lower inequality. In the established democracies we study in this book, average income has approximately doubled since 1975. In the United States, average inflation-adjusted income increased from USD 22,886 to USD 45,710. German incomes went up from USD 19,559 to USD 39,219, while British and Swedish ones grew from USD 19,772 to USD 40,231 and USD 25,438 to USD 45,588, respectively (World Bank 2015). Clearly, a rising tide does not lift all boats to the same extent (for a similar conclusion, see Palma 2011: 126). Second, the substantial cross-country variation in changing inequality indicates that there is no single master-factor that drives developments across national contexts. To understand why inequality goes up more in some places than in others, we must study the institutional and political characteristics of individual countries.

Since the heydays of Thatcher and Reagan in the 1980s, the United Kingdom and the United States have seen sustained pro-rich policies in the form of tax cuts, deregulation of labour markets and welfare state retrenchment, much more so than in the Nordic and continental European countries (for overviews of policy developments, see Korpi and Palme 2003; Jones and Williams 2008; Hacker and Pierson 2010; Clasen and Clegg 2011; Scruggs et al. 2014). It is, therefore, noteworthy that it is exactly where these pro-rich policies have gone furthest that inequality has increased the most. This flies in the face of the prediction of trickle-down economics. Given the empirical evidence, it is not surprising that a number of prominent economists have criticized the idea of wealth trickling down the income ladder.

Galbraith noted several decades ago that trickle-down economics requires you to believe that businessmen and business executives, because of their tax bracket, are now idling away their time – in the forthright language of my Canadian youth, are buggering off. Tax reduction will put them back to work. And they will save and invest the income so released – even in Dallas and Palm Springs. I have a far better view of the American businessman: I judge him to be working very hard now, and I believe him to be decently ensconced in the American dream. Given more money, and with the help of his wife and family, he will spend and enjoy most of it. (Galbraith 1982: 10)

Three decades after Galbraith, Quiggin (2012: 152–67) takes stock of the empirics, observing that '[a]ll the evidence supports the common-sense conclusion that policies designed to benefit the rich at the expense of the poor have done precisely that' (see also Jones and Williams 2008: 85; Stiglitz 2013: 8–9; Prillaman and Meier 2014).

The Pessimistic View

'We can't have our cake of market efficiency and share it equally', said Okun (1975: 2), summarizing the view of the pessimists, whose fundamental claim is that there is a trade-off between equality and economic growth. Okun tries to illustrate his point by likening redistribution to transport with a leaky bucket. When money is moved from one group of people to another, inevitably some of it will get lost because it seeps from the bucket *en route*. The bucket of redistribution is leaky for a number of reasons (ibid.: 96–100). One concerns the administrative costs of setting up a bureaucracy to handle the operation. Another is the reduced willingness to save and invest in a situation where government is carrying much of the risk of social failure, although this 'is the leakage most widely cited and confirmed least convincingly' (ibid.: 98). A third negative effect stems from the detrimental consequences on work efforts when taxes are high and the benefits from performing well are diminished. Lazear and Rosen (1981) have formalized this intuition in a widely known article: the likelihood of providing the extra – winning – effort increases with the incentives available. Fourth and finally, there can be an effect on the attitudes of the public, culminating in a drop in the entrepreneurial spirit of a country's population.

None or all of these mechanisms may be at play, but it turns out that whether or not they are has no bearing on the overall economic performance of countries. The core contention of the pessimists is that countries with a lot of equality get lower growth and, hence, end up poorer than the less equal countries. A straightforward way to evaluate this claim is to look at countries' GDP per capita. GDP per capita measures the average income of all citizens and is the conventional way to capture societal affluence. Figure 6.1 ranks the countries with the highest

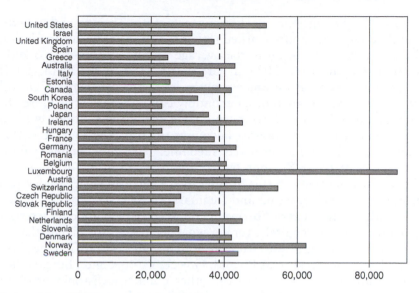

Figure 6.1 *GDP per capita in 2013*

Note: GDP per capita in USD corrected for purchasing power parity (PPP). Mean of all countries is USD 38,563. Countries are ranked according to their latest Gini coefficient, with the country with the highest Gini at the top. The dashed vertical line is the average across all countries.

Source: The World Bank (2015).

Gini coefficient at the top and the lowest at the bottom, using the latest data available. For each country, the figure displays GDP per capita for the year 2013. In this way, it immediately becomes possible to assess whether there is a correlation between inequality and GDP per capita. If the pessimists are right, GDP per capita should be high in unequal countries and low in equal countries. It transpires that no correlation exists. With USD 51,340, the United States scores above the mean of all countries in the figure, which is USD 38,563 (represented by the dashed line), but from then on things get messy. Seven of the ten most unequal countries have below-average GDP per capita. Some of these have only recently become democratic, which might explain their low level, but also long-established systems such as Israel (USD 31,028), the United Kingdom (USD 37,017) and Italy (USD 34,167) underperform. At the other end, only three out of ten of the most equal countries score below the average. It is clear from Figure 6.1 that even if we look at the old democracies, the only country with a high Gini coefficient that really performs well economically is the United States. A number of countries with low Gini coefficients, by contrast, have a GDP per capita above the average, including the Netherlands (USD 44,944), Denmark (USD 41,990), Sweden (USD 43,741) and Norway (USD 62,448).

To get at the efficiency of different economies, it is arguably better to look at GDP per hours worked rather than the yearly accumulation. There is a lot of variation in the average numbers of hours worked – in 2013, ranging from 2037 in Greece to 1380 in the Netherlands. An economy that can produce a given level of GDP per capita with fewer hours spent than another economy can be regarded as more efficient. Figure 6.2 reports how much GDP is produced per hour worked, with the most unequal countries again at the top. The average is USD 41.39, marked with the vertical dashed line. The United States is above the average with 56.88, but Israel, Spain, Greece and Italy all fall below. The top three in terms of equality all perform well. Sweden produces 46.30, Norway 62.63 and Denmark 46.88 USD per hour. In several southern and eastern European countries, which are characterized by a low GDP per capita, average working hours are higher than in more affluent places in western Europe. This entails that GDP per hour worked in countries such as Poland, Greece, Estonia and Hungary ends up even lower compared with the other countries. Estonia produces least per hour, with only USD 22.71. In sum, Figure 6.2 shows that there is little support for the pessimists' view of an equality–efficiency trade-off.

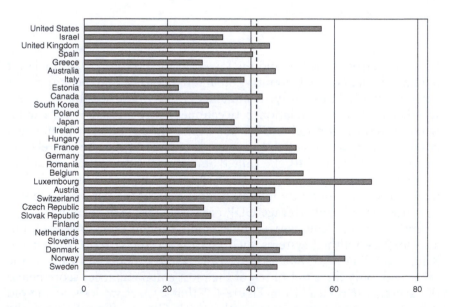

Figure 6.2   *GDP per hours worked in 2013*

Note: GDP per capita are constant 2005 USD. The dashed vertical line is the average across all countries.

Source: OECD (2015a).

GDP per capita captures the level of wealth that is available for a population to enjoy. Strictly speaking, it does not measure the speed at which an economy expands, but only the absolute level it has reached. We should, therefore, also look at the annual growth rates in GDP per capita. We begin by looking at the most equal and the most unequal country, namely, Sweden and the United States. Figure 6.3 traces annual growth in GDP per capita from 1975 all the way to 2013. The United States is represented by the dashed line and Sweden is represented by the full line. The year-on-year percentage change in GDP per capita, adjusted for inflation, is recorded on the vertical axis. Both countries have had a few dips with a shrinking economy, most severely during the Great Recession in the late 2000s. Despite these short, but hurtful, periods, the economies have grown at a steady pace of 1.8 per cent on average in the United States and 1.6 per cent in Sweden. The 0.2 per cent difference stems from the fact that Sweden has suffered slightly worse recessions than the United States. Conversely, outside periods of recession, Sweden has outperformed the United States during the last 20 years, although again the margins are minor. It is also apparent from the figure that both countries have lived through the same cycles of booms and busts, at least since the 1980s. After some years of high growth rates, both endured a crisis in the early 1990s, followed by more than a decade of expansion until a new and deeper crisis hit. The two most diverse countries in terms of equality, which, according to

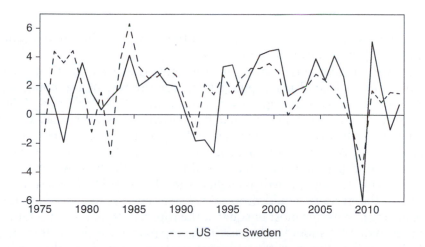

Figure 6.3 *Annual growth in GDP per capita in Sweden and the United States*

Note: Annual percentage growth rate of GDP per capita in constant USD (with 2005 as base year).

Source: The World Bank (2015).

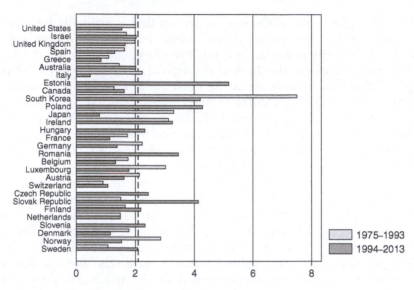

Figure 6.4   *Annual growth in GDP per capita*

Note: Annual percentage growth rate of GDP per capita in constant USD (with 2005 as base year). The mean for the 1975–1993 period is 1.8 per cent, and for the 1994–2013 period it is 2.1 per cent. Countries are ranked according to their latest Gini coefficient, with the country with the highest Gini at the top. The dashed vertical line is the average growth rate from 1994 to 2013.

Source: The World Bank (2015).

the pessimists, ought to perform very differently, have had remarkably similar trajectories over the past 40 years.

To see whether this is true for other countries as well, Figure 6.4 displays annual GDP per capita growth for the rest of the countries. The growth rates are averaged over two periods, 1975–1993 and 1994–2013, to get an impression of changing growth rates over time. In the first period, the average growth rate is 1.8 per cent, and in the second, 2.1 per cent. A number of countries from eastern Europe only appear in the second period due to lack of valid data on the first, which is the reason why average growth is higher after 1994. Without these new-comers, the average would drop to 1.7 per cent. Again, the countries are arranged with the most unequal at the top, reflecting the expectation that growth rates should be highest in the top part of the figure. It is, first of all, worth noting that the countries performing best are those with the lowest GDP per capita in Figure 6.1. This is not surprising, because it reflects a catch-up effect whereby smaller economies – all else equal – grow more quickly than bigger ones. Yet, even disregarding such obvi-ous outliers as South Korea (a whopping 7.5 per cent in the first period and a still-impressive 4.2 per cent in the second), Poland (4.3 per cent) and the Slovak Republic (4.2 per cent) does not alter the conclusion: the prediction of the pessimists is not borne out by the data. Since 1994, the United States and the United Kingdom have grown 2 per cent and 1.7 per cent, respectively, which is matched by the growth rates of Sweden (2.1 per cent) and Finland (2.2 per cent), and only a little better than the Netherlands and Norway, which both grew at an average rate of 1.5 per cent. Virtually all the affluent and established democracies have seen growth rates in the 1–2 per cent range.

Our conclusion – that there is nothing to indicate that the pessimists are correct about the equality–efficiency trade-off – mirrors that of other researchers. Neither Alesina and Rodrik (1994), Clarke (1995), Deininger and Squire (1998), Cingano (2014) nor Thewissen (2014) – using a variety of statistical techniques and data – find any positive correlation between inequality and growth. Indeed, several of the researchers actually find a negative correlation, suggesting that more inequality can hurt growth, at least at high levels of inequality. Cingano states that '[f]ocusing on a 25-year horizon, for example, the estimated coefficients imply that a 1 Gini point reduction in inequality would raise average growth by slightly more than 0.1 percentage points per year, with a cumulative gain in GDP at the end of the period of around 3%.' How might it be possible that inequality can hurt growth? To answer this, we need to take a step back and consider a different perspective on growth.

Wage-Led versus Profit-Led Growth and the Decline of Labour's Income Share

Economic growth is, in the broadest sense, a function of the human capital of the employees (their skills and knowledge) brought to bear on the employers' physical (machines, equipment, etc.) and structural capital (patents, trademarks, etc.). The value that this collaboration between employees and employers creates is shared between the two parties. The employees get a wage, while the employer gets a profit, which can be invested into more physical capital, saved for later use, or paid out to the owners. If we sum up all the wage shares of employees in firms within a country, we get labour's income share: that is, how much of the income created in a given year in a country is going to employees rather than to employers. The proportion going to the employers is called 'capital's share', a term that refers to the fact that it goes to the owners of the physical and structural capital. A standard measure of a country's yearly income is GDP, so the common way to measure labour's income share is to calculate the ratio between wages and GDP.

Figure 6.5 reports labour's income share as a percentage of GDP (on the vertical axis) from 1960 to 2014 (on the horizontal axis) in four countries representing different types of market economies and welfare state models (cf. the next two chapters). The overall trend, however, can be found in most of the European and Anglo-Saxon countries, for which we have data

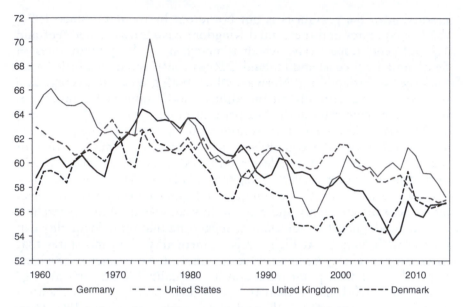

Figure 6.5   *Labour share of income as a percentage of GDP*

Note: Labour income share is defined as compensation per employee as percentage of GDP at market prices per person employed.

Source: European Commission (2015).

all the way back to 1960. Labour's income share is above 50 per cent in all four countries, but has exhibited a roughly curvilinear trend over time. At least in Germany and Denmark, labour's share rose through the 1960s and early 1970s, but then began a long, though uneven, decline. German labour's share increased from 58.9 per cent in 1960 to an all-time high of 64.4 per cent of GDP in 1974 and then fell back to 56.7 per cent in 2014. In Denmark, labour's share went up from 57.2 per cent in 1960 to 62.7 in 1975 and back to 56.7 per cent. In the United States, the maximum share going to labour was 62.7 per cent, in 1970, while today labour's share is 57 per cent. British labour's income share rose from 64.5 per cent in 1960 to 70.2 per cent in 1975 as the British economy collapsed (in the following year the British government had to ask the IMF for a loan to keep the economy floating), and then fell to 57.2 per cent.

The fall in labour's income share is a central cause behind the rising inequalities in market income during the past couple of decades. It points to the fact that ordinary wage earners are getting a smaller and smaller cut of the income produced, whereas the owners of physical and structural capital are capturing a larger and larger share. Even disregarding the tendency towards larger disparities between wage earners, with low-paid workers growing in numbers in many countries, the proportion of all national income available to the wage earners has decreased.

The pie is not only being cut into more and more uneven pieces, it is also shrinking in size. The fact that labour's income share has declined in Denmark, where inequality in disposable incomes – as we saw in Chapter 4 – has stayed roughly stable, hints at the important role that government intervention can have in modifying market forces (to be discussed in Chapter 8).

Changes in the range of 6–8 percentage points may appear minute, but they are in fact huge. The American GDP in 2014 added up to a colossal USD 17.348 billion, so if labour's income share had stayed at 62.7 per cent, American wage earners would have been paid USD 989 billion *more* than they are today. With a population of just under 319 million, that would yield around USD 3100 per person living in the United States if the extra wage was distributed evenly across the populace. Based on a similar back-of-the-envelope computation, German wage earners would have had USD 3650 more to spend, while Danish ones could have taken home USD 2700 more. The biggest gap is found in the United Kingdom, with USD 5360, but that is mostly due to the exceptionally large labour share per cent in 1975. If we use the more normal 1974 as baseline, the lost income share is 'only' worth USD 3710.

The declining share of GDP going to wages is important because it limits the amount of consumption in society as the purchasing power of the middle class and the less well-to-do gets squeezed. Marglin and Bhaduri (1990) were the first to formulate the argument systematically, at that time to understand better the slowdown of the economies from the mid-1970s (a topic to which we return in Chapter 11), observing that

> wages [...] have a dual character under capitalism. On the one hand, wages are costs to the capitalists. On the other hand, wages, or more precisely, the wages of the employees of other businesses, are a source of demand. High wages are bad for the capitalist as producer but good for the capitalist as seller.... (Marglin and Bhaduri 1990: 183)

Or, as the Berkeley economist Robert B. Reich recently put it pointedly with reference to the American experience,

> [c]onservatives believe the economy functions better if the rich have more money and everyone else has less. But they're wrong. It's just the opposite. The real job creators are not CEOs or corporations or wealthy investors. The job creators are members of America's vast middle class and the poor, whose purchases cause businesses to expand and invest. (Reich 2014)

In all economies, the bulk of consumption – and, hence, demand for goods and services – comes from the large masses of ordinary people.

If the share of GDP going to firms and their owners rises, neither the firms nor the owners are suddenly going to consume much more than they already did; and certainly not more than the wage earners would. At the end of the day, this lack of consumption can depress economic growth just as a lack of sufficient investments into new physical capital would.

Several empirical studies have shown that aggregated demand – which consists of private consumption, private investment, government expenditure and net export – in most rich democracies increases when labour's income share increases (or capital's share decreases). By one estimate, the GDP of the 20 richest countries in the world (the G20) declines by 0.36 per cent in reaction to a worldwide 1 per cent decline in labour's income share (Lavoie and Stockhammer 2013: 30). Another study estimates that a 1 per cent increase in labour's income share in the 15 Eurozone countries would raise GDP by 0.30 per cent (Onaran and Obst 2015: 16). It is important to appreciate that many factors apart from the generosity of wages help determine economic growth. These other factors include technological innovation, governments' fiscal and monetary policies, human capital formation, housing and stock market bubbles, etc., so there will never be a one-to-one relationship between the size and changes in labour's income share, on the one hand, and growth, on the other. Yet, it underscores why we definitely should not expect to see a positive relationship between inequality and growth, and also why inequality, if it gets out of hand, can slow down an economy.

Alternative Measures of Prosperity

So far in the chapter we have focused exclusively on GDP as the measure of economic growth and prosperity. To use GDP is entirely within the norms of the literature, but it is important to be aware of the limits of the concept (for an introduction, see Coyle 2014). GDP measures the final value of all goods and services produced in a country over a period of time. There are, therefore, first of all, a number of technical, but consequential, questions of what to count as part of the national economy and how to calculate the value of less tangible activities such as financial and public services. For instance, publicly funded services such as education, police, road maintenance or health care are normally not sold on the free market. It is, therefore, not possible to measure the value public services create in any traditional sense of the word; i.e. how much people are willing to pay for them minus the cost of producing them. Even so-called private health care is normally so heavily subsidized and regulated that it makes no sense to talk of a free market. Instead, the wages spent producing public services are used as a measure of the value they create. This means that the wage *costs* of public services are equated with their added *value*. This solution to the tricky measurement problem probably underestimates the value of public services. If all the value created by public services had gone to wages, it is difficult to see why almost all modern societies would have been willing to organize and fund them in the first place.

Another, more fundamental critique of the GDP measure is that it includes goods and services that do not contribute to the welfare of citizens. Kuznets, the economist who fathered the positive view on inequality, in the 1930s worked for the American government to devise a measure of national wealth before GDP became the all-dominant measure. GDP won out, but Kuznets was an ardent opponent of it, because it confuses economic activities that generate value for citizens with activities that do not. In his own, knotty words,

> It would be of great value to have national income estimates that would remove from the total the elements which, from the standpoint of a more enlightened social philosophy than that of an acquisitive society represent dis-service rather than service. Such estimates would subtract from the present national income totals all expenses on armament, most of the outlays on advertising, a great many of the expenses involved in financial and speculative activities, and what is perhaps most important, the outlays that have been made necessary in order to overcome difficulties that are, properly speaking, costs implicit to our economic civilization. All the gigantic outlays in our urban civilization, subways, expensive housing, etc., which in our usual estimates we include at the value of the net product they yield on the market, do not really represent net services to the individuals comprising the nation, but are, from their viewpoint, an evil necessity in order to make a living. (Kuznets, as cited in Coyle 2014: 13–14)

We should, in sum, according to Kuznets, only include activities into the GDP measure that make people happy. This view proved too radical, if for no other reason than that it is also important to know how many 'evil necessities' a society produces. Building a road may not make most of us happy, but to argue that it has no value to society is probably a step too far. Yet, Kuznets foreshadows later periods' search for better measures of prosperity and affluence. One is happiness, which has become something of an intellectual fashion vogue. The country of Bhutan even runs a Gross National Happiness (GNH) index, while the UN has included happiness among its developmental goals.

Given the prominence of the happiness measure, a natural question is whether it correlates with inequality. Proponents of equality will probably intuitively expect equality to create happiness, although that intuition hinges on several assumptions. First of all, happiness is an individual-level phenomenon. It is something that people feel themselves. GDP, by contrast, is a country-level phenomenon. It only exists at the national level and is therefore meant to be measuring a single, national statistic. It is unclear whether happiness can be aggregated meaningfully in an identical way to the national level. You as a person may be happy, while everybody else feels miserable. A second assumption is that rising equality increases the poor's happiness more than it decreases the rich's happiness. If equality makes the poor happy, why should it not make the rich unhappy as they lose their relative position? Both these points emphasize that exploring the relationship between inequality and happiness is best done by using individual-level data that allow the study of how the effect of inequality can vary across people with different incomes.

One such study employed survey data from the United States from 1972 to 2008, a total of 27 yearly surveys with nationally representative samples, in which the respondents were asked, among other things, whether they were very happy, pretty happy or not too happy (Oishi et al. 2011). The study found that higher inequality, measured with the Gini coefficient, on average leads to lower happiness. However, the overall finding is conditioned in two ways. First, the effect works through reduced feelings of generalized trust and fairness. That is, higher inequality makes the respondents less inclined to believe that other people are trustworthy or will treat the respondent in a fair way – and these negative feelings then reduce happiness. Second, higher inequality does not have these effects among the richest 20 per cent of the respondents. This makes sense to the extent that this is the group that either has gained from, or at least has not been made worse off by, the past decades' rising inequality in the United States. It is mainly among those adversely affected by increasing inequality that feelings of happiness have been depressed.

Delhey and Dragolov (2014) supplement these results by analysing nationally representative survey data from 30 countries collected in 2007. In this way, it is possible to see whether cross-country differences in inequality, again measured as the Gini coefficient, can explain individual-level feelings of happiness and life satisfaction. The authors find the same negative effect as Oishi et al. (2011), meaning that respondents living in countries with a high Gini coefficient on average report being less happy and satisfied with life than respondents living in countries with a low Gini coefficient. Moreover, the effect of inequality appears through a reduced belief in the trustworthiness of others and an increased feeling of being marginalized. This mirrors the findings from the American surveys well.

Conclusion

We ended this chapter by discussing an unconventional measure of prosperity, namely happiness. Using such a measure is not only unconventional, but it also takes us from the realm of economic growth to subjective feelings of well-being (and back to the issues discussed in Chapter 3). It also takes us away from the substantial critique of inequality made by many fiscal conservatives: that fighting inequality is bad for growth and/ or that growth will eventually lead to lower inequality. The main conclusion from the empirical evidence summarized above is that inequality definitely is no prerequisite for sustained economic growth. When we look at the aggregate patterns, both between countries and over time, there is little, if anything, to substantiate such an argument (for similar conclusions, see Lindert 2004; Pontusson 2005). A recent literature has begun to suggest that inequality may, on the contrary, actually be bad for growth because it reduces the purchasing power of the large majority of ordinary people – but the effects from this have so far not manifested themselves in the aggregated patterns either.

The most balanced conclusion is, in our view, that there is no universal relationship between inequality and growth. One reason for this is probably that most countries do not venture too far towards the extremes, or have only recently begun to do so. If an economy became extremely equal, it might plausibly dampen growth, just as an economy becoming extremely unequal may hurt growth. However, even countries such as Denmark, Norway and Sweden still exhibit substantial inequality, and it is only recently that the United States and, to a lesser extent, the United Kingdom have seen really soaring levels. Another reason is that, even within the range of observed inequality, there are different ways to organize the economy. It turns out, as the next chapter will detail, that there is more than one road to affluence.

Chapter 7

What are the roads to riches?

How is it possible for some countries to maintain fairly equal income distributions without having to suffer any severe economic consequences? The answer lies in the fact that growth can be achieved in different ways, and that a high level of inequality is a necessary by-product in only some of these. History shows, as we saw in the last chapter, that it has been possible in several European countries to combine decent growth (that is, as good as elsewhere) with decent equality (that is, much better than elsewhere). This chapter explores how that is doable.

We begin by introducing the New Institutional Economics. The New Institutional Economics is the intellectual backdrop for much of the research into different types of market economies and how these generate growth and inequality. Today's market economies differ on at least three dimensions: first, the form and extent of their human capital formation; second, the way in which wages are decided; and third, the business environment more broadly. In combination, these three dimensions demarcate three types of market economies – the social, the liberal and the statist – each of which performs distinctly in terms of both growth and inequality. This chapter explores these different market economies in detail.

New Institutional Economics

There is, in fact, nothing particularly 'new' about New Institutional Economics. The term was coined by Oliver Williamson in his 1975 book, *Markets and Hierarchies*, but the basic idea dates back to Ronald Coase's influential essay *The Nature of the Firm* from 1937. There is also nothing controversial or fanciful about New Institutional Economics, as the term 'new' might perhaps suggest. Four of the field's founding fathers and mothers have so far won the Nobel Prize in economics. Apart from Coase in 1991 and Williamson in 2009, these are Douglass North in 1993 and Elinor Ostrom in 2009 (together with Williamson). New Institutional Economics, in short, is one of the most well-established and productive fields in economics. The reason? It provides a credible account of why and how social context matters for economic behaviour in ways previous theories had difficulty providing.

Social context matters because it affects what is the best course of action for individuals and firms in an economy. Given a certain set of formal and informal rules – what the literature calls institutions – it may or may not be smart to invest time and money in a particular way. Big public subsidies may make it profitable to invest in windmills or solar energy, while tougher laws on smoking may make it less attractive to buy stocks in companies making cigarettes. However, institutions not only affect behaviour within markets; institutions create markets. Some of the most fundamental institutions are property rights and money. Without rules governing who owns what and what constitutes a valid medium of exchange and storage of value, there would be no basis for a market economy of any sort. Other basic, although less fundamental, institutions govern how and under what conditions an employer can hire an employee and how people can acquire and document skills relevant for the labour market.

Over the duration of human history and across the world today, there is great variation in the rules of the game. There are several reasons for that. One is that humans often are not able to maximize their utility very well, even though they may try to, meaning that even if there is a single most-rational choice to be made across social contexts, people will typically opt for different things anyway. In the words of North,

> Human behavior appears to be more complex than that embodied in the individual utility function of economists' models. Many cases are ones not simply of wealth-maximizing behavior, but of altruism and of self-imposed constraints, which radically change the outcomes with respect to the choices that people actually make. Similarly, we find that people decipher the environment by processing information through preexisting mental constructs through which they understand the environment and solve the problems they confront. (North 1990: 20)

People and firms evaluate new information based on prevailing norms about good and appropriate behaviour (which can rule out utility-maximizing choices because they are regarded as morally wrong) as well as ideas about what will work in a given situation (ideas that can be mistaken). These mental constructs can be deep-seated and virtually cut in stone within a country, but vary between countries or across cultural regions. What is, for instance, the appropriate solution to a prolonged labour shortage like the one the European economies lived through in the 1960s and early 1970s? Since women everywhere had a substantially lower labour force participation rate than men, one solution was to get more females into the labour market. That turned out to be acceptable in some places, such as the comparably secularized Nordic countries, but out of bounds in the Catholic countries of continental

Europe. The consequences of this particular choice were huge for the women concerned and the national economies, and can still be felt today; yet the choice had little to do with utility maximization and a lot to do with cultural norms (Lewis 1992; Esping-Andersen 1999; 2009; Huber and Stephens 2001).

Another reason for the variation in institutions across time and countries is path dependence. Path dependence means that past decisions or events narrow the range of viable choices available. David (1985) provides the famous example of the QWERTY keyboard, i.e. the one all computers and smartphones in most countries – Germany has QWERTZ and France has AZERTY – are equipped with. QWERTY refers to the first six letters on the keyboard and was the sequence originally chosen for Remington typewriters back in 1873. The QWERTY system was intended to get the optimal speed on typewriters without jamming the typebars. Yet, with the emergence of the computer and other electronic platforms, the QWERTY system is no longer the optimal one, because there are no longer any physical typebars that can jam. However, by the time the typewriter was out of date, the QWERTY keyboard had already become deeply embedded. Millions of people knew the QWERTY system by heart, and shifting to another would have required an effort no one cared to organize or pay for.

More specifically, path dependence occurs because of four self-reinforcing mechanisms (North 1990: 94). The first is large set-up or fixed costs and falling marginal costs. To move from one technology or production mode to another typically demands a large investment in new equipment or retraining of the workers, which will pay off only later. In contrast, over time, the unit price will fall if you stick to the existing technology or production mode. This militates against moving from the existing path. The second mechanism is learning effects. The longer you stick to a technology or production mode, the better you master it. The third mechanism is coordination effects. It is easier for both individuals and firms to interact when everybody knows what to expect from each other, which entails that radical change is often not welcome. The fourth and final mechanism is adaptive expectations, meaning that there is a natural tendency to assume that if a certain technology or production mode dominates today, then it will probably also do so tomorrow. This, of course, often becomes a self-fulfilling prophecy, since the belief makes even more people adopt the technology or production mode.

A crucial insight from New Institutional Economics is that not only do the rules of the game vary between countries, as distinct solutions to roughly similar problems are chosen and later became entrenched via path dependence, but that more than one of these may lead to high economic performance. There are multiple ways in which the institutions that create and regulate the market economy can facilitate growth and prosperity, and over time, different countries have followed quite distinct pathways. The reason is precisely that both individuals and firms try to adapt and specialize to match the institutions, which again reinforces the existing path. This means that seemingly small nuances in how economies work gradually can turn into dramatic differences. The lesson is not, however, that all institutional paths yield high-performance results; far from it. The lesson is, rather, that some paths are successful, but that all are persistent even in the face of failure.

Three Types of Market Economies

So, how is it possible for some countries, notably the Nordics, to maintain fairly equal income distributions without having to suffer any severe economic consequences? The answer is that the low levels of inequality of the Nordic countries to a large extent are by-products of the way the institutions regulating the capitalist system operate here. These *social market economies* combine a number of important features to produce competitive capitalist systems while maintaining comparably low levels of inequality. The core elements of the social market economies' growth strategies are, first of all, extensive investment in their citizens' skills, or human capital, which in particular takes the form of early childhood education and vocational training at the secondary level. The high skill levels make it possible to compete on the global markets with high-quality products, while the fact that human capital investment is aimed at the whole populace, and not just the middle class and affluent, justifies relatively generous wages for the majority of workers. The second element is centralized wage-setting. When wage-setting occurs at the national or industry level, wages tend to get compressed compared with a situation in which wages are set at the individual firm, or in negotiations between the employers and the individual employee. The third and final element is a generally business-friendly environment, including limited red tape when dealing with public authorities as well as a flexible labour market in which it is easy to hire and fire workers.

The *liberal market economies* comprise the Anglo-Saxon countries and, to a varying degree, Israel, South Korea and other East Asian tigers. The liberal market economies all share a reluctance to use public money to invest in the skills of their citizens. Investment is instead left to people themselves, entailing that those at the bottom increasingly lose out because they are unable to pay for their own or their children's education. This creates a workforce that on average is highly skilled, but with large differences between the well-educated top and the under-educated bottom. For the latter group, the only option is often to accept so-called *junk jobs*, i.e. low-paid work in restaurants, domestic services and so on. The bifurcation of the labour market is underlined by the lack of any wage centralization that could have counter-balanced the tendency to pay low-skilled workers very low wages. The third feature of liberal market economies is a very business-friendly environment, which, as in the social market economies, facilitates smooth dealings with the public authorities and a flexible labour market.

The *statist market economies* are found in southern and continental Europe and include countries such as Belgium, France, Greece, Italy, Spain and, to varying extents, Germany and the Netherlands. The term *statist* has a negative ring to it, and we intentionally use it to describe these countries because government here often is part of the problem rather than the solution. In the social market economies, governments are heavily involved in human capital formation, but largely stay out of businesses' way. In the statist market economies, the reverse is true. Most importantly, this means that the business environment is generally bad, with a lot of bureaucracy and too little labour market flexibility. This, in turn, leads to a dualization of the workforce into insiders and outsiders. The insiders tend to enjoy high levels of job security and other benefits such as generous pension schemes, while the outsiders move from one low-paid temporary job to another. Several of the statist market econo-mies, in addition, have settled on an unhealthy mix of limited human capital investment and a high degree of wage centralization, making companies less competitive on the world market. It is no surprise, then, that several of the statist market economies, including heavyweights such as France and Italy, during the past couple of decades have grown at a modest pace compared with the social and liberal market economies.

The fourth cluster of countries consists of the new democracies of eastern Europe. These *post-communist market economies* share relatively low levels of inequality and a not-too-business-friendly environment. Both features presumably stem from their communist past. Communism as an ideology emphasizes economic equality, and it is plausible that this has left an imprint on today's inequality levels. Communism in eastern Europe was also characterized by ineffective government and production systems, and this, too, is plausibly still evident in the business environ-ment. However, apart from communist legacies, the new democracies of eastern Europe are a diverse bunch of countries, with little in com-mon except their past. Even when it comes to the level of inequality, there is, moreover, quite a bit of variation, with Slovenia and the Slovak Republic being almost as equal as the Nordic countries and Poland and Hungary being more like Ireland. With so few commonalities, it makes little sense to analyse them as a single group.

The rest of the chapter goes through the three dimensions of human capital formation, wage centralization and business-friendly environ-ment one by one. A core takeaway is that how you organize one dimen-sion of the economy affects the workings of the others. This is what Hall and Soskice (2001: 17) refer to as the institutional complementari-ties of a capitalist system. Because of such complementarities, market economies tend to stick with the social, liberal or statist recipe. That is, market economies are path dependent. Despite a string of reforms since the 1990s, the Nordic countries, for instance, remain social market economies in much the same way as the Anglo-Saxon countries remain liberal market economies, or the southern and continental European ones statist. New policies are layered on top of existing arrangements for the combined reason of not disrupting the economy and not upsetting vested interests. Path-breaking reforms, as a result, rarely happen (Pierson 2004: 17–53; Streeck and Thelen 2005; Palier 2010). This is a key reason why the social market economies have stayed highly equal, as shown in Chapter 5, whereas the liberal market economies have spiralled towards ever more inequality. Both outcomes are natural effects of the way the capitalist system is organized.

Human Capital Formation

To appreciate the role of education in inequality, take a look at Figure 7.1. The figure plots countries' public spending per pupil on the horizontal axis against the Gini coefficient on the vertical axis. Spending

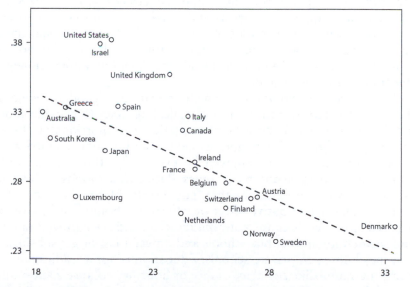

Figure 7.1 *Public education spending and the Gini coefficient*

Note: Spending is measured as public expenditure per pupil at all levels of schooling as a percentage of GDP per capita. Reported figures are the average since the year 2000. The Gini coefficient is from 2010 to 2013.

Source: LIS (2015) and The World Bank (2015).

is measured as a percentage of GDP per capita and is the average for the years 2000–2012 to make it robust to yearly fluctuations that are irrelevant when comparing countries. The Gini coefficient is the latest available. It is evident that there is a negative correlation between the amount of public spending on education and inequality: the more public spending, the less inequality. To get an idea of the strength of the correlation, we can calculate Pearson's r. Pearson's r ranges from –1 (a perfect negative correlation) through 0 (no correlation) to 1 (a perfect positive correlation) and is a conventional measure of the strength of statistical correlations. In Figure 7.1, Pearson's r is –0.65, which is considered a strong negative correlation. The dashed line is the trend-line that illustrates the association between the two variables.

Luxembourg stands out by achieving low inequality with a modest spending effort, but this is a function of the extremely large GDP per capita in this specific country: USD 25,000 more than the second highest. Since spending is measured as a percentage of GDP per capita, this automatically makes the monetary input appear smaller than it really is in a situation where one country is so much richer than the rest. If Luxembourg is excluded from the sample, Pearson's r increases from –0.65 to –0.72. The United States and Israel, conversely, stand out as exhibiting even more inequality than their low levels of public spending on education justify. Still, the deviation is marginal, and excluding the United States and Israel from the sample reduces Pearson's r by less than 0.02. The same applies to Norway and Sweden, which – compared with Denmark – manage to get a lot of equality for little educational spending. The point we want to make is straightforward, but crucial: no matter how you cut into the empirical evidence, spending public money on education is good for equality.

Now, there are two ways in which education is good for equality. The first is the redistributive effect of collecting taxes to provide education free of charge. Because taxes are paid disproportionately by the well-to-do, and free primary and secondary, and in some countries also tertiary, education can be enjoyed by everybody, this will inevitably reduce inequality in disposable incomes. Public education is in this sense just another social programme that, put starkly, bleeds the rich to feed the poor. The redistributive effect of education should not be overemphasized, however, because many middle-class and even affluent families send their children to public schools and universities, or get subsidies to send the children to private schools. Education is not a traditional pro-poor programme like social assistance or housing, because a substantial part of the tax revenue is spent on the families that pay the most taxes in the first place. The special value of education lies less in redistribution and more in investment in the skills of the population. It is this skills investment that makes education a key programme everywhere – but in remarkably different ways across the various types of market economies.

Human capital is the knowledge and abilities that make workers able to add value in the production process. In all economies throughout mankind's history, human capital has been a central ingredient of enterprise. Without it, the other central ingredients, physical capital (machinery, buildings and tools) and structural capital (patents, know-how), would have had no value at all. Education creates human capital by enhancing people's innate skills. It can, of course, also do many other things, such as training people to become good democrats or to hate a country's minorities, but the reason why topics such as mathematics, science and reading virtually always take up the bulk of the curricula is their importance for human capital formation. It is a testament to the role of human capital that the better educated you are, the more money your employer is willing to pay you for your efforts (OECD 2014a: 132–49).

Yet, there is more to human capital than these cognitive skills. As shown in a series of studies, non-cognitive skills such as the ability to lead other people, communicate effectively and plan ahead are critical too (e.g. Cunha et al. 2006; Heckman 2011; Heckman and Mosso 2014). One reason why non-cognitive skills are important is that they affect the likelihood that children will acquire cognitive and more advanced non-cognitive skills down the road. Making sure that children have sufficient non-cognitive skills early on is, therefore, vital. As summed up by Heckman (2011: 32), '[a]dverse impacts of genetic, parental, and environmental resources can be overturned through investments in quality early childhood education that provide children and their parents the resources they need to properly develop the cognitive and personality skills that create productivity.'

The Nordic countries are home to some of the world's best, and most expensive, childcare arrangements. In many ways, this is the defining characteristic of the Nordic welfare states (Jensen 2008). As Figure 7.1 makes clear, these countries also spend substantial sums on public education more broadly, as do the Netherlands, Austria and a few others. The extensive public investment in education increases the skills among those with the lowest formal education. One way to see this is from data on the mathematical skills of adults 15–64 years old collected by the OECD for 16 of the countries we study. Based on a test, respondents were placed into five proficiency categories, with Category 1 containing the respondents with the weakest skills and Category 5 containing those with the strongest. With this information, it is possible to see how large a share falls in each category conditional on the respondents' highest achieved educational level. Figure 7.2 displays on the horizontal axis the percentage of people with less than upper secondary education who belong to Category 3, 4 or 5, i.e. the fairly to really good categories. The Gini coefficient is displayed on the vertical axis.

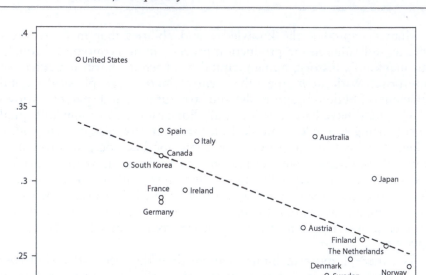

Figure 7.2 *Mathematical proficiency among early school leavers and the Gini coefficient*

Note: The horizontal axis reports the percentage of people with less than upper secondary education who belong to one of the three best proficiency categories in mathematics. See OECD (2013c) for details about measurement and survey methodology. The Gini coefficient is from 2010 to 2013.

Source: OECD (2014b) and LIS (2015).

There is a strong negative correlation between the two variables. Pearson's r is –0.73. In the right-hand side of the figure, we see that Denmark, Finland, Norway and Sweden are all clustered near the bottom, together with the Netherlands and Austria. In these countries, 22–31 per cent of those with less than upper secondary education, which in most countries means that they stopped school when they were in their mid-teens, belong to one of the three top categories. This is still less than for the well-educated, of whom typically around 55–60 per cent belong to the top category, but considerably better than the situation in most of the liberal and statist market economies. In Canada, France, Germany, Ireland, Italy, South Korea and Spain, a mere 10 per cent of the poorly educated belong to the top category, and in the United States, a tiny 3 per cent do. This matches the higher inequality in these countries. Australia, in contrast, stands out with its medium level of inequality and skilled population. Apparently, other things are at play in the home of Crocodile Dundee than simply a compressed skills structure. This is also the case for the United States, which boasts even more inequality than expected from its badly trained early school leavers.

Education plays a more complex part than making the least educated better skilled. In countries with an encompassing vocational training system, the wage-earning potential of manual workers increases. Vocational training is often aimed at developing skills that are specific to one industry or even one company, and that are highly sought after by companies, especially in western Europe, where production, at least since World War II, has been geared towards high-quality industrial products (Hall and Soskice 2001: 24–6; Eichengreen 2008). In countries such as Denmark, Germany, France, the Netherlands, Norway and Sweden, employers depend on a workforce with specific skills, and they are willing to pay for it. In the liberal market economies, production is less dependent on such specific skills, and consequently little vocational training exists (Hall and Soskice 2001: 30–1). The result is a labour market with many university-educated generalists, many low-educated, and comparably few with specific skills from upper secondary vocational training programmes. The middle of the educational spectrum is, in other words, small, and given that earnings increase with educational level, this creates inequality in wage earnings. In contrast, where a large share of upper secondary students are enrolled in vocational training programmes, wages get spread out more evenly, entailing that inequality drops (Estevez-Abe et al. 2001: 177; Busemeyer 2014: 190–5).

Centralized Wage-Setting

Wage-setting can take place at many different levels in society. It can be a negotiation between the individual employer and employee, between the employer and all her employees collectively, between associations of employers and employees at either the industry or the national level, or, finally, an act of government. To the employees, there is strength in numbers. This is because the individual employee normally can be easily substituted with another, whereas it is more difficult for employees to substitute one employer for another. If a worker commands very specific, perhaps even unique, skills, or if a shortage of labour supply makes moving from one firm to the next easy, the position of the employer is less favourable. When wage-setting occurs at the individual level, a lot of variation between employees therefore manifests itself. Some will be able to secure generous pay, while others will get much less. Such wage inequalities will occur within individual companies, depending on the bargaining position of the individual employees, but also across sectors of the economy, depending on whether labour is in short supply or not. Much the same effect is likely if the employer negotiates with the entire firm, or a part thereof, for instance, a production plant. Here, inequalities within the firm or plant will tend to get reduced, because employees will get similar pay for similar work, yet substantial wage inequality could persist within and across industries.

Both of these first wage-setting modes can be said to reflect the classic way of negotiating wages since the Industrial Revolution in the 19th century. On balance, wage-setting like this is to the benefit of the employers, who can either squeeze wage costs or create powerful monetary incentives by rewarding valuable employees. In much of Europe, wage-setting became centralized during the 20th century, meaning that negotiations were lifted to the industry or national level. The movement was caused by the rising power resources of employees, not least after World War II, when labour supply was at an all-time low, making it difficult for employers to resist demands for both centralization and wage increases (Eichengreen and Iversen 1999: 124–30; Korpi 2002: 382–9). Centralization tends to make wages more alike because it makes those interest groups representing low-pay occupations more powerful. When wage-setting is centralized, these groups often become *de facto* veto players, because they are the ones getting the lowest wages to begin with and therefore have least to lose if negotiations come to nothing. In this scenario, it is not difficult to imagine that the prize for the veto player's acceptance is a relatively higher wage increase for the low-pay worker segment. Centralization can also affect wage inequality because those representing the well-paid workers believe it is fair. This is particularly likely if the representatives are members of the same peak-level organization as those representing the employees with low pay (Wallerstein 1999: 674–6; Rueda and Pontusson 2000: 360–1; Visser and Checchi 2009: 24–5).

Unions often play an important role in centralized wage bargaining. This is most obvious in the social market economies, where union density, i.e. the percentage of the workforce who are members of a union, traditionally has been very high. Historically, this meant that to negotiate with the workers, employers had to go to the peak-level union that coordinated most union activities. To match the employees, the employers organized into their own peak-level associations. This created highly centralized wage-setting because the deals struck between the two peak organizations automatically covered large segments of society. Since the 1980s, negotiations have been decentralized slightly to the industry level, but unions remain crucial players in wage-setting. In the statist market economies, union density is generally lower than in the social market economies, but centralization is nevertheless high.

As pointed out by Pontusson (2005: 100), there are two reasons for that. The first one is that some governments, in line with the statist tradition, extend deals that only cover a small group of workers or companies to the rest of the industry, or even the nation. The other is that wage settlements between an employer association and a union often require that both union and non-union members are covered by the agreement.

Coverage rates are, therefore, much higher than union membership rates. By one estimate (Visser 2013), the percentage of the workforce that were members of a union in 2010 in Germany was 18.6 per cent, whereas the wage bargaining coverage was 61.1 per cent. In France, only 7.6 per cent were union members, but bargaining coverage was a full 92 per cent. This should be compared with a union density of 68.9 per cent and bargaining coverage of 91 per cent in Sweden, and 11.3 per cent and 13 per cent, respectively, in the United States. In both the latter countries, which exemplify the social and liberal market economies, union density and wage bargaining coverage roughly match each other.

Figure 7.3 illustrates the effect of wage centralization on inequality. The horizontal axis reports an index of wage centralization. Countries get the value 1 if bargaining is fragmented, i.e. confined to the firm or plant. The value 5 is for highly centralized wage bargaining via either peak organization agreements or government action. On the vertical axis, the Gini coefficient is reported. Notice that we stick to inequality in disposable income, even though it is market inequality that wage centralization directly affects. Apart from ensuring comparability with the previous figures, the reason is, as explained in Chapter 4, that it is

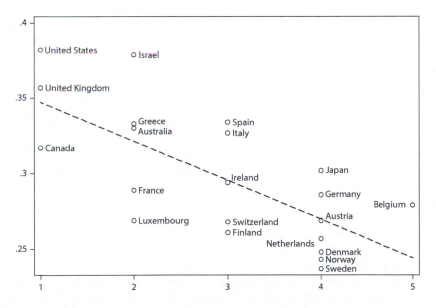

Figure 7.3 *Wage coordination and the Gini coefficient*

Note: The Wage Coordination Index ranges from 1 to 5; 1 means that wage coordination is fragmented and largely confined to individual firms or plants. 5 means that wage coordination is highly centralized at either the national or the industry level. Data on wage coordination is for the year 2009. See Figure 5.1 for details on the Gini coefficient.

Source: LIS (2015) and Visser (2013).

inequality in disposable income that is the truly interesting phenomenon. So, if wage centralization has an effect here, this adds to its importance. The wage centralization index is for the year 2009, and the Gini coefficient covers 2010–2013, but both variables are slow-moving, so that the exact years chosen do not matter for the result, which is that there is a strong negative correlation between the two variables. Pearson's *r* is –0.60. Using more advanced time series–cross section regression techniques and data on market inequality going back to 1980, Wallerstein (1999) and Rueda and Pontusson (2000) reached the same conclusion. Figure 7.3 shows that there is no country that seriously deviates from the trend, although Israel has 'too much' inequality given its level of centralization, whereas Luxembourg has 'too little'.

Scheve and Stasavage (2009) argue that centralized wage bargaining does not affect inequality, as the conventional wisdom would have it. According to this study, there is actually no association between wage centralization and inequality. Interestingly, however, in the study the authors use the World Top Incomes Database, presented in Chapter 4. Doing so allows an exploration of long-term trends in the income share of the rich, but not of the structure of inequality further down the ladder. This is crucial, because the effect of wage centralization is all about raising the earnings of those at the bottom compared with those in the middle. This will reduce the distance between the bottom and the middle, as measured by the 50:10 ratio, and overall inequality in society, as measured by the Gini coefficient. It will not, in all likelihood, reduce the share of all income going to the very top, since these typically are not even covered by wage agreements. The findings of Scheve and Stasavage, in sum, at one and the same time lend additional credibility to the assumed mechanism of wage centralization and show how important choosing the right measures can be.

The past decades have seen a lot of change in how wage-setting is done. As already mentioned, the social market economies have moved away from the pure centralized model they had perfected around 1980. This is why Denmark, Norway and Sweden score 4, not 5, on the wage bargaining index, and Finland only 3. In spite of this, bargaining coverage remains high, with the lowest coverage found in Norway at 74 per cent in 2008. In the liberal market economies, conversely, coverage has plummeted. In Australia, for instance, it fell from 88 per cent in 1980 to 45 per cent three decades later, while British coverage collapsed from 80 per cent in 1979, when Thatcher entered office, to 31.2 per cent in 2011. In the United States, coverage was never extensive, but still has fallen from 23.9 per cent in 1981, the year Reagan became president, to 13 per cent in 2011 (Visser 2013). The point to appreciate here is that this alone may account for a substantial portion of the rising inequality in the liberal market economies, on the one hand, and the relative stability in the social market economies, on the other.

The Business Environment

The availability of human capital and the mode of negotiating wages are hugely important for firms. They influence the type and quality of the workforce as well as how much it costs. Neither of them, however, relates directly to how easy or difficult it is to do business in a country. It is an often-heard complaint in countries with big governments that there is too much red tape, obstructing entrepreneurs' efforts to create the new wealth that ultimately will benefit the country. Employees may be well educated, and wages being decided with only the employer and the individual employee in the room, but if day-to-day operations are slowed down by a vast bureaucracy and arcane rules, what good does that do? Research, unsurprisingly, documents that when business is heavily regulated, economic growth suffers as a result (Djankov et al. 2006; Justesen 2008). The thing to be aware of is that, contrary to common sentiments, it is not the case that big government equals bad government. It sometimes does, but frequently it does not (Hopkin and Blyth 2012).

To illustrate this, consider Table 7.1. It contains the Ease of Doing Business Index constructed by the World Bank. The index is meant to measure how easy it is to run a firm in a country. It contains information on 11 essential activities that cover a firm's lifecycle: starting a business, employing workers, dealing with construction permits, getting electricity, registering property, getting credit, protecting investors, enforcing contracts and resolving insolvency (for details, see World Bank 2014). Countries vary widely. To exemplify, in the worst-performing countries it can take 3 months and cost almost 140 per cent of GDP per capita to register a firm, while this is done in a matter of days and virtually free of charge elsewhere (ibid.: 73). Based on the 11 activities, each consisting of several sub-activities, countries are ranked from the easiest place to do business to the worst. Columns 1 and 2 in Table 7.1 report the rank of the countries we have studied so far, with the first column giving the rank among our sample and column 2 giving the rank among all 189 countries on which the World Bank has data. The subsequent columns contain the rank on some of the 11 activities to get a fuller picture of countries' performance.

Of the 22 countries in the table, Denmark comes out as the easiest place to do business in 2014. This flies in the face of any notion that big spending necessarily means a poor business environment. Indeed, Norway (no. 3), Finland (no. 6) and Sweden (no. 8) are right on Denmark's tail. This impressive showing does not mean that small government is bad either. Performing just as well are the liberal market economies of South Korea (no. 2), the United States (no. 4), the United Kingdom (no. 5), Australia (no. 7), Ireland (no. 9) and Canada (no. 11). The countries that perform poorly are consistently the statist market economies. France, for instance, is no. 17 in the 22-country sample and

Table 7.1   *Ease of doing business in 2014*

	Rank	Overall Rank	Starting a Business	Construction Permits	Registering Property	Getting Credit	Paying Taxes	Trading across Borders
Denmark	1	4	11	1	3	7	3	5
South Korea	2	5	7	3	24	12	11	1
Norway	3	6	10	9	2	20	4	17
United States	4	7	18	11	10	2	18	11
United Kingdom	5	8	17	5	22	5	5	10
Finland	6	9	13	10	13	12	8	9
Australia	7	10	3	7	18	3	15	28
Sweden	8	11	16	6	7	20	14	2
Ireland	9	13	8	29	17	7	1	3
Germany	10	14	31	2	25	7	21	12
Canada	11	16	2	27	19	4	2	16
Estonia	12	17	12	8	5	7	12	4
Switzerland	13	20	23	12	6	16	6	15
Austria	14	21	29	17	12	16	22	13
Netherlands	15	27	9	23	20	22	10	8
Japan	16	29	27	19	23	22	30	14
France	17	31	14	20	28	22	26	6
Poland	18	32	28	30	14	5	25	26
Spain	19	33	24	24	21	16	23	21
Slovak Republic	20	37	25	25	4	12	28	31
Israel	21	40	21	28	29	12	27	7
Belgium	22	42	5	18	31	27	24	18
Czech Republic	23	44	30	31	11	7	29	30
Romania	24	48	38	140	63	7	52	65
Slovenia	25	51	6	22	26	30	16	29
Hungary	26	54	57	103	52	17	88	72
Italy	27	56	18	26	15	27	31	23
Luxembourg	28	59	26	13	30	31	7	22
Greece	29	61	20	21	27	22	19	27

Note: Column 1 (Rank) refers to the ranking of each country compared with the other countries in the table, while Column 2 (Overall rank) refers to the rank of each country compared with all the 189 countries included in the World Bank's Ease of Doing Business Index. The ranks in Columns 3–8 similarly refer to all 189 countries. Columns 3–8 only represent a selection of the indicators that go into the Ease of Doing Business Index.

Source: The World Bank (2014).

no. 31 overall, just behind Macedonia. Italy, Luxembourg and Greece show even lousier performance at the bottom in the unglamorous company of Jamaica, Belarus and Tunisia. Germany and the Netherlands are partial exceptions to the poor performance, which fits the impression that these countries have less blatant government intervention in the economy. When we look across the various activities, there is a lot of variation within countries. Denmark does well when it comes to getting construction permits, registering property or paying taxes, but less well for start-ups. In the United States, the paperwork needing to be done before launching a firm is even worse than in Denmark, and you are also bothered by bureaucracy when you want to pay your firm's taxes. The variation within countries hints at the fact that no country is perfect in the fight against wasteful procedures, and that even the best performers have room for improvement. Still, the core insight is that whether government is big or small has no bearing on the business environment.

Another important aspect of a business-friendly environment is the degree of labour market flexibility. Employers generally prefer a high level of flexibility in terms of hiring and firing. This makes it possible to adapt to new market conditions quickly by off-loading workers during downturns, or shifting emphasis from one product market to another. Strict employment rules make such flexibility difficult, and that can, in turn, have a negative effect on the willingness of firms to take on new employees even during booms. When a firm is uncertain about whether it will be able to shed workers down the road if the good times end earlier than expected, it will be more hesitant to hire in the first place. There is a substantial amount of evidence that employment legislation that makes firing difficult, or in some cases even impossible, lowers overall employment levels in society (Bradley and Stephens 2007) and depresses productivity (Bassanini et al. 2009). Furthermore, in countries with rigid employment legislation – notably the statist market economies – a group of labour market outsiders is created, who are either unemployed or work on short-term and low-pay contracts. Inequalities, as a consequence, increase between those with secure jobs and generous benefits and those without (Esping-Andersen 1999; Häusermann and Schwander 2012).

Conclusion

How the economy is organized matters profoundly for inequality. The relationship, however, defies both the optimistic and pessimistic accounts that were introduced in the previous chapter. It is not the case that growth will automatically lead to lower inequality, as the optimists would have it, or that inequality inevitably is bad for growth, as the pessimists claim. All advanced democracies have experienced sustained growth for many decades, but it has been achieved in radically different ways. All countries are, of course, unique, yet some clear country clusters are visible. The liberal market economies have pursued a small-government approach with lots of room for private initiative. This has been a success in terms of growth, but a failure in terms of equality. The statist market economies have followed an interventionist approach with a highly regulated labour market and business sector, but with relatively limited investment in citizens' human capital. The result has been sluggish growth and a mounting insider–outsider divide, leading to gradually rising inequality. The social market economies, finally, have embraced an investment strategy with a lot of resources being spent on human capital formation, but with wage-setting left to the partners of the labour market and a hands-off approach towards firms. This formula has made it possible to combine growth with equality.

The optimist and pessimist accounts are basically a political. They view the relationship between growth and inequality as purely economic in nature. Realizing that there are different capitalist systems makes us aware that how the economy is organized fundamentally is a choice – and that means that it is a question of politics. Clearly, capitalist systems are slow-moving things, and revolutionary change virtually never happens, but over the long haul, the preferences of powerful actors will leave an imprint. One decision after the other can gradually transform an economy. All countries have seen reforms ever since their births in the aftermath of World War II that have morphed them continuously. Take Denmark as an example from the picture-perfect social market economies. From the 1990s onwards, the social rights of the unemployed have been systematically curtailed, while the stiff tax rates on firms and high personal incomes have been trimmed (Green-Pedersen and Klitgaard 2009; Andersen 2011; Jensen 2014: 102–11). Given the starting point, these are real changes, and explain why the income of the poorest has stagnated compared with the rest of the population (see Chapter 5). In the next chapter, we focus on the redistributive role of the welfare state, which differs widely according to the type of organized capitalism. To the extent that the setup of the capitalist system and the institutionalization of the welfare state are choices, the question becomes who influences those choices and what they want to achieve. This is the topic of Chapters 9 and 10.

Chapter 8

Does the welfare state reduce inequality?

Many people spontaneously associate the welfare state with equality, reasoning that the welfare state implies redistribution and that redistribution means more equality. At first sight, this seems to make perfect sense. In fact, one of the earliest students of the welfare state, Harold L. Wilensky, tellingly titled his book *The Welfare State and Equality* and concluded that 'taxes and benefits taken together have a *highly* egalitarian effect on income distribution' (1975: 94, original emphasis). A whole generation of researchers then empirically tried to document the intuition that the bigger the welfare state (in terms of public social spending), the more egalitarian the income distribution tended to be (for a review of this early literature, see Esping-Andersen and Van Kersbergen 1992).

In this chapter, we first present an overview of public social spending data and show that, compared with people's intuition, the picture turns out to be much more complicated. There does not seem to be a clear and strong (negative) relationship between the size of the welfare state and inequality. We turn to the theory of welfare state institutions to explain why this is the case. We find that the main reason is that there is no such thing as *the* welfare state that can be measured with spending data. There are different *kinds* of welfare states, whose different qualities have systematically different social consequences (Esping-Andersen 1990). We also explain that the different kinds of welfare states are closely associated with the different kinds of market economies discussed in Chapter 7.

With the help of this insight, we then continue with the presentation of empirical data, demonstrating that welfare states reduce inequality to varying extents; some welfare states actually reinforce inequality. Redistribution of income is one major function of the welfare state, but it does not always go from the rich to the poor, nor is the size of the welfare state (in terms of social spending) necessarily a good indicator of the welfare state's redistributive power. This is because some welfare states tax back substantial amounts on their social spending. Others rely strongly on the tax system and private social spending for social purposes. If one looks at the picture as a whole, it turns out that the differences between welfare states in net social spending are not that big, and yet their levels of inequality still diverge widely. By looking at the qualitative features of welfare states, we can explain why some welfare states redistribute relatively more to the poor than to the rich, others target the poor but are not very redistributive, whereas still others actually reinforce existing inequality via the tax–benefit system.

Does the Size of the Welfare State Matter for Inequality?

Total public social spending is usually the first thing people look at to gauge the size of the welfare state and to see what, if any, is the relationship between the welfare state and income inequality. Although we will argue that exclusively looking at public social spending is problematic if one is interested in the welfare state's redistributive impact, expenditure data can nevertheless be argued 'to measure the total commitment of society to the public provision of income support and social services' (Huber and Stephens 2001: 40). With that in mind, it makes sense to start by delving into public social expenditure data.

Figure 8.1 shows the association between public social spending as a percentage of GDP, on the vertical axis, and inequality expressed

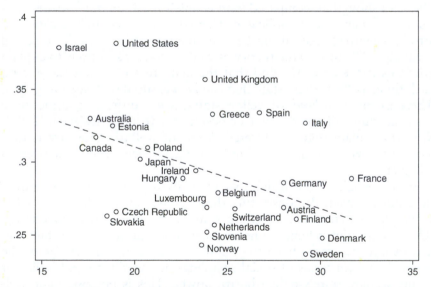

Figure 8.1   *Public social spending as a percentage of GDP and the Gini coefficient*

Note: Public social spending includes both public and mandatory private spending and is calculated as a percentage of GDP.

Source: OECD (2013a) and LIS (2015).

in the Gini coefficient, on the horizontal axis, and demonstrates that there turns out to be a relationship, but that it is a far from perfect one (Pearson's $r = -0.45$). This implies that not all welfare states with similar levels of social spending have similar levels of inequality. Some smaller welfare states actually perform better than some of the bigger ones in this respect. It is plausible that the structure (where the money is spent) and the financing of the welfare state are more important factors than plain spending.

In the upper left corner of Figure 8.1 (< 25 per cent spending and Gini > 0.28), we find all the Anglo-Saxon countries plus Israel, Estonia, Poland, Japan and Greece. These are the welfare states that confirm the intuition about social spending, to the extent that these countries combine low social spending with high inequality. Note, however, that the variation within this group of countries is still considerable: Greece and the United Kingdom have comparable levels of spending, but diverging levels of inequality, whereas Australia has about the same level of inequality as Greece, but much less social spending. The United States and Israel have the highest levels of inequality, yet differ somewhat in spending levels.

In the upper right corner of Figure 8.1 (> 25 per cent spending and Gini > 0.28), we find Italy and Spain, which defy expectations about the size of the welfare state because they combine a medium to high level of social spending with high inequality. Apparently, these countries' public social spending does not create a lot more equality. In fact, big spender Italy has about the same level of inequality as the much leaner welfare states of Australia, Estonia and Canada. In the bottom right corner of Figure 8.1 (> 25 per cent spending and Gini < 0.28), we find the major continental European countries (except Belgium and the Netherlands, which spend slightly less), and all the Nordic countries (except Norway) that live up to the expectations. These countries have relatively modest inequality and medium to high levels of spending. Also here, however, we note considerable within-group variation: France is by far the biggest spender, but its level of inequality is comparable with that of Hungary and Ireland, countries that spend approximately 9 to 10 per cent less than France.

Finally, in the bottom left corner of Figure 8.1 (< 25 per cent spending and Gini < 0.28), we find all the post-communist countries (except Poland), the Benelux countries and Norway. These countries also defy our intuition, because they roughly have moderate to low levels of inequality, but do not spend as much as the big spenders. Again, there is substantial variation within this group of countries: Slovakia, for instance, has the lowest level of spending, but takes a middle position on inequality in this group.

Norway is an interesting case, because of all the Nordic countries it has the lowest level of public social spending, yet still a comparably low level of inequality. Note, however, that this might be partly a denominator effect, because the level of expenditure is expressed as a percentage of GDP. Norway (like Switzerland and Luxembourg) is a comparatively rich country, and although the amount of GDP the Norwegians devote to social goals can be argued to reflect their society's political choices, expressing public social expenditure as a percentage of GDP could still be somewhat misleading. If we look at total social expenditure on social protection per head of the population for European countries, we find that Norway and Switzerland are much bigger spenders than the data in Figure 8.1 suggest. It is really the southern welfare states that stand out, spending a meagre less than EUR 7000 per capita. Norway, for example, spends EUR 15,870 on social protection per head of the population, which is twice the sum spent by Italy (EUR 6884) and more than four times as much as Portugal (EUR 3769) (Eurostat 2015). Of course, the differences level off somewhat if one takes into account the different price levels in these countries, but still, public social spending expressed as a percentage of GDP does not always precisely capture a society's social commitment.

The point is that, more generally, the use of public social spending data for evaluating explicitly the size of the welfare state (or welfare *effort*, as Wilensky (1975) called it) and implicitly its quality is notoriously fraught with the danger of misinterpretation. There are several reasons for this. Importantly, public social spending data hide the impact of the tax system on social transfers and do not reveal the various other important policy instruments that welfare states employ for social protection purposes, such as, for example, tax breaks (see OECD 2014b). Moreover, to get the full picture, one should also look at non-mandatory private social expenditures, such as benefits that employers grant to their employees and private collective or individual social schemes (e.g. pension, childcare, health) that governments promote by allowing them special tax treatment.

Figure 8.2 summarizes some of the relevant information. The light grey bars show the so-called net tax effect. This is the amount that the state gets back from recipients of social benefits. In many countries, recipients have to pay tax on the benefits they receive, which obviously reduces the real value of the benefits, but how much recipients have to pay varies a lot between countries. The net tax effect is measured as a percentage of GDP. The most eye-catching fact concerns the net tax effect in Denmark (–9 per cent), Finland (–6.1 per cent), Sweden (–5.8 per cent), Austria (–5.4 per cent) and Luxembourg (–5.1 per cent), on the one hand, and the small difference in South Korea (0 per cent), the United States (–1 per cent), Japan (–1.2 per cent), Australia (–1.2 per cent) and Canada (–1.3 per cent), on the other. Thus, if one wished to use social expenditure as an indicator of a society's commitment to the public provision of income support and social services, one would, at a minimum, need to correct for how much the welfare state actually claws back again in taxation.

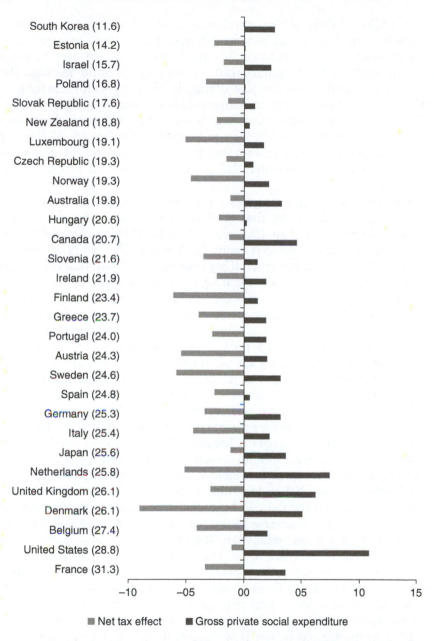

Figure 8.2   *From gross to net social spending, as a percentage of GDP, 2011*

Note: Countries are ranked according to net social spending. Net tax effect includes direct taxes and social contributions, indirect taxes and net tax breaks for social purposes similar to cash benefits (TBSPs). TBSPs can also include favourable tax treatment of household pension saving, tax relief for employers, and private funds that ultimately benefit households, e.g. favourable tax treatment of employer benefits provided to households and favourable tax treatment of private funds.

Source: OECD (2013a).

In addition, there is the phenomenon of private social spending, which is defined as 'social benefits delivered through the private sector (not transfers between individuals) which involve an element of compulsion and/or inter-personal redistribution, for example through the pooling of contributions and risk sharing in terms of health and longevity' (OECD 2014b: 6). The most important categories of private social spending concern private social health spending, and particularly pensions, which could be (mandatory and voluntary) employer schemes or individual pension arrangements that benefit from tax breaks. On average, OECD countries devoted 2.7 per cent of GDP to private social spending in 2011.

If we look at the data for gross private social spending, the dark grey bars in Figure 8.2, we see that the United States is by far the biggest spender, with no less than 10.9 per cent of GDP being devoted to private social spending, followed by the Netherlands (7.4 per cent) and the United Kingdom (6.2 per cent). If we take the gross public spending (as used on the horizontal axis in Figure 8.1), subtract the net tax effect and then add the gross private social spending, we get the *net social spending*: that is, social spending as a percentage of GDP taking both taxes and private social spending into account. In the figure, net social spending for each country is reported in the brackets, and the countries are ranked according to how much they spend. Surprisingly, net social spending in the United States is 28.8 per cent, *de facto* ranking this country as the second biggest spender after France. Countries such as Finland, Norway and Sweden are found way down on the list.

Traditionally in the welfare state literature, the United States has been labelled a welfare state laggard because of its relatively small welfare state, measured in terms of public social spending, but this view can be challenged if one, for example, includes public education in the picture (see Garfinkel et al. 2010). Including education might stretch the concept of public social spending – because it is not meant to protect against a risk, but, rather, to increase young people's human capital – but even if one leaves out public education, it turns out that large parts of the American welfare state are invisible in public expenditure data. In the United States, the tax system plays an important welfare state role, because it offers various types of tax breaks for social purposes. In fact, such tax expenditures – taxes that citizens should have paid if it were not for various deductions – accounted for almost 6 per cent of GDP in 2013 in the United States. If we aggregate all tax expenditures that make up this 'hidden' American welfare state, we find that they account for even more spending than Medicare (3.1 per cent of GDP) and Social Security (5 per cent of GDP), two of the biggest social programmes in the American welfare state (Congressional Budget Office 2013; see also Howard 2007).

It is important to understand that tax expenditures tend to be regressive, i.e. they are more favourable to higher- than to lower-income groups. This is intuitively understandable if one realizes that in order to qualify for a tax reduction, one needs to have something to deduct and enough money to buy something to which a tax break applies. To benefit from a tax break on private health insurance, one has to be able to buy it first; and the more expensive the insurance is, the more one can deduct. The Congressional Budget Office (2013) of the United States estimated that in 2013 more than 50 per cent of tax expenditures went to households with incomes in the highest quintile of the population, whereas no less than 17 per cent went to households in the top 1 per cent of the population. In sharp contrast, 13 per cent of tax expenditures went to households in the middle quintile, and only 8 per cent to the households in the lowest quintile.

The American tax system overall is regressive: in all 50 states, low- and middle-income families pay higher taxes than the wealthy. In fact, the lower a family's income, the higher the effective state and local taxes are. In the ten most regressive American states, families in the bottom quintile pay seven times more of their income in taxes than those in the top quintile. On average across all states, there is a clear income gradient in how much tax families pay: almost 11 per cent in the bottom 20 per cent, about 10 per cent in the second quintile, 9.4 per cent in the middle quintile, 8.7 per cent in the fourth quintile, 7.7 per cent in the next 15 per cent of the income distribution, 7 per cent in the next 4 per cent, and 5.4 per cent in the top 1 per cent (Institute on Taxation and Economic Policy 2015).

But even in Denmark, where tax expenditures account for much less, such provisions tend to be regressive too. Table 8.1 shows the percentage of people within specific income groups who use a special tax deduction for house and garden maintenance. It clearly shows a double income gradient: the higher the income, the larger the share of the income group that benefits from the tax provision, and the larger the amount deducted.

If we include all information on the impact of gross public social spending, private social expenditure and taxation, we can conclude that in reality, levels of net social spending in modern welfare states do not differ all that much. As can be seen from Figure 8.2, most countries spend between 20 and 25 per cent of GDP on social goals, with South Korea at the low end, with only 11.6 per cent net social spending, and France at the high end, with 31.3 per cent of GDP net social spending.

But we also conclude that, even though it seems to make intuitive sense to look at public social spending if one wishes to understand the size of the welfare state and its redistributive role, public social spending data, in fact, tell surprisingly little about this. If net social spending level does not vary that much cross-nationally, it follows that there can be

Table 8.1   *Housing/garden improvement tax deductions according to income group in Denmark, 2013*

Personal income (USD)	People using tax break (% of total in income group)	Average amount (USD)
Under 30,000	5.4	1288
30,000–51,000	12.7	1300
51,000–73,000	19.7	1365
73,000–100,000	29.1	1442
Over 100,000	38.8	1600

Source: The Danish Ministry of Taxation (2014).

no strong relation with the level of inequality, which does vary widely. One important reason, most clearly exemplified by the American case, is that the institutional setup of the tax–benefit system can actually be and raise, rather than moderate, inequality.

Welfare State Models and Inequality

This finding indicates that we should look beyond public social spending figures and ask how the institutional features of the welfare state may affect the distribution of income. Why is it that there is no straightforward relationship between the size of the welfare state (public social spending) and equality? Why do some welfare states redistribute more than others? Why do some welfare states actually reinforce, rather than moderate, inequality?

As we have said, the main reason why the biggest welfare states are not necessarily also the most redistributive ones is that there are different *kinds* of welfare states, which have systematically different social consequences. More specifically, most welfare states are simply not designed to create more equality; their purpose is, first and foremost, to offer protection against social risks (old age, unemployment, disability, etc.) and to help maintain income (see Van Kersbergen and Vis 2014). The egalitarian effect of the welfare state, therefore, depends on the design and generosity of the tax–benefit and social service system, with only some systems being capable of producing more equality.

Two dimensions of welfare state systems are particularly relevant for explaining the widely diverging social outcomes that different welfare states produce: the quality of social rights that the state guarantees, and the intended and implied social stratification that a welfare state creates and maintains. First, the dimension of the quality of guaranteed social rights refers to the extent to which individuals and families can uphold a decent life in case of sickness, unemployment or old age independently of what they bring home from the (labour) market. This quality is high if it is relatively easy to qualify for a benefit, for example, when the required contribution period is short and there is no means test. Similarly, a social right is of high quality when a benefit's replacement rate is high (how much of a wage or salary a benefit replaces) and its duration is long.

Second, as Esping-Andersen (1990: chapter 3) has famously emphasized, the welfare state is not only providing social protection and income security, but is also itself a system of social stratification, sometimes intentionally upholding class and status differentials. Welfare states 'are key institutions in the structuring of class and the social order' (ibid.: 55), and, depending on their institutional setup, they have widely divergent outcomes in terms of social structure. Welfare states 'may be equally large or comprehensive, but with entirely different effects on social structure', and they come in three shapes: 'One may cultivate hierarchy and status, another dualisms, and a third universalism. Each case will produce its own unique fabric of social solidarity' (ibid.: 58).

The conservative or corporatist welfare state model features social insurance programmes that are differentiated and segmented along occupational and status distinctions. In addition, in countries such as Germany and Austria, state employees (civil servants) receive privileged treatment in social insurance, particularly pensions. In this model, people qualify for a provision or benefit to the extent that they have contributed to a social scheme. Employment record is decisive for acquiring social rights, and employees pay contributions to social insurance funds and receive benefits that are earnings-related and depend on contribution period. This model is typically social service-lean and transfer-heavy. These features of the conservative system imply that the existing stratification system and income inequality are largely left untouched and, in fact, tend to magnify rather than moderate existing differences in status and income. The employed, especially those working for the state, are well-protected insiders, whereas those without a strong attachment to the labour market are outsiders.

The liberal welfare state is market-oriented, and public provisions for income maintenance and relief mainly cater to the poor. Most people in countries such as Australia and the United States are obliged to find social protection for themselves and their families in the private market. Low and flat-rate tax-financed benefits characterize the system, and access to benefits is restrictive because benefits are means-tested. Private social insurance is encouraged via tax exemptions and allowances, which favour the middle class and the rich. The liberal welfare state is also service-lean, and transfers are modest. The inequalities generated in the private market are not countered in this system, and those who can afford it are well protected, whereas others come to depend on means-tested assistance.

The social democratic welfare state grounds social rights in citizenship or residence, and hence, to a substantial extent, does away with status differentials. This model, as found in the Nordics, is generally tax-financed, but access to social provisions is much more open and benefits and services are more generous than in the liberal model. The model provides social services for all without qualifying conditions. The role of the market in service and benefit provision is played down.

These welfare state models, in short, differ substantially in how much they are committed to spend, but what matters most for social outcomes such as inequality is on what specific social purposes that money is spent, how the programmes are organized, taxed and financed, and how transfer- or service-oriented they are.

Welfare State Generosity

By measuring empirically such indicators as replacement rates, duration of benefits, qualifying demands, waiting days and coverage, researchers (Esping-Andersen 1990; Korpi and Palme 2007; Scruggs et al. 2014) have devised measures that capture the extent to which social services and benefits are social rights and allow people to 'maintain a livelihood without reliance on the market' (Esping-Andersen 1990: 22). The initially most widely used indicator of the quality of the welfare state was Esping-Andersen's decommodification index. This measure had the drawback that it did not take into account national guaranteed social minima. Closely following Esping-Andersen's methodology, Scruggs and his collaborators amended this shortcoming and developed an index that more fully captures the generosity of old age pensions, unemployment insurance and sick pay insurance (Scruggs 2014).

In Figure 8.3, we report this index for the countries for which data were available for both 1980 and 2010. The countries are ranked (high to low) according to their generosity index in 1980. The higher the score on this index, the more generous the entitlements are. Because the index combines information on programme replacement rates, social insurance coverage (the proportion of the working-age population entitled to a benefit) and take-up rates, the duration of a benefit, and various qualifying conditions (such as waiting days in sickness insurance or contribution period in pensions), the numbers have no direct and intuitive meaning. The Swedish welfare state had a generosity score of 44.1 in 1980, which – taken by itself – cannot be readily interpreted. However, comparing generosity levels between countries or over time is

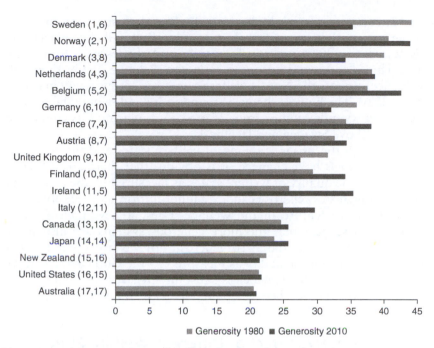

Figure 8.3 *The generosity of welfare states, 1980 and 2010*

Note: Countries are ranked (high to low) according to their generosity score in 1980. Figures in brackets refer to (1) the country's ranking in 1980 and (2) its ranking in 2010.

Source: Scruggs et al. (2014).

meaningful. In fact, we can say that in 1980 the Swedish welfare state's entitlements were much more generous than those of Australia.

The 1980 classification of welfare states according to their generosity very much reproduces Esping-Andersen's decommodification index, which used data from the same year. The Nordic countries (except Finland) clearly had the most generous welfare states in 1980, closely followed by the continental European countries. The liberal welfare states of Canada, New Zealand, the United States and Australia can also be clearly distinguished at the bottom of Figure 8.3. Italy's welfare state in 1980 was more like the liberal than the continental European welfare model, whereas the United Kingdom, often considered a liberal welfare state, was closer to Austria and Germany than to any of the liberal welfare states.

Figure 8.3 also reveals that there has been both stability and change in the worlds of welfare. As one can see from the bars and the country ranking numbers, the liberal welfare states have remained squarely within their own cluster, whereas the United Kingdom has dropped from place

9 to 12, coming now much closer to the liberal cluster than in 1980. Sweden, the world's generosity champion in 1980, falls five places and ends at rank 6 in 2010, whereas Denmark similarly descends from place 3 to 8. Three continental European countries (Belgium, the Netherlands and France) surpass the Nordic welfare states (except Norway) in generosity in 2010. The biggest change is found in Ireland, where the welfare state generosity index jumps from 25.8 to 35.3, placing this country at rank 5, i.e. above Sweden and Denmark.

Even though the precise ranking of welfare states and the composition of the models have changed, it is obvious that there are still clear differences in the quality of welfare states as measured by the generosity index. Although the generosity index cannot inform us precisely about the redistributive feature of the welfare states, it nevertheless seems reasonable to suspect that the more generous systems are also more egalitarian. If we relate the 2010 generosity of welfare states to their post-tax-and-transfer inequality as measured by the Gini coefficient, we get a Pearson's r of -0.62, which is substantially stronger than the one we found for the relation between public social spending and inequality.

The Redistributive Effect of Different Welfare States

One way of getting an idea of how, and how much, welfare states redistribute is by tracing more directly who benefits most from transfers. The OECD provides data on the percentage of public cash benefits that flows to different income groups measured as quintiles. As Figure 8.4 shows, welfare states vary substantially in which income group profits most from transfers. The countries in Figure 8.4 are ranked according to the difference between the share of the lowest quintile and the share of the top quintile.

One group of countries (placed in the bottom part of Figure 8.4, from France downwards) clearly transfers a higher proportion of cash benefits to the highest quintile than to the lowest one. Portugal leads a group of southern European countries (plus Luxembourg, Austria and France) where the lowest income group clearly receives less than the top. These countries have double-digit 'redistribution deficits'. Portugal has a difference of -29.1 between what goes to the bottom and what goes to the top. This country also has one of the highest levels of inequality, with a Gini of 0.35 in 2010 (OECD 2015b).

There are two important causes for this phenomenon of 'redistribution deficit'. First, most transfers in these countries are simply not *meant* to help the poor exclusively, but are to cover the social risks of all social strata. Second, benefits for the retired, disabled and unemployed are often linked to contribution period and are earnings-related, so that relatively more goes to the well-off than to the poor. This is especially true

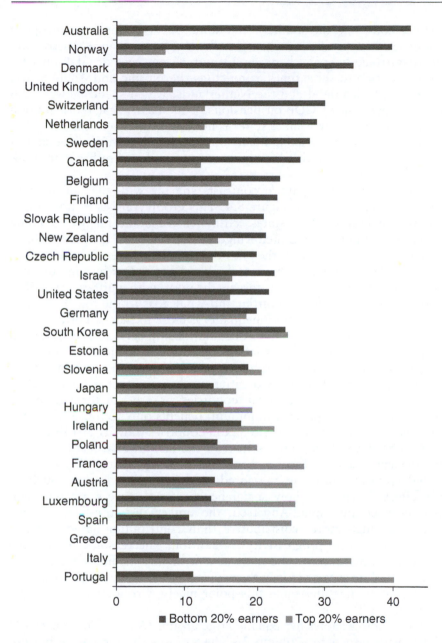

Figure 8.4 *Percentage of all cash benefits going to the top and bottom earners*

Source: OECD (2013a).

for pensions, and the southern and some of the continental European countries are typically pension states: Italy, Greece, France, Austria and Portugal roughly spend between 13 and 16 per cent of GDP on pensions, i.e. two to three times as much as the Nordic and Anglo-Saxon countries, Switzerland and the Netherlands, which spend between 3.6 and 7.4 per cent of GDP on pensions. This means that redistribution in the pension-heavy welfare states is not from the rich to the poor, but primarily from one period in life to another. In other words, inequalities produced during working life are directly reproduced rather than moderated in retirement.

This redistributive pattern contrasts sharply with the one we find for a group at the top of Figure 8.4. This group consists of liberal and social democratic welfare states, led by Australia and further including Norway, Denmark, the United Kingdom, Switzerland, the Netherlands, Sweden and Canada. Here, the bottom group clearly receives more than the top. These countries have a double-digit 'redistribution surplus'. Australia, for instance, clearly targets the poor, with a difference of 38.6 between what goes to the bottom and what goes to the top. However, given that Australia's level of inequality is close to that of Portugal, it is also clear that there is no one-to-one relationship between the allocation of public benefits to different income groups and inequality. The main reason is that the relatively high level of transfers to the bottom income group can be an effect of two different things: either a high level of overall spending, as in the Nordic countries, or targeting through means testing, i.e. offering (usually minimum) benefits only to those who have no other means, as in the Anglo-Saxon countries (OECD 2014b).

Another important reason – next to the institutional features of the tax–benefit systems – for the absence of a strong relationship between social spending, however measured, and inequality is that much of the effect depends on how social benefits and services are financed. As described by Esping-Andersen, the universalist, tax-financed systems are much more redistributive than contribution-based systems, even if there is no progressivity in taxation. The reason is that while every individual receives the same benefit, higher-income groups pay a larger absolute sum of money than lower-income groups. Bo Rothstein (1998: 147ff) has illustrated this point nicely with a stylized example (see Table 8.2).

The example shows five equally large groups (A to E, Column 1) and their average income (Column 2). The ratio of the top to the bottom income groups is 5 to 1, i.e. the top group gets five times more than the bottom. The tax rate in this imaginary country is set at 40 per cent for all, so there is no progressive taxation. Although every group pays the same *percentage*, each pays different *amounts* (Column 3). All social benefits and services (transfers) are distributed according to the principle of universalism: every group on average receives the same amount, namely,

Table 8.2 *The redistributive effect of the universalist welfare state*

Group	Average income	Tax 40%	Transfers	Income after taxes and transfers
A (20%)	1000	400	240	840
B (20%)	800	320	240	720
C (20%)	600	240	240	600
D (20%)	400	160	240	480
E (20%)	200	80	240	360
Ratio between groups A and E	5/1	(= 1200)	(1200/5)	2.33/1

Source: Adopted, with kind permission, from Rothstein (1998: 147, table 6.2).

240 (Column 4). If we now subtract taxes from income and add transfers, we get the groups' income after taxes and transfers (Column 5). We see that a considerable redistribution of income has occurred. The bottom group's income has increased by 80 per cent to 360, whereas the top group's income has decreased by 16 per cent to 840. The top group now only gets 2.33 times as much as the bottom group.

This is quite a drastic implication of universalism for inequality, but it should be nuanced in two ways. First, a fully means-tested system with the same tax level and with a disproportional amount of benefits going to the poor would be much more redistributive. However, means-tested systems tend to be tight-fisted, whereas universal systems distribute much larger sums of money; as a result, the latter come out as much more redistributive than the more targeted and means-tested systems (Korpi and Palme 1998). Second, the distributive effect of the service-heavy social democratic welfare state in reality is probably less than suggested in this stylized example, because even though in-kind services are redistributive, high-income groups also profit from services, especially health care and education.

Figure 8.5 summarizes the redistributive effect of the welfare state, measured as the percentage difference through transfers and taxes between inequality in market income and inequality of disposable income in 2010. This effect is the outcome of public spending on cash benefits, how much the tax–benefit system is targeted at the poor, and the progressivity of the tax system. The countries are listed according to highest distributive effect.

The first observation is that all welfare states redistribute and lower inequality, at least to some extent. However, the cross-national

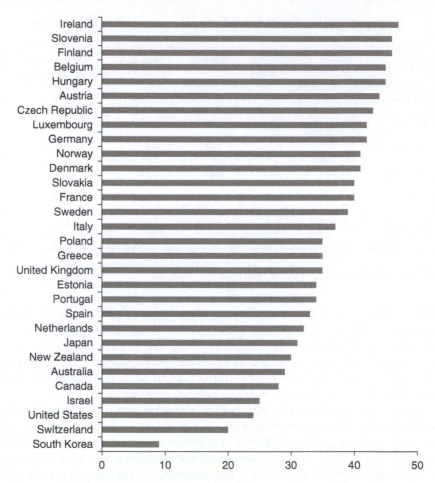

Figure 8.5 *Redistributive effect of the welfare state: percentage difference through transfers and taxes between Gini at market income and disposable income, 2010*

Source: Adema et al. (2014a: 17/18, table 2) and OECD (2015b). Countries are ranked according to the redistributive effect in 2010 (high to low).

differences in the welfare states' redistributive effects are large, varying from 9 to 30 per cent in South Korea, Switzerland, the United States, Israel, Canada, Australia and New Zealand to 45 to 47 per cent in Ireland, Slovenia, Finland, Belgium and Hungary. Most of the countries that top the list also have a relatively low post-tax-and-benefit Gini. In other words, if we look at the redistributive effect of the tax–benefit system, we find that there is a negative relationship between the redistributive predisposition of the tax–benefit system and inequality

(Pearson's $r = -0.57$), which turns out to be a stronger association than the one we found in the case of social spending (see Figure 8.1), but a weaker one than for welfare state generosity.

In any case, the relationship is again not perfect, as the Irish case illustrates: this country's tax–benefit system has the highest redistributive effect, but its Gini coefficient is more or less the same as that of South Korea (around 0.31 in 2010), the country that is placed at the bottom in Figure 8.5, with a redistributive effect of the tax–benefit system of only 9 per cent.

A second, and perhaps surprising, observation is that the countries with the lowest Gini coefficients, namely, Sweden, Norway, Finland and Denmark, are not among the countries with the top redistributive tax–benefit systems. This, in fact, reveals a weakness of the focus on cash benefits and taxation, as we also discussed in Chapter 4. The redistributive impact of the welfare states that offer extensive social services financed via taxation, the Nordic countries, is simply not captured in Figure 8.5 and is therefore underestimated (see also Adema et al. 2014a: 19). This is particularly relevant for Denmark and Sweden, two countries that spend significantly more than other countries on public social services, namely 13.8 and 14.1 per cent of GDP respectively (OECD 2013a).

All western countries spend a lot on health care (Jensen 2008; 2014), so it is not this in-kind service that makes Denmark and Sweden stand out. As Figure 8.6 illustrates, it is, rather, the non-health services. On average, our countries spend 2.4 per cent of GDP on non-health services (i.e. childcare and elderly care), whereas this figure is 7 per cent in Denmark and 7.5 per cent in Sweden. The only two countries that come near these high non-health social service spending levels are the other Nordic countries, Finland (4.8 per cent) and Norway (4.9 per cent). Although in-kind services are generally less redistributive than cash transfers, they nevertheless do reallocate to some extent, an effect that is not picked up in the redistributive effect data presented in Figure 8.5.

Welfare State Models and Types of Market Economies

It is no coincidence that the three welfare state models correspond closely to the three market economies examined in Chapter 7. The Anglo-Saxon countries have liberal market economies and liberal welfare states; the continental and southern European countries have statist market economies and conservative welfare states; and the Nordic countries have social market economies and social democratic (or universalist) welfare states. Although it is not possible to reduce a country's welfare state and its capitalist system to a single factor, there are powerful synergies

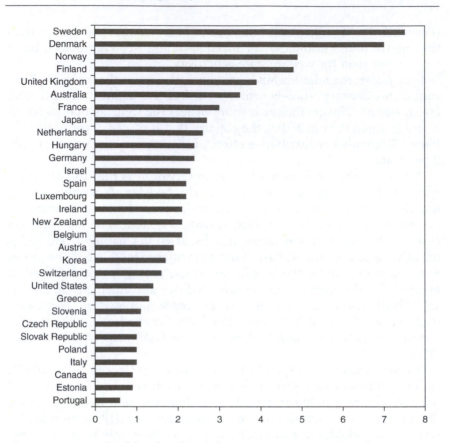

Figure 8.6   *Non-health-related social services as a percentage of GDP, 2012 or latest year available*

Source: OECD (2013a).

between the two. As pointed out by Estevez-Abe et al. (2001: 146), 'the shape of social protection has bearings on national competitive advantage in international markets and choice of market strategies'.

The institutional characteristics of the liberal welfare state go together with the form of market economy in these countries. The combination of means-tested and meagre benefits with extensive tax breaks means that there is maximum incentive for private initiative. Because the liberal market economy is based on a highly polarized workforce, in terms of both education and salary, there is little basis for generous public education or unemployment protection that could raise the reservation wage of workers (i.e. the minimum wage they would accept for a job).

The same applies to the conservative and social democratic models. The contribution-based and earnings-related schemes of the conservative welfare state fit the skills-specific industry production that these countries traditionally excelled in and where long-term employment was of great value to both employee and employer (although this setup is currently less successful than it used to be). In the social democratic welfare state, free-of-charge and generous education facilitates a well-educated workforce, and heavily subsidized childcare creates exceptionally high employment rates among women. Because the workforce is comparably well educated, it becomes possible to finance fairly high wages also for manual workers and others, who earn very little in any of the other types of welfare states.

As we touched upon in Chapter 7, and will return to in more detail in the next, the fact that a country's welfare state matches its market economy means that both get stabilized. Welfare state institutions like those discussed above entail that both wage earners and employers not only are induced to behave in a certain way, but also begin to adapt their expectations about the future, and perhaps even their normative values, accordingly. If companies know that there is a ready supply of high-skilled but pricey manual workers, they organize the production so as to make the best of this fact. And if they know manual workers are cheap, but with fewer qualifications, they will decide how to organize production so as to maximize profit under these conditions. This adaptive behaviour, in turn, makes it harder to alter the welfare state institutions, because change will affect previous production decisions. Yet, while the linkage between welfare state models and market economy is strong, it is not deterministic. Change happens. In Chapters 9 and 10, we take a look at how such change comes about and, more broadly, who decides in the politics of inequality.

Conclusion

The empirical overview of this chapter has shown the following. Although all welfare states redistribute from the rich to the poor and decrease market inequality to some extent, there is no straightforward negative relationship between the size of the welfare state (measured as public social spending) and inequality. Taking into account the impact of the tax system on social transfers, tax instruments for social provision, and private social spending, welfare states are more alike in terms of net social spending than is often assumed. Welfare states come in different kinds, and their qualitative differences, expressed in the generosity index, are substantial. Some welfare states, especially the conservative ones that have contribution-based and earnings-related social schemes, redistribute relatively more to the rich than to the poor. The liberal welfare states exclusively target the poor and rely relatively more on tax expenditures. They are not very generous and tend to be more regressive than others. The social democratic welfare states tend to be generous and also the most egalitarian.

Most welfare states are finding it increasingly difficult to maintain the level of redistribution that they have historically fostered. Large-scale economic processes – globalization, technological change and large sectoral shifts in the structure of employment – have increased the demand for highly educated, high-skilled and more productive workers, and reduced the demand for poorly educated, low-skilled and less productive workers. The former group's market income has risen, whereas the latter group has seen its income decline. In addition, the emergence of new social risks associated with post-industrial society has augmented inequality, because the traditional welfare state was ill equipped to manage these.

Simply maintaining the same level of income equality under conditions of rising market inequality would, therefore, already have required a huge increase in the generosity and redistributive effort of the welfare state, and – judging by the rising inequality in many welfare states in the last decades – this apparently has not happened.

Apart from the question of whether this would have been politically feasible, the room for more redistributive policies has most likely been extremely limited anyway, as most welfare states, in the same period as they had to deal with rising market inequality and new social risks, also had to find a solution to the financial predicament – caused by population ageing – of their pension and health care systems. In fact, and in this context, welfare state reforms and adaptations very often aim at austerity and have the effect (if not the intention) of decreasing generosity, hence offering less protection and income security and reinforcing, rather than offsetting, the already considerable inegalitarian tendencies. Even in the strongly equality-focused Nordic region, some countries, notably Denmark and Sweden, have substantially decreased the generosity of their welfare state and have not been capable of entirely upholding their relatively flat income distributions.

Most political systems will have difficulties in coping with the huge pressures resulting from these big challenges, whether stemming from outside (say, globalization) or from inside (say, ageing). Given their existing commitments, governments have very limited room to manoeuvre. On the one hand, the institutional resilience against a radical overhaul of the welfare state is strong, as is the popular resistance against it. On the other hand, increasing the effort to reach a higher level of redistribution and equality is already difficult and would require either higher taxation or radical redistribution of resources within the public sector, or both. Even if this were possible, and assuming no negative effects on economic growth, it would require exceptional political conditions to push through.

Chapter 9

Does economic inequality lead to political inequality?

Chapters 6, 7 and 8 asked how the economy and the welfare state relate to inequality. Although inequality influences how both the economy and the welfare state work, our focus was mostly on how inequality is *caused* and shaped by the structure of the economy and welfare state arrangements. The overarching argument of the two chapters was that the degree to which the economy and the welfare state create inequality is fundamentally a political decision. In that sense, both chapters were concerned with how politics affects inequality. This and the next chapter, on the other hand, take a more sustained look at how inequality affects politics. The key question that we want to know the answer to is whether *economic* inequality leads to *political* inequality.

Political inequality occurs when the preferences of some citizens systematically are given more weight in the political process than those of other citizens. In this book, we are, of course, especially interested in whether or not those with more economic resources have a greater say than those with fewer. For many people, such political inequality is normatively wrong, because it seems to fly in the face of our intuition about how democracy ought to work. In the words of Almond and Verba (1963: 180), '[d]emocracy is a political system in which ordinary citizens exercise control over elites'. This highlights how democracy requires that ordinary people control the elite, not the other way around. Just as importantly, political inequalities may help explain why economic inequalities persist or widen. If those with most to win from pro-rich policies also disproportionately influence policy-making, it is easy to imagine that there will be a bias towards keeping or expanding these kinds of policies. In this way, economic inequalities may create political inequalities that, in turn, maintain or increase the existing economic inequalities, and so on.

We can think of the process by which citizens' preferences for equality get transformed into policies as a ladder with a number of steps that must be climbed. The first step is *preference formation*. What do people want when it comes to equality and redistributive policies, and, relatedly, do the well-off want something different from those with fewer resources? If the well-off and the less well-to-do agree, it is hard to argue that there is a problem in terms of political inequality, even if the affluent make all the decisions, exactly because everybody is in agreement anyway.

The next step is *preference articulation*, i.e. the degree to which citizens voice their opinions and participate in the political process. Such articulation will typically manifest itself as participation in civic associations (unions, parties, but also more broadly various social organizations) and demonstrations. The most vital form of articulation, however, is participation in elections, because it is here that ordinary people get a chance to influence directly the composition of a country's legislative bodies and government. If people do not articulate their preferences in one or more of these ways, it is less likely that their views will be taken into account at a later stage in the decision-making process. The key question, again, is whether the prosperous participate more than others, because this could create a bias in whose preferences are heard.

The third step is *preference aggregation*. How do elite actors – above all else, political parties – respond to the input from citizens? Do all parties react in similar ways, and do some segments of the citizenry carry more weight than others? The fourth and final step is *policy-making*. At the level of policy-making, people's preferences only matter indirectly via the strategic actions of parties and other elite actors. Even if no inequalities exist at the previous steps, there is no guarantee that public preferences will matter much for policies. Policies can be decided behind closed doors under the influence of lobbyists, or as a bargaining chip in a larger compromise – effectively turning participatory democracy into what Lane (1959: 226) called a democratic illusion, with serious consequences for ordinary people's willingness to engage in politics. It does not have to be like that, naturally, and Chapter 10 explores whether this is the case by mapping what we know about political inequalities in preference aggregation and policy-making.

In the current chapter, we look at the two first steps, which together can be called the *input* into the political system. The first section presents a summary of some of the key facts about public preferences for equality and redistributive policies. In the next section, the main competing arguments on preference articulation are outlined, whereas the subsequent section summarizes the empirical evidence. A core message of the chapter is that there are, indeed, big differences between the economically powerful and the less well-off. The well-to-do are more interested in politics, they believe that they are better able to influence the political process, and they vote much more frequently in elections. When it comes to the input into the political system, it is, in sum, pretty clear that there are not only differences in preferences, but also substantial inequalities in the articulation of these preferences.

Public Preferences

As formulated by Robert A. (1971: 1), '[a] key characteristic of democracy is the continuing responsiveness of the government to the preferences of its citizens, considered as political equals'. If governments are immune to the wishes of the populace, it is difficult to see how one in any meaningful way can call a political system democratic. As we will explain in Chapter 10, it is far from obvious how public preferences more precisely map onto government policies, but there is little doubt that from a normative viewpoint there should be at least some connection. To evaluate the scope of political inequality, we first need to get an impression of what the public actually wants. More specifically, we need to know whether there are differences in public preferences that correlate with the economic status of individuals. Do the poor and the rich hold the same preferences for inequality and redistribution?

We have solid knowledge about the main characteristics of public preferences for equality as well as for some of the core policies that typically create redistribution. Let us look at opinions about equality itself first. Figure 9.1 can help us get a good impression of what goes on. The

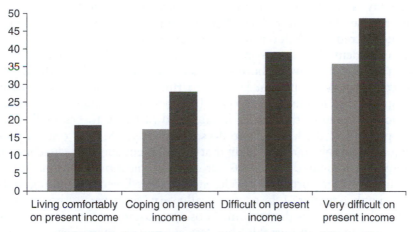

■ For fair society, differences in standard of living should be small
■ Government should reduce differences in income levels

Figure 9.1 *Opinions about equality and redistribution*

Note: Respondents were asked how they were feeling about the household's income nowadays. The reported percentages on the vertical axis are those within each of the four answer categories saying that they strongly agree with the two statements: 'for a fair society, differences in standard of living must be small' (the light grey bars) and 'government should reduce differences in income levels' (dark grey bars). Post-stratification and population size weights have been applied to correct for sample bias, as recommended by the European Social Survey.

Source: European Social Survey Round 4 Data (2008).

figure is based on surveys conducted by the European Social Survey in 2008 in 29 European countries with more than 56,000 respondents in total. The European Social Survey has fielded more recent survey waves, but the 2008 round contains some particularly appropriate questions pertaining to the issues of equality, redistribution and the government's role in providing social protection to those in need. Later in the chapter, we use the newer data from 2012, but for the moment we stick to the 2008 data, because these are the best available for our current purpose.

As in Figure 3.2 in Chapter 3, respondents are grouped into four categories according to their household's economic status: are they living comfortably on present income (19.5 per cent of the population); coping on present income (43.8 per cent); finding it difficult on present income (25.8 per cent); or finding it very difficult on present income (10.9 per cent)? This measure has the great quality that it sums up the entire situation of the household, i.e. not only whether the household enjoys a certain income, but also whether that income is sufficient for making ends meet. On the vertical axis, the percentage of the population is reported that agrees strongly that 'for a fair society, differences in standard of living must be small' (the light grey bars) and 'government should reduce differences in income levels' (dark grey bars). The first question concerns whether, and how much, inequality is acceptable. It is the more normative of the two, because it concerns the ideal society. The other question asks whether action should be taken to reduce whatever inequalities exist today.

It is evident that the proportion of the public that strongly agrees increases dramatically for both statements as we move from those who live comfortably on present income to those who find it very difficult to cope. In the former group, only 10.7 per cent strongly agree that a fair society requires differences in standard of living to be small, while 35.8 per cent of the latter group do so. Similarly, 18.5 per cent of those living comfortably agree strongly that government should reduce income differences, compared with 48.6 per cent among those who find it very difficult. It is noteworthy that preferences change linearly, meaning that it is not simply a matter of the economically very secure versus the very insecure or the top versus the bottom. Those just coping are more supportive than those living comfortably, but less supportive than those finding it difficult to manage, who again are less supportive than those finding it very difficult to cope. This is a general feature of all the associations we go through in this chapter, and something we will get back to later. In sum, the better off people are, the less likely they are to believe that inequality is a problem or that government should take action to do anything about it.

The basic correlation between economic situation and preferences for equality and redistribution has been documented extensively. The conclusion is not dependent on how the respondents' income is measured. Whether using a subjective measure of the household's overall situation as in Figure 9.1, a more objective measure such as placement in income deciles, or broader measures of socio-economic status such as occupation, the results are the same (e.g. Cusack et al. 2006; Svallfors 2012; Guillaud 2013; Tóth et al. 2014). This is not surprising, because earnings are, to a large extent, a function of a person's education and occupation. Chapter 7 highlighted the importance of education for future earnings, while Chapter 3 showed that the more people earn, the more economically secure they feel (cf. Figure 3.1). That is not to deny that some academics are unemployed or work in low-paid service jobs, or that people without formal training can become successful, but in the larger picture these are exceptions to the general rule.

The next question is what concrete policies people prefer. Chapter 8 showed that the redistributive potential of welfare states varies substantially. Not least the continental European ones combine big social budgets with relatively limited equality. Still, there is no doubt that the social policies in place in a country constitute an important instrument of redistribution. Without them, many jobless, old and sick people would be destitute, even in countries where work and contribution history determines the generosity of benefits. This is because those who have accumulated little over the life course normally are still entitled to some minimum protection, which is paid for by those with a larger income via the tax system. Social protection, therefore, almost inevitably creates some amount of redistribution, although the amount can vary greatly.

Figure 9.2 replicates the setup of the previous figure, but this time looking at the percentage of the population who believe it is the

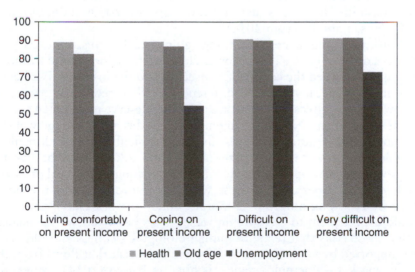

Figure 9.2 *Support for government involvement in social protection*

Note: See Figure 9.1 for details.

Source: European Social Survey Round 4 Data (2008).

government's responsibility to ensure 'adequate health care for the sick', 'a reasonable standard of living for the old' and 'a reasonable standard of living for the unemployed'. These are the three dominant activities of most welfare states, although in some countries, notably the Nordics, childcare and other services aimed at the old and the disabled take up a sizeable part too (see Chapter 8). Between them, the three areas consume the vast bulk of the welfare state budget. The scale used to measure public support for all three areas ranges from 0 (not government's responsibility at all) to 10 (entirely government's responsibility). The percentages reported in Figure 9.2 are those who chose to tick in 7, 8, 9 or 10, i.e. indicating clear support for a statement.

Several things are worth noting in Figure 9.2. First of all, there is generally a lot of support for public provision of social protection. On average across the three areas, and taking into account that there is an unequal proportion of the population in each of the four economic status categories, 78.4 per cent expressed support. Although the exact definition of support we have opted for is arbitrary, there is no doubt that the welfare state, broadly speaking, is popular among a majority of the populace. Second, there are clear differences between the areas. Health care and old age as a government responsibility enjoy backing from 89.7 and 87.1 per cent, respectively, whereas a more modest 58.3 per cent support government responsibility for the living standards of the unemployed. This finding agrees with a substantial amount of research showing that the sick and the old are considered more deserving than the jobless, and that this affects whether or not people think government has a responsibility for their situation (Van Oorschot 2000; 2006; Slothuus 2007; Jensen and Petersen 2016).

Third, there might be other things going on than just moral assessments of deservingness. This becomes clear when we look at the variation in support between the economically secure and the insecure. For health care and old age, it makes no difference whether people are secure or not; everybody agrees that these are risks that deserve to be taken care of by the government. Not so for unemployment, because here the well-off are much more hesitant than those finding it difficult and very difficult to cope on their present income. In the latter group, 72.8 per cent believe it is the government's responsibility to ensure an adequate standard of living, while only 49.4 per cent of those who live comfortably say the same. If we were dealing purely with moral evaluations of deservingness, we would expect them to be more universal in scope. What we see instead is that those risks that relate to human biology – sickness and old age – are supported by virtually everybody, while the risk that flows from the labour market – unemployment – is not. As Jensen (2014) argues, the reason is that the former risk type is perceived to pose a threat no matter what the economic situation is, whereas the latter is not. Everybody is afraid of getting old without dignity, living in pain or dying prematurely.

No amount of wealth and no government transfer, no matter how generous, can – by most people's standards – compensate for such misery. In contrast, if you are doing fine economically, perhaps owning a house or having a substantial amount of savings, you can overcome losing your job; and with a good education, chances are that you will find a new one quickly (see also Jensen and Petersen 2016).

The disagreement between the haves and the have-nots over equality and labour market-related policies goes together with assessments about the wider consequences of government-provided welfare. In Chapter 6, we discussed whether there is such a thing as a free lunch when it comes to the relationship between equality and growth. When you get more of one, do you then have to get less of the other? The answer seems to be no: if the economy is organized wisely, it is possible to have both. Figure 9.3 gauges public opinion about the potential bad effects of generous welfare. The European Social Survey's respondents were asked whether they agreed with the statement that 'social benefits/ services place too great a strain on the economy' and 'social benefits/ services make people lazy'. The questions, in other words, get at the perceived negative consequences of providing generous welfare for the functioning of the economy and people's incentives to make an effort. The percentages reported in Figure 9.3 are those who agree or strongly agree, i.e. the proportion of people who unambiguously believe that social benefits cause problems. Once again, a clear economic gradient

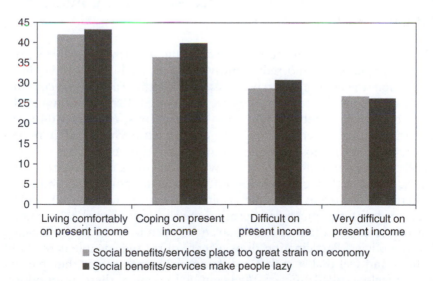

Figure 9.3 *Assessment of the negative consequences of social benefits*

Note: See Figure 9.1 for details.

Source: European Social Survey Round 4 Data (2008).

appears. Among those living comfortably on present income, 42 and 43.3 per cent, respectively, believe that social benefits cause problems in terms of putting too great a strain on the economy or making people lazy. Those numbers decrease to 26.8 and 26.3 per cent for those people finding it very difficult to cope on present income. Although the gradient is slightly less pronounced than for opinions about equality and redistribution (in Figure 9.1) and unemployment protection (in Figure 9.2), it is still marked, with a 15–17 percentage point difference.

Taken together, Figures 9.1, 9.2 and 9.3 give us a solid overview of public preferences. Overall, the better-off tend to be comparably accepting of inequality and oppose redistribution. This is not surprising, given that they – all else being equal – must expect that redistribution will hurt them. In line with this, the belief that the government must ensure a decent standard of living for the unemployed is lowest among this group. The better-off are also more likely to believe that generous benefits hurt the economy and make people lazy. People's motivation is most pervasive on these issues. Conversely, the risks of bad health and old age are perceived as more equally distributed. Even though poorer individuals actually tend to have poorer health as well, the seriousness of the risks neutralizes the effect, so to speak. An important lesson, therefore, is that one cannot draw a direct line from support for equality and redistribution to support for the welfare state in any general meaning of the term.

Empirical Patterns in Preference Articulation: Interest, Efficacy, Participation

Having established that there is an economic gradient in people's preferences for equality and redistributive policies such as unemployment protection, the next question becomes whether there also is an economic gradient in how these preferences are articulated. Participation – in the form of voting, membership of social associations, etc. – is vital input into the political system. Elections, by design, settle who will sit in parliament, and are the most straightforward way to influence what goes on. Public demonstrations or work in civic associations can have the same effect, because they can provide information to politicians about the preferences of citizens. If people's opinions about how society should be organized differ as much as appears to be the case, then there are good reasons to expect them to use the avenues open to them for influencing future policies. Participation, however, requires that people care about politics and feel that it makes a difference whether or not they participate: a feeling called *efficacy*. We begin by looking at these more subjective beliefs and feelings first, before moving on to people's behaviour.

Figure 9.4 mirrors the setup of the three previous figures. This time, however, the percentages reported are those saying that they are 'not

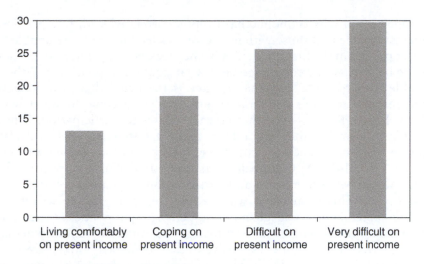

Figure 9.4 *Percentage not at all interested in politics*

Note: See Figure 9.1 for details.

Source: European Social Survey Round 6 Data (2012).

at all interested in politics'. On average, 20 per cent of the population entertain this opinion, but economic hardship strongly conditions it. Among those living comfortably on present income, 13.1 per cent have no interest in politics at all, whereas more than twice as many, 29.7 per cent, feel the same among those finding it very difficult to cope on present income. At the other end of the scale, 58.7 per cent of those living comfortably on present income are either 'very' or 'quite' interested in politics, compared with only 34.1 per cent of those finding it very difficult to cope.

That economic status, broadly defined, influences political interest is old news. In their classic study *The Civic Culture*, Almond and Verba (1963: 94) explore, among many other things, the political interest of people from different educational backgrounds in five countries: the United States, the United Kingdom, Germany, Italy and Mexico. Respondents were asked whether they followed politics regularly or from time to time. Among those with at least some university training, between 87 (in Italy) and 100 per cent (in Germany) reported that they did, while between 24 (in Italy) and 69 per cent (in Germany) of people with primary schooling or less reported that they did. Virtually all studies since then have shown the same pattern of lower-educated people being less interested in politics than the well-educated, whether using data from a single country, often the United States, or from a number of countries (e.g. Solt 2008).

One reason why economic hardship is correlated with low political interest may be that those with few resources feel that they are unable to affect politics in the first place, that is, they lack efficacy. Internal efficacy is the belief that one can understand what goes on in politics and, thus, is able to participate. External efficacy is the belief that governments will respond to one's demands if one decides to come forward with them. It is well established that efficacy relates to participation. When people believe that they are able to make a difference, they will also have a greater tendency to actually get involved in the political process (Lane 1959: 147–55; Campbell et al. 1960: 101–10). Importantly, the relationship between efficacy and participation is, in all likelihood, self-reinforcing. This means that while a high sense of efficacy will make people more likely to engage in politics, engaging in politics at the same time makes them believe more in themselves, especially about whether or not government will be responsive to their demands (Finkel 1985).

Figure 9.5 illustrates the level of efficacy across degrees of economic hardship. The light grey bars report the percentage of people saying that politics 'regularly' or 'frequently' is 'too complicated to understand'. This is a standard measure of internal efficacy. The dark grey bars are the percentage of respondents believing that governing parties are not punished in elections when they have done a bad job. The original scale of the variable ranges from 0 (they are not punished) to 10 (they are punished), and the percentages reported are those who chose one of

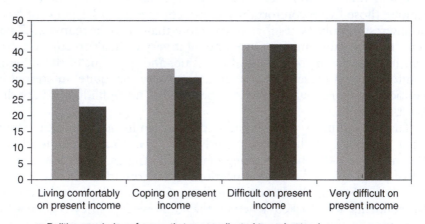

■ Politics regularly or frequently too complicated to understand
■ Governing parties are not punished in elections when they have done a bad job

Figure 9.5   *Percentage of people with low efficacy*

Note: See Figure 9.1 for details.

Source: European Social Survey Round 4 Data (2008) was used for the question on whether politics is too complicated. European Social Survey Round 6 (2012) was used for the punishment question.

the four lowest categories. The measure is meant to capture an important aspect of external efficacy. If people do not believe parties get punished for doing a bad job, it makes no difference whether they articulate their protest against them. Among those living comfortably on present income, 28.4 per cent say that politics regularly or frequently is too complicated, and 22.9 per cent claim that governing parties are not punished for bad performance. Depending on the viewpoint, this may be a lot or a little, but it is unquestionably smaller than the percentages among those finding it very difficult to cope. Of these, a full 49.3 per cent believe that politics regularly or frequently is too complicated to understand, and 45.9 per cent do not believe governments are punished for doing a bad job. These are massive numbers, and they suggest that roughly half of all those in dire economic straits do not believe that they can influence what happens in politics. No wonder, then, that political interest in the group is low.

Looking at the depressing numbers in Figures 9.4 and 9.5, it is important to remember, first of all, that only around 10 per cent of the population on average falls into this category according to the European Social Survey, although typically another 25 per cent find it difficult to cope on present income (the exact percentage varies a bit from one year to the next). It is also worth noting that the proportion of people who fall into the different categories of economic hardship varies between countries. For example, in the Nordic countries, a majority of all citizens report living comfortably on present income. In 2012, a whopping 65.5 per cent of all Danes said they lived comfortably, while a still impressive 58.8 and 54.9 per cent of the population reported to be living comfortably in Norway and Sweden. To a large extent, the high number of people living comfortably reflects the redistributive effort of these egalitarian societies. By comparison, only 37.7, 28.8 and 35.8 per cent claim to be living comfortably in the United Kingdom, France and Germany, respectively. This is despite the fact that all six countries are equally wealthy, as we saw in Chapter 5. Put differently, while the economic living conditions always affect people's efficacy, the living conditions themselves are not constant between countries.

Having established that there is an economic gradient in political interest and efficacy, it is less surprising to find that an identical gradient exists for turnout. As early as 1937, Tingsten published his *Political Behavior*, which reported how disadvantaged social groups voted less than more advantaged ones in a number of elections in several countries from which he had obtained data. These included Prussian elections from 1893 to 1913, Swiss canton elections in 1908 and 1933, and local elections in Copenhagen in 1909 and 1913. In practically all the elections Tingsten (1937: 120–81) studied, he found a gradient. The data on the two Danish local elections are particularly informative, because here he had data not only on the occupation of voters, but also on their income.

That allowed him to conclude that turnout increases with income within all the occupations on which he had data. For example, in 1909, male workers earning DKK 800 to 1000 had an average turnout rate of 65.2 per cent, which increased to 79.3 per cent for those making DKK 1000 to 1200, and so on. Even earlier than Tingsten, Arneson (1925) had conducted interviews with 4930 residents of the town of Delaware in the American state Ohio. He found that on average non-voters were much less educated and lived in worse neighbourhoods than voters.

It is fascinating to observe how the insights of a hundred years ago are still valid today. Figure 9.6 summarizes the average abstention rate across 29 European countries. It is clear that economic hardship power-fully conditions the extent of non-voting. For those living comfortably on present income, the average abstention rate is 15 per cent, while it is 33.3 per cent for those finding it very difficult to cope. The same pattern emerges if we turn to other activities. Twice as many of those living comfortably had participated in legal demonstrations in the past year prior to the survey than those finding it very difficult to cope (10.5 versus 5 per cent), while being four times more likely to have worked in civil associations (22.1 versus 5.7 per cent).

Anderson and Beramendi (2008) and Solt (2008; 2010), using more advanced statistical methods, find the same, but also show that the effect is amplified by a high level of inequality in a country. Figure 9.7 illustrates the point by focusing on turnout in Sweden and the United Kingdom: the least and most unequal European country, respectively.

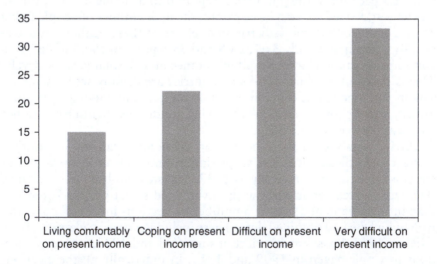

Figure 9.6 *Percentage of the electorate who are non-voters*

Note: See Figure 9.1 for details.

Source: European Social Survey Round 6 Data (2012).

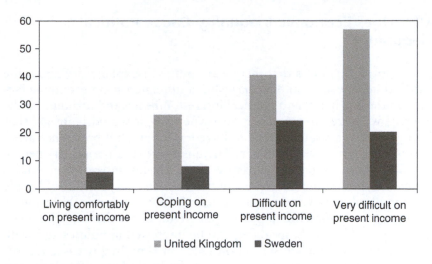

Figure 9.7 *Percentage of the electorate who are non-voters in the United Kingdom and Sweden*

Note: See Figure 9.1 for details.

Source: European Social Survey Round 6 Data (2012).

In both countries, economic hardship is associated with abstention, but the magnitudes are dissimilar. For those living comfortably on present income, there is a 16.8 percentage point margin between the countries. That margin has grown to a stellar 36.6 percentage point for the group of people finding it very hard to get by on their present income. The implication of this point is important. It is not just that some countries – such as Sweden, Norway or Denmark – have fewer people experiencing severe economic hardship; it is also the case that the low inequality in these countries reduces the negative effect of hardship for those – comparably few – who belong to the category. This is a crucial insight. Being poor is less bad for the likelihood of voting if one lives in an egalitarian country.

An 18.3 percentage point gap in turnout, as is evident in Figure 9.6, is very substantial, especially because opinions about the appropriate level of inequality and redistribution vary as much as they do. If people abstain from voting, their preferences are less likely to matter, because candidates advocating policies to match them are less likely to get elected. Moreover, since the gap in turnout between the economically secure and insecure widens as inequality increases, this underrepresentation of the less well-off will tend to be particularly bad exactly where the underprivileged need redistribution the most. In principle, this is one (of several) reasons why highly unequal countries remain so. But how policy-making on inequality and redistribution occurs more precisely, and how this relates to political inequality, is the topic of Chapter 10.

Why Does Economic Inequality Cause Political Inequality?

It is important to stress that there is nothing self-explanatory about the association between economic hardship and related socio-economic factors, on the one hand, and political interest, efficacy and turnout, on the other. If we were talking about car ownership, it would be trivial that those with fewer resources tend to have fewer cars, but preference articulation does not cost any money. There is no reason per se why people who find it difficult to make ends meet should be less interested in politics or abstain from voting in greater numbers than everybody else. People living in absolute poverty might not own or have access to television or the internet, and therefore might be unable to follow the news, but even then they could, strictly speaking, still be interested in politics and walk down to the local polling station on Election Day. In any case, according to the European Social Survey, people finding it very difficult to cope on their present income watch television substantially more often than those who are doing better economically. For example, 31.8 per cent in the former group report that they watch television for more than three hours per day, compared with only 15.8 per cent in the latter group. Clearly, the dissimilarities we observe are not simply down to crude differences in access to information.

It is, relatedly, also relevant to underscore that political inequality is not something only the poor experience. Across the entire gradient of economic hardship, preference articulation decreases. Those reporting to be coping on present income – which in most countries constitute the majority of the citizenry, the middle class if you will – exhibit less political interest and efficacy and lower turnout than those saying they are living comfortably. The people saying it is difficult to cope on present income likewise exhibit less preference articulation than those coping, but more than those saying it is very difficult to cope. The point is that in most countries, the majority of citizens suffer from this form of political inequality, in the sense that they are outperformed by those who are economically better off than themselves. This is a conclusion that is corroborated by most of the research that has been conducted on the issue. To understand the mechanism behind these political inequalities is, in sum, neither trivial nor marginal.

One explanation may be called the inheritance theory. It posits that political inequalities in preference articulation are a result of two closely related factors (Easton and Dennis 1967; Verba et al. 1995: 416–60; Jennings et al. 2009; Schlozman et al. 2012: 177–98). The first is socialization in the family. Well-heeled parents – well educated and economically secure – are on average more engaged in politics than less wealthy parents. This means that children brought up in these families will be exposed to politics during a period of their life when their personality is still impressionable. The more engaged the family, the more engaged the child will end up. The second factor is that children with well-educated and high-earning parents tend to become well educated and high earning themselves. This is important, because education makes people more aware of society and politics. The more education you have, the more interested you become. Both these factors, in short, can help understand why economic inequalities are transformed into political inequalities in preference articulation.

In a study from the 1960s, Easton and Dennis (1967) provide early, but very convincing, evidence on the role of family background. The researchers surveyed the political efficacy of 12,052 American children in the third to eighth grades. They found that political efficacy emerges gradually as the children get older, exactly what one would expect if childhood is where people's basic feeling of efficacy is formed. The socio-economic status of the child's family also plays a role. Political efficacy is substantially higher with higher status, but mainly among the older children. The age of the child and social background apparently go together, which makes sense. The children first have to develop their cognitive skills sufficiently before they are able to form beliefs about a rather complex phenomenon such as efficacy – and it is only then that the advantages that some children enjoy kick in for real.

In a statistically very demanding investigation, Prior (2010) explored the stability of political interest over the duration of people's lifetime. To do so, Prior employed so-called panel surveys, i.e. surveys where the same person was interviewed several times. The longest of the panels covers 32 years, and consists of interviews conducted in 1965 with high school students who were then re-interviewed in 1973, 1982 and 1997, but several of the other panels also cover decades. The panels came from several different countries, including the United States, the United Kingdom and Germany. In all the panels, the respondents were asked about their interest in politics. Using the panels, Prior could therefore see how stable the political interests of the individual respondents were over time as they got older and their life situation changed. Prior concluded (ibid.: 763) that '[p]ut together, these analyses indicate exceptionally high absolute stability in political interest both from year to year and in the long run [...] political interest behaves like a central element of political identity, not like a frequently updated attitude'. This stability is what we would expect to see if preference articulation, at least in part, reflects family background and educational choices (for other studies finding substantial intergenerational transmission of preference articulation, see Jennings et al. 2009; Schlozman et al. 2012: 177–98).

While there is much to indicate that economic inequality maps onto political inequality because of the socialization that occurs in the families of the economically secure, there may still be other factors at work.

One alternative explanation is that it is simply rational for the disadvantaged to stay out of politics. In the formulation of Pateman,

> [t]here is a simple and straightforward explanation for the low rates of political participation of ordinary citizens. Given their experiences of, and perception of the operation of the political structure, apathy is a realistic response; it does not seem worthwhile to participate. This explanation, it should be noted, is in terms of adult, not childhood experiences, and in terms of cognitive, not psychological factors. (Pateman 1971: 298)

If people experience that their opinions carry little or no weight, the rational response is to stop wasting time trying to make them heard. Such sobering learning, moreover, has nothing to do with family upbringing or where one went to school, but is something that adults conclude when experiencing how the world of politics really is. On the basis of this conjecture, Goodin and Dryzek (1980) proposed the relative power theory. With their theory, they go one step further than Pateman and argue that political inequality can be explained by systematic differences in the relative power of groups in society. As they put it,

> [t]hose with relatively few political resources and little hope of outbidding likely opponents should, if they are rational, save their resources for another time or another market in which they might bring better returns. Those relatively rich in resources, and who therefore feel they have a reasonable chance of winning the competition, have a far better reason for entering. (Goodin and Dryzek 1980: 278)

Power resources, to Goodin and Dryzek, cover a range of things from soft cultural to hard economic capital (although both the authors themselves, and later research testing their theory, mainly relied on economic position). Interestingly enough, these are the same sort of resources that the inheritance theory argues are important. This implies that the key distinction between the relative power theory and the inheritance theory is less about the source of political inequality, and more about the mechanism by which it gets transformed into low preference articulation. According to the inheritance theory, children and young adults develop an interest in politics and a belief that they can make a difference if they are brought up in an environment that puts an emphasis on such things. If a child is brought up by well-educated and economically secure parents, the child will tend to become interested in politics and have a high degree of efficacy. It is, so to speak, the resources of yesteryear rather than the resources of today that matter. The relative power theory, in contrast, argues that it is precisely the resources of today that play the bigger role. To put it bluntly, it does not matter whether your upbringing made you believe that you can make a difference. If you are short on relevant resources now, that is what counts.

The two theories on the sources of inequalities in preference articulation are less at odds with each other than one might think at first. It is, indeed, quite possible that both are correct. There is, first of all, no reason why resources could not matter both during childhood and adolescence and in adulthood. Assuming that both the inheritance and the relative power theory are correct, we can expect adults with few resources, and therefore a bad impression of politics, to pass this negative impression onto their children. In this way, the rational reaction of adults who cannot make their voice heard is converted into the socialization of children who are taught that politics is not for them.

The initial link is reinforced in two ways. First, social mobility is, as we saw in Chapter 3, often low, meaning that children from disadvantaged backgrounds tend to end up being disadvantaged themselves. Even in high-mobility countries this is true. A child brought up in an environment with few resources will tend to be socialized to believe that it cannot make a difference. As a low-resource adult, the child will then get first-hand experience that in actual fact it cannot make a difference, essentially confirming its childhood knowledge. Second, assuming that it takes energy and stamina to participate in politics, it is plausible that people who believe less of themselves become less effective in pursuing political influence in the first place, which makes them even more impotent. All of this suggests that the connection between economic inequality and political inequality in preference articulation is extremely stable even over the course of generations.

Conclusion

If it is true, as postulated by Almond and Verba (1963: 180), that democracy requires ordinary citizens to control the elite, we must conclude that not all citizens are equally likely to do so. Some, the economically well-off, generally speaking, exhibit a high degree of political interest, a strong belief in their own abilities and a correspondingly high propensity to participate in elections and other political activities. Others, those with few resources, exhibit the opposite tendency. Assuming that political elites are not able to govern without some sort of reliance on the input from the citizenry, such disparities can be consequential. This is not least because the rich not only articulate their preferences more, but also hold different opinions about the appropriateness of equality in society, the amount of redistribution necessary, a government's responsibility for the living standards of the jobless, and the possible negative effects all of this might have on the economy. If these opinions are taken more seriously in policy-making than those of people with fewer resources, policies will be biased against people who are already marginalized.

Some observers, for example Robert A. Dahl (1989), argue that it is normatively wrong that some citizens' opinions count for more than those of others. Whether one agrees with that position depends on one's belief about to the extent to which humans can control their own situation. To be brought up in a disadvantaged family means that some core material and immaterial resources will be lacking, and much research indicates that this will leave a lasting mark on many as they grow into adulthood. Some might argue that since people do not choose their parents, they cannot be blamed for these negative effects. Yet, on the other hand, being born in the 'wrong' family does not absolve people from a fundamental responsibility to engage with society and behave as good citizens. If we accepted that view, criminals with a poor upbringing should not be punished for their crimes either, something very few people would accept. Because there is no way of objectively, or scientifically, settling which of these arguments must carry most weight, we return – once again – to the realm of politics. It is a political decision whether or not those in disadvantaged circumstances are to be helped so as to compensate for their suboptimal starting point in life, and, if so, how much.

There are at least two ways governments can provide such help. One is to let public childcare and education substitute, as much as they can, for an affluent home. In countries such as Denmark, Norway and Sweden, political elites have for decades accepted a responsibility for delivering such substitution. Extensive childcare, as noted in Chapter 7, raises the skills of those with a weak background, but it is especially primary schools that have been instrumental in turning small children into democratically minded citizens. While frequently called into question because it takes time away from topics such as mathematics and science, the effort, in all likelihood, is part of the explanation for why socio-economic inequalities do not turn into political inequalities in preference articulation nearly as much as in other places. In many other countries, much less attention is paid to such soft skills, which effectively means that society lays responsibility firmly on the shoulders of the individual citizen.

The other avenue is to fight the root cause of it all: economic inequality. There is huge variation across countries in the level of inequality that is tolerated. The previous two chapters looked at the connection between the economy and the welfare state, on the one hand, and inequality, on the other. It was a central lesson from these chapters that the design of the economy and the welfare state, to a large extent, is based on political decisions. Yet, how are these decisions made? We would intuitively expect public preferences to matter somehow, although perhaps with a bias towards those who most keenly express their preferences. But is it really that simple? As we detail in the next chapter, things quickly get complicated when one begins to think seriously about the politics of inequality.

Chapter 10

Who decides in the politics of inequality?

At its heart, politics is about the power to decide over society's resources. In the formulation of Lasswell (1936), politics is about who should get what, when, how. Redistribution of income and wealth from the rich to the poor is, in this sense, all about politics. There is no unbiased, or neutral, way of organizing the tax system, the labour market or the welfare state. Conflicts are everywhere. How high should the top marginal tax rate on income be? What about corporate tax rates? What balance should be struck between the ability of companies to hire and fire and the job security of employees? Should the welfare state be arranged to facilitate the needs of the poor and marginalized, or to the advantage of the middle class? Policies benefitting some groups in society will inevitably leave other groups worse off, at least in the short run.

In Chapter 9, we studied the input into the political system, i.e. the preferences of the citizens and their participation in legal demonstrations, associations and elections. It was clear that economic status matters a lot for both preferences and the likelihood that these preferences will be articulated. So, already at the early stages of the political process, biases exist. Yet, there is a long way to go from articulated public preferences to policies regulating things such as taxes or employment protection. In this chapter, we want to know how democracies make decisions about inequality and redistribution. We begin by presenting the most straightforward and analytically elegant explanation, the so-called Meltzer–Richard model (Meltzer and Richard 1981). The model rests on the assumption that the median voter decides how much redistribution there should be in a country. The political process is biased towards the preferences of the median voter, and the median voter wants more redistribution as long as mean income is higher than the median voter's own income.

The Meltzer–Richard model leads to the prediction that the more market inequality there is in a country, the more the median voter can gain from redistribution, and the more redistribution there actually will be. The Meltzer–Richard model has been criticized because this 'more inequality, more redistribution' prediction does not seem to hold. It is more the other way around, meaning that countries that have a lot of market inequality redistribute a little. As Lindert (2004: 15) has it, 'history reveals a "Robin Hood paradox," in which redistribution from rich to poor is least present when and where it seems to be most needed'. Several alternatives exist to the Meltzer–Richard model that potentially can account for the puzzle. At the most basic level, the different theories vary according to who they argue are the principal actors in politics, i.e. who is able to dominate decision-making. While the alternatives are clearly distinct, we believe that they supplement each other to a large extent. Viewed in connection with each other, they provide a nuanced picture of the politics of inequality. An important lesson is that politics appears to be biased against those with the least resources, but not always and everywhere to the same extent. Trying to understand the circumstances under which biases do occur and how strong they are, as well as when and how they can be reduced or eliminated, is a vital goal of the chapter.

The Meltzer–Richard Model and the Robin Hood Paradox

The Meltzer–Richard model assumes that all voters wish to maximize their income. Voters with a market income below the mean wish to impose taxes on those with a market income above the mean, although they take into account that at some point too much taxation would hurt mean market income (because it implies a work disincentive for the rich) and, hence, ultimately also their own interest. Those with market incomes above the mean prefer no taxation. The median-income voter, then, wishes to redistribute as much income as possible on the condition that mean income does not decline. The implication of the model is that the more unequal the market income distribution in a country, the higher the median voter's demand for taxation and redistribution will be.

Figure 10.1 shows two countries – A and B – that have the same mean income, but different income distributions (Pontusson and Rueda 2007). Country B's market income distribution is more skewed to the right (more unequal) than country A's. As a result, the distance between the median voter's income and the mean income is bigger in B than in A (D2 > D1). The median voter in B, therefore, wants more redistribution than the median voter in A for the simple reason that there is more to be gained in B than in A. In the Meltzer–Richard model, the median voter is decisive for getting a majority. Parties wanting to win office, therefore, compete for the decisive median voter by bringing their policy proposal closer to the median voter's preference. That is why the Meltzer–Richard model posits not only that the median voter in B wants more redistribution, but also that the government in B will deliver what is demanded. Countries with a lot of market inequality will redistribute a lot.

The Meltzer–Richard model is a stylized, elegant and highly influential explanation of why the demand for redistribution among median-income

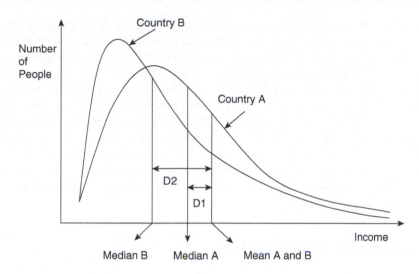

Figure 10.1 *Right-skewed income distributions and the median-income voter*

Source: Adapted, with kind permission from the authors, from Pontusson and Rueda (2007).

voters should be higher in more unequal capitalist democracies than in more equal societies. There are several problems with the model, however. The most important one is the Robin Hood paradox. The paradox exists because the countries that have the lowest levels of market inequality redistribute the most, and the countries that have the highest levels of market inequality redistribute the least (Lindert 2004: 15; Kenworthy and Pontusson 2005: 456–7; Iversen and Soskice 2009: 440–41; Luebker 2014). This is the exact opposite of the expectation of the Meltzer–Richard model. Apparently, the median voter is least supportive of redistribution where she could gain the most from it – or some other factor is stopping the median voter from getting what she asks for.

The debate on how to solve the Robin Hood paradox has yielded a variety of alternative explanations. The rest of the chapter discusses proposed solutions to the paradox. The first of these stays within the median voter framework, but asks whether the median voter really is motivated by a preference for redistribution, or whether other motives are more or just as important. The next set of solutions leaves the median voter framework behind altogether. Here, the argument is that political parties are not driven by what the median voter wants, but by what their core constituencies want. Left parties have pro-redistribution voter constituencies and will therefore pursue redistributive policies, while right parties have anti-redistribution voter constituencies and will therefore pursue less redistributive policies. However, pure left or right parties seldom win a majority in parliament, and therefore need to enter into coalitions with other parties. That makes coalition-making central to understanding what policies government enact. A third explanation is less concerned with why countries originally decided to redistribute, or not, but focuses on how redistributive welfare state policies can become self-reinforcing and, as a result, persist even when the conditions that gave rise to them have changed or completely disappeared. The fourth and final account focuses on perhaps the most worrisome solution offered to the Robin Hood paradox, namely, that government simply does not, or does only in a very limited way, respond to the preferences of ordinary people – and that this unresponsiveness is bigger in some countries than in others.

Insurance or Redistribution?

Market inequality per se may be not that relevant for the politics of redistribution after all. Voters may want something else (or more) than just redistribution. The Meltzer–Richard model assumes that the median voter only worries about how high her income is compared with the average income. However, wage earners are not just concerned about the size of their income, but also – and perhaps even in the first instance – about whether they will have an income at all. To the extent that wage earners depend on the ability to sell their labour power on the market, not being able to work due to unemployment, sickness, disability or old age implies loss of income. So, next to level of income, workers and employees are likely to seek a higher level of protection against such risks via social insurance.

When people decide on how much redistribution they prefer, they look both at their income situation and at the risk that they will lose their job. If the risk of unemployment is higher among low-income groups, political struggles over social policy and redistribution will be fierce (Cusack et al. 2006; Rehm 2011; Rehm et al. 2012). This has important ramifications for the politics of inequality:

> To the extent that citizens lower on the economic ladder are also most likely to experience the risks that the welfare state buffers, social policies will be characterized by (1) greater and more intense opposition, (2) greater opinion polarization, and (3) lower average support. (Rehm et al. 2012: 386)

Conversely, if the risk of unemployment is spread out more equally across the income distribution, so that also more well-off people are exposed to the risk, opposition to generous social policies will be less intense, opinions more consensual and average support higher. This proposition is backed by solid evidence. Using survey data from 20 European and Anglo-Saxon democracies, Rehm (2011), for example, shows that as the unemployment rate in a respondent's occupation increases (i.e. not the entire country, but only in the respondent's potential job market), preferences for government involvement in unemployment protection rise too. The size of the effect matches that for household income, which, as we have seen in Chapter 9, can be substantial. Rehm then calculates how unequally unemployment is distributed across occupations. In some countries, for example Portugal, there is comparably little variation in unemployment between different occupations. In other countries, for example Ireland, there is a lot of variation. Higher unemployment inequality is associated with lower unemployment protection. This is what one would expect to find if generous protection requires that a large voter bloc is roughly equally exposed to the risk of unemployment.

Other studies have added credibility to the notion that the economic situation in a country affects mass preferences. Owens and Pedulla (2014), for example, use an American panel survey to explore the effect of economic shocks on people's preferences for redistribution. Because of the panel survey setup – whereby the same person is interviewed several times – it is possible to study the changing preferences of respondents as their personal situation changes. This allows very robust statistical conclusions. Summing up their findings, Owens and Pedulla note:

> [w]hen individuals experience unemployment or a loss in their household income, they increase their preferences for government redistribution [...]. We also find that the effect of changing material circumstances on changing political preferences is rather delimited, affecting only attitudes toward redistributive social policies and not more general attitudes toward government spending, such as spending on social security, mass transit, or parks and recreation. (Owens and Pedulla 2014: 1104)

Similarly, Margalit (2013) employs another American panel survey and finds that losing one's job makes people more supportive of government help to the jobless. However, the effect tends to wear off quickly when people find a new job. In addition, it turns out that the effect is biggest for centre- and right-wing voters. The reason is presumably that left-wing voters already are supportive of government help, whereas the centre- and right-wing voters normally would not endorse that sort of government involvement, but make an exception when they themselves are in need of assistance. This result points to the next type of explanation, which focuses on the role of partisanship and parliamentary coalitions.

Core Constituencies and Class Coalitions

The works of Meltzer and Richard (1981), Rehm (2011) and Rehm et al. (2012) explicitly or implicitly assume that parties compete for the vote of the median voter by delivering the policies that she favours. The expectation is that parties, and certainly the big mainstream ones, will move towards the centre of the political spectrum and become relatively indistinct in terms of the policies they advocate. In contrast to such median-voter-oriented theories stands the power resources approach, which holds that wage earners and employees organize in labour unions and social democratic and socialist parties to represent and defend their material interest in decent wages and employment, goods that are permanently at risk in market economies. The better organized workers are in the economy and the better their interests are represented in politics, the more likely it is that policies will be adopted and pursued which protect workers' incomes both in and outside the market (Korpi 1978; 1983; 1989; 2006; Stephens 1979; Huber and Stephens 2001; Bradley et al. 2003).

The power resources approach posits a direct causal link between, on the one hand, how many and how well workers are organized in unions and social democratic and socialist parties and, on the other hand, the level of wage compression in the economy and the extent of redistribution through the political system. Where unions and left parties are strong, wage-setting becomes centralized, reducing earnings inequality, as we saw in Chapter 7, while social benefits become more generous and taxes get heavier. Obviously, from the perspective of the power resources approach, the empirical fact that the more equal countries redistribute the most – the Robin Hood paradox – is not particularly puzzling. The labour movement's strength explains a relatively equal distribution of wages and salaries as well as a high level of redistribution (McCarthy and Pontusson 2009: 673).

The strength of the labour movement stems from its power over various types of capital in the production process. Production is a function of physical capital, such as machines and buildings, in combination with human capital, in the form of skills and knowledge about how to use the physical capital. Employers (or their banks) typically own the physical capital, while the wage earners own the human capital, in the sense that they have the skills and knowledge needed for using the physical capital. This means that wage earners and employers need each other to generate income. Employers need the wage earners' human capital, while wage earners need the employers' physical capital. Hence, the physical capital of employers and the human capital of workers become a power resource for both that can be used against each other.

This suggests that the power balance between the employers and wage earners is roughly equal, but it is, in fact, fundamentally asymmetric.

The reason for this asymmetry is that physical capital can be concentrated in a relatively small number of hands. It is, indeed, the general rule that most economic assets are owned by a select minority of wealthy individuals and firms. In contrast, human capital – the power resource of wage earners – is necessarily attached to the individual wage earner and cannot be concentrated. This is important for the balance of power between employers and wage earners. An employer just needs *someone* to man the machines to generate profit, while the wage earner is dependent upon that someone being *him or her*. The employers can almost always pick and choose among a large pool of potential employees, whereas the wage earner normally has a much smaller selection. Except in periods of very high or full employment, or if the wage earner has unique skills, employers have the upper hand in negotiating with wage earners (see also Chapter 7 on wage-setting). This asymmetry is only counter-balanced if wage earners organize into unions that deny employers the access to *any* wage earners. This is why strikes – or more often the threat of strikes – are a crucial weapon for the labour movement, but also why strikes are only effective if unions organize a lot of wage earners and all participate in the action.

Organized conflicts in the labour market are one way in which wage earners can compensate for their baseline weakness. Another is to form the country's government. To be in government is often the best way to have ideology turned into political reality. In government, left parties are able to influence the legislation passed in parliament and oversee its implementation in society. Based on an extensive historical study, Huber and Stephens (2001: 10) conclude that office power, in fact, has been the most important way for the labour movement to ensure redistribution. In countries with strong unions, but infrequent left governments, redistribution never got very far. Unions are not necessarily always struggling to create more equality, because they defend the interests of their members, not society at large, and union members are not by definition benefitting from redistribution (e.g. Nijhuis 2009; Pontusson 2013). But even if they do push in the direction of equality, without government power it is difficult to transform union pressure into policy.

The traditional power resources approach, as noted, views parties' core constituencies as defined by their economic class position. However, there are other sources of social and political identity than economic class, including religious denomination and ethnicity, that can have an impact on collective action and distributional struggles and outcomes (Van Kersbergen 1995). Still, class-related distributional struggles prevail. 'The extent to which cross-cutting cleavages are mobilized is affected by structural factors', says Korpi (2006: 173), 'but distributive strife is also focused on influencing the relative importance of these competing lines of cleavages.' Empirically, a great number of studies time and again have demonstrated that a relatively equal distribution of wages and salaries and a high level of redistribution are, indeed, associated with a powerful presence of the left in politics, especially when the political party was backed by well-organized and disciplined unions (e.g. Bradley et al. 2003; Iversen and Soskice 2006: 174–5; Brady 2009: 114–15).

One problem with the traditional version of the power resources approach is that virtually nowhere did the left ever become so well organized and politically strong that it could pursue its redistributive programme without political alliances and, hence, compromises. In other words, egalitarian redistributive policies could only come about if the left parties were able to find coalition partners in parliament that supported the programme. And this implied wooing the middle class and its representatives, because the middle class typically contains the median voter, who can secure a majority in favour of redistribution (Esping-Andersen 1985; Przeworski 1985). But why would the middle class be interested in joining forces with the left to increase redistribution? Why not forge a coalition with the high-income groups to protect their own interests against the redistributive demands of the lower-income groups?

Iversen and Soskice (2006) explain under what conditions the middle class allies with the working class to support redistribution and equality. The empirical observation is that multi-party systems seem much more conducive to left governments than two-party systems, whereas the right seems to profit much more from a two-party system than from a multi-party system. This is explained by how the middle class protects its material interests. The middle class has more to lose if the left governs in a two-party system, but more to gain if it enters a coalition with the left in a multi-party system. If the left is in power in a two-party system, it may be tempted to tax only the upper and middle classes and redistribute the revenues exclusively to the lower class. In that case, it is safer for the middle class to vote for the right, which promises no (or low) taxes and no redistribution. Certainly, the middle class would not receive any benefits, but it would not have to pay (much) tax either.

Under proportional representation and a multi-party system, the middle class faces a different political choice. Middle-class voters can now vote for a party that exclusively represents their interests and that can be trusted and held responsible. If the middle-class party allies with the left, it will allow the middle class and the rich to be taxed, but only on condition that the benefits will flow to the middle class too. Alternatively, the middle-class party can ally with the right, in which case there will be no, or low, taxation, but no benefits either. To the extent that middle-class voters develop preferences for receiving benefits and services (say, health care or education), they can now support a centre-left coalition from which they will profit too. In short, under proportional representation and multi-party democracy, the centre-left will be in power more often and redistribution and equality will be higher than under majoritarian, two-party democracy.

The Iversen–Soskice model explains very well the difference between the non-redistributive regimes in the Anglo-Saxon countries and the redistributive systems in the Nordics, but seems to fall short of explaining the in-between countries on the European continent, such as Germany. This shortcoming can be remedied by appreciating the fact that majoritarian electoral rules and two-party systems really only leave room for the articulation of the labour–capital cleavage that dominates politics. Here, the model works well. Under proportional rules, however, more conflict dimensions can be articulated and represented by multiple parties. The redistributive outcome then becomes dependent on which other cleavages are present in the system, how the middle class's political behaviour is affected by this, and which coalitions emerge in favour of or against redistribution.

The varying national histories of political class coalitions explain the variety of redistributive regimes. In countries with a majoritarian electoral system and a politically dominant class cleavage, the middle class allies with the right against redistribution and equality. If, as in the Nordics, the farmers and their parties ally with the workers and social democracy, the result is a universal and highly redistributive regime. If, by contrast, cross-class parties of religious defence (Christian democracy) enter a coalition with the workers and social democracy, more diverse middle-class interests have to be catered for in a much more particularistic and less redistributive manner (Van Kersbergen and Manow 2009). The result is the three models of welfare state that we presented in Chapter 8.

Changing Patterns of Participation and Power Resources

Civic participation, the topic of Chapter 9, links directly to the ability of the left to maintain its power resources. Two forms of participation have turned out to be particularly important: turnout and union membership. Much of the left parties' effect on redistribution hinges on the extent of turnout (Pontusson and Rueda 2010). Increasing inequality triggers a leftist response among both left voters (rather than the median voter) and left parties relative to centre-right voters and their parties. However, this translates into a more redistributive stance of parties and – when in power – into more redistributive policies of left governments, if and only if low-income and poor voters actually show up at the polling station.

In contrast to the Meltzer–Richard model, but in line with the power resources approach, the assumption here is that left parties, rather than exclusively focusing on the median voter, primarily look at their core constituencies, which comprise relatively well-defined lower-income groups that have an interest in redistribution. When inequality rises, left parties need to maintain a workable compromise between the increasing redistributive demands of their core low-income constituencies and the demands from the median voter. How this balancing act works out depends on the extent to which the core constituencies actually plan to vote. The less they are likely to show up at the polls, the more left parties must cater to other voter groups to do well in elections. Because we know that political participation declines when income inequality is on the rise (see Chapter 9), a low electoral turnout moderates or even completely offsets the willingness of left parties to adjust their political programme towards more redistribution. To put it bluntly, when turnout is low, the parties of the left stop fighting as vigorously for the poor as they otherwise would have done. Having a left government in a low-turnout country is, in other words, less likely to have the same redistributive impact as having one in a high-turnout country.

The other form of participation, union membership, also matters. It matters, first of all, in the straightforward sense pointed out by Korpi's (1978) and Stephens' (1979) classic works in the power resources tradition, namely, that high union density makes it easier to pressurize the employers into compromises over salary and benefits. Just as important is the effect strong unions have on the behaviour of left governments. Strong unions amplify left governments' redistributive effect (Garrett 1998; Kwon and Pontusson 2010). One mechanism by which this is accomplished is that strong unions are able to secure moderate wage increases as compensation to employers for accepting generous social policies. In this way, welfare state expansion does not have as negative an effect on the economy as it might have had. Another mechanism is that strong unions can put political pressure on left governments by threatening to reduce or stop funding for electoral campaigns and similar activities. Both processes plausibly account for how and why unions are vital for redistribution even in a situation where the left occupies the cabinet. Note that neither of these mechanisms contradicts Huber and Stephens' (2001) finding that left governments are a necessary condition for extensive redistribution; they only specify that having a left government is not sufficient for extensive redistribution to occur, but requires the additional impetus from unions.

In sum, it appears quite plausible that both turnout and union membership are ways for the disadvantaged to make their voices heard. For the politics of inequality and redistribution, it is, therefore, crucial to realize that both have seen a dramatic decline during the past decades, as evident from Figure 10.2. The figure displays average union density (measured as a percentage of the labour force that are members of a union, on the left-hand side) and average turnout (the percentage of the eligible population that voted at the last election, on the right-hand side) from 1960 until 2012 for the 23 countries that we look at in this book and that have been democracies long enough to exhibit long-term

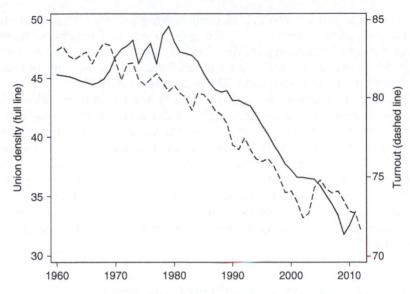

Figure 10.2 *Union membership and turnout since 1960*

Source: Armingeon et al. (2014).

patterns. From 1960 to 1980, nothing much happened; union density hovered around 45–50 per cent and turnout around 80–83 per cent. From the 1980s onwards, a steep decline is visible. Union density sank to less than 35 per cent, and turnout went the same way, ending at just above 70 per cent.

The decline is an almost universal phenomenon, although the magnitude of the decline varies across countries. In many Anglo-Saxon countries, union membership has virtually collapsed. In the United Kingdom, it fell from 51.7 per cent in 1980 to 27.1 per cent three decades later, in Australia from 49.6 to 18.9 per cent, in New Zealand from 69.1 to 28.8 per cent – the biggest fall anywhere – and in the United States from an already low 22.1 to 11.4 per cent. In other places, unionization rates hold up better, although they still trend downwards. In Italy, union density dropped from 49.6 to 35.5 per cent, in Belgium very slightly from 54.1 to 50.6 per cent, much the same as in Norway, where it fell from 58.3 to 54.6 per cent, while in Finland it stayed around 69 per cent. Sweden and Denmark, the frontrunners in terms of unionization, saw declines from 78.6 and 78.0 to 68.5 and 68.9 per cent, respectively. In the Nordic countries, unions have, additionally, lost some of their sway in wage-setting and have more frequently been sidelined in national political compromises, where they used to play a major role. The relatively benign trend in membership, thus, masks bigger losses in the integration of unions into the decision-making process. When it comes to the decreasing turnout rates, the most prominent exception to the general rule of backsliding are the Nordics, where turnout has remained high. In Denmark, Finland, Norway and Sweden, average turnout was 79.3 per cent around 1980 and 79 per cent around 2010.

The historical differences in union density and turnout can, along the lines of the power resources approach – both the classic version by Korpi (1978) and Stephens (1979) and the newer versions by Garrett (1998), Pontusson and Rueda (2010) and Kwon and Pontusson (2010) – explain why the Nordic countries have introduced much more redistributive policies than the Anglo-Saxon ones. Yet, the decline in the left's power resources even here raises the intriguing question of why inequality has not increased by more than the minor hikes we saw in Chapter 5. What sustains the low inequality regime in the face of a weakened labour movement?

Feedback and Institutionalized Preferences

One reason why some countries maintain their low inequality is that it has turned out to be relatively efficient to do so, as we explained in Chapter 7. Social market economies such as Sweden host a combination of extensive human capital formation, centralized wage-setting and a reasonably business-friendly environment that facilitates growth and equality simultaneously. The fact that equality does not seriously hurt growth means that the model has been sustainable in an economic sense over the past decades. There is an additional, political reason that complements the economic explanation, however. In a nutshell, policies generate their own public support. Even when the actors who created social policies lose power, it can be very difficult to cut them back. Policies introduced today affect what policies can be introduced tomorrow. Policies are, in this way, said to create feedback. As formulated by Skocpol,

> Once instituted, policies have feedback effects in two main ways. In the first place because of the official efforts made to implement new policies using new or existing administrative arrangements, policies transform or expand the capacities of the state. They therefore change the administrative possibilities for official initiatives in the future, and affect later prospects for policy implementation. In the second place, new policies affect the social identities, goals, and capabilities of groups that subsequently struggle or ally in politics. (Skocpol 1992: 58)

The first mechanism implies that in countries and policy areas where, for whatever reason, policies have been introduced, it will be easier to continue to introduce new and perhaps more expansive policies. In countries that traditionally intervene in the distribution of income and wealth, the bureaucracy and politicians will have the experience and know-how to make further interventions. In fact, not only will they have the skills to continue down the existing path; they will typically be strongly biased to do so. In the words of Maslow (1966: 15), 'if all you have is a hammer, everything looks like a nail'. Plenty of research shows that old ideas can be very sticky, because replacing them with new ones requires that both politicians and bureaucrats accept that the old ones are defunct and that they have to become familiar with something novel and perhaps very complicated (e.g. Hall 1993; Blyth 2001).

The second mechanism concerns how new policies reshape the preferences and powers of those who designed and deliver the benefits and services and those who receive them. The welfare state has created a lot of vested interests among recipients and public employees that are all dependent on the continuation of social programmes. 'Welfare states create their own constituencies', in a famous formulation by Pierson (1996: 147). But the feedback effect extends beyond pure self-interest. Existing policies also influence how people perceive themselves – their social identity – and, thus, how they react to new policy proposals.

Let us give one simple and stylized example of the second type of feedback mechanism, which is the most tricky to understand. Before there were pension systems, there were no 'pensioners'. Certainly, there were old people, most probably poor, who could not work any longer, but no 'pensioners'. The category 'pensioner' is created by the rules of the pension system. These rules specify the pension age of entitlement, the contribution period, the generosity of the benefit, and so on. Once created, pensioners develop an interest in the system that accords them their money to survive without having to work on the labour market. They might also derive their social status and identity from the institution: they are pensioners. Pensioners, moreover, often mobilize in interest organizations of the elderly that have as their goal the defence of their legal and moral right to a pension. Finally, pensioners are, of course, also voters, and parties need to take their wishes into account if they wish to win elections; especially because the group of pensioners is expanding in an ageing society, and older voters tend to be very loyal voters. Those who run the pension funds also have an interest in the continuation of pension policy, if only because their jobs, and hence their incomes, depend on it. So, the institution of a pension system creates pensioners and pension administrators who defend pensions economically, morally and politically.

Social policies, once institutionalized, create and reinforce their own support base by altering the preferences, norms and interests of those affected by them. This makes social policy programmes exceptionally resilient. If a pension system comes under pressure from increasing ageing, and even if it is clear that if nothing is done (no radical reform of the system) the system will collapse financially, it still does not follow that there will be a radical pension reform. PAYGO (pay-as-you-go) pension systems, for instance, are systems whereby the current generation in employment pays premiums and taxes that finance the pensions of the people currently on a pension. With decreasing fertility and increasing life expectancy, this system becomes unaffordable, as a shrinking number of contributors have to pay for a growing number of beneficiaries.

The solution to the PAYGO problem would be to move to a fully funded system, i.e. a system where those currently employed pay into a capital-funded pension system, out of which their own pension will be paid once they retire. This unfortunately creates the double payment problem, because when one introduces the transition from a PAYGO to a funded system, there has to be at least one generation that has to keep on paying for the current pensioners, while at the same time saving for their own pension. It would also upset normative expectations as to the rights and obligations created by the current system. One can imagine that the people affected will resist this transition, for instance by expressing their discontent politically via their organizations and their vote (for an empirical analysis of the political problems of retrenching PAYGO pension systems, see Myles and Pierson 2001).

The pension example can be extended to many other social policy areas (e.g. Skocpol 1992; Pierson 1994; 1996; 2004; Streeck and Thelen 2005; Palier 2010). Once in place, policies create their own support base that will fight for their continuing existence or expansion. This mechanism probably helps to explain why attitudes towards existing policies are not only relatively positive and stable, but also cross-nationally variable. Some institutional setups generate more positive feedback effects than others. It turns out that the bigger and more comprehensive redistributive social policies are, the more public support they tend to generate. Support for equality, redistribution and state intervention is strong in the Nordic and continental European countries and weak in the Anglo-Saxon countries (e.g. Brooks and Manza 2007; Larsen 2008; Svallfors 2012; Larsen and Dejgaard 2013).

Figure 10.3 provides an example of these differences. Focusing on the United Kingdom and Sweden, the figure displays the proportion of the population living comfortably on present income who agree that the standard of living of the unemployed is the government's responsibility and that social benefits make people lazy (see Chapter 9 for details on the measures). The differences between the two countries are revealing. In Sweden, many more people agree with the two statements than in the United Kingdom. In Sweden, even the economically secure believe that the living conditions of the jobless are the government's responsibility and that social benefits do not make people lazy. In the United Kingdom, the picture is the opposite.

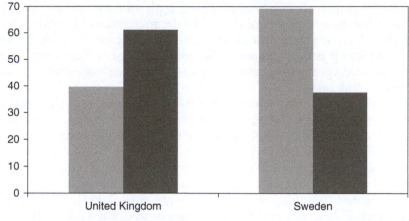

Figure 10.3 *Public preferences among the economically secure in the United Kingdom and Sweden*

Source: European Social Survey Round 4 Data (2008).

Policy feedback is, in conclusion, one possible explanation for why the declining power resources of the left do not translate into rising inequality everywhere. Where encompassing redistributive policies were introduced before the power resources began to drop from the 1980s onwards, public preferences have taken over as the main force maintaining the status quo (Pierson 1994; 1996; Brooks and Manza 2007; Jensen 2010; 2014). Politicians who care about their election results will be particularly careful about suggesting cutbacks in countries that already redistribute a lot. If they are too eager to retrench the welfare state, they risk upsetting large segments of the voters. Where redistribution never got very far in the first place, there is, conversely, more leeway for cutbacks without causing uproar.

What If the Preferences of the Voters Do Not Matter at All?

The previous accounts of the politics of inequality all ascribe a central role to the voters. It may be uncertain which voter segments carry the most weight – the median voter or some class-based constituency. And there may be no one-to-one relationship between voters' preferences and the resulting policies, for example because of the need for coalitions to secure a parliamentary majority. But even though politicians and other elite actors are constrained significantly in their actions, policies nevertheless to a large extent do reflect the preferences of a substantial amount of *some* voters. In this sense, all these arguments view politics as a bottom-up process whereby the preferences of citizens-cum-voters are expressed via elections and the agitation of mass organizations such as unions and parties.

The alternative view, which is the focus of attention in this section, sees politics as a top-down process in which voters' preferences matter much less, and perhaps not at all. One reason why democratic electoral politics may not always produce egalitarian outcomes is that some democracies are 'captured' or 'constrained': economic elites here have accumulated non-electoral power resources that can block responsive governments from redistributing (Acemoglu et al. 2013). Even though democratic politics undermines the *de jure* power of the elites, they may respond with 'investments in de facto power (e.g. via control of local law enforcement, mobilization of non-state armed actors, lobbying, and other means of capturing the party system) in order to continue to control the political process' (ibid.: 2).

Similarly, but mainly analysing the political causes of rising inequality in the United States, Hacker and Pierson (2010) have argued that political scientists have too one-sidedly, and hence wrongly, focused on the role of electoral and parliamentary politics and the median voter in explaining distributional politics and rising inequality. Instead, what really drives developments is the kind of politics that they typify as 'organized combat': organized interest groups, especially big corporate and financial interests, determine public policies and redistribution (tax, industrial relations, corporate governance and executive compensation, and financial deregulation). The dramatic rise in inequality in the United States in the past decades is a result of intentional policy drift, whereby policies have not been updated to meet the needs of growing groups such as single-parent households and immigrants. As formulated by Hacker and Pierson,

> policy change often occurs when groups with the ability to block change effectively resist the updating of policy over an extended period of time in the face of strong contrary pressure and strong evidence that policy is failing to achieve its initial goals [...]. (Hacker and Pierson 2010: 168)

Policy drift, then, is the 'politically driven failure of public policies to adapt to the shifting realities of a dynamic economy and society' (ibid.: 170). Unlike simple inaction, which may stem from, for example, unawareness of the changed social and economic circumstances, policy drift assumes knowledge of policy failure and implies that 'policy makers fail to update policies due to pressure from intense minority interests or political actors exploiting veto points in the political process' (ibid.: 170). As the needs of large parts of the population have changed, policies have not followed suit. The narrow electoral democracy view already reveals that inequality has political causes, but may very well seriously underestimate the strong extra-parliamentary political forces at work.

The general point to take from this is that the theories and approaches that we have discussed so far all, in some way, try to make sense of how politicians and other elected representatives determine how and to what extent income inequalities in capitalist societies are dealt with. While some citizens may have more influence than others because they are part of the median voter segment or of some vital core constituency, the basic point is always that voters induce politicians to act in certain ways. As noted, this is a bottom-up perspective on politics. Yet, what if voters and governments do not really matter all that much in systems that combine a predominantly capitalist market economy with a democratic polity? In other words, what if voters do not exert the kind of power over governments that the theories assume? Or what if governments are much more constrained in pursuing redistributive policies than has been suggested? There are actually two long-standing, but until recently somewhat underrated, theoretical perspectives, Marxism and neo-pluralism, that provide arguments explaining why in capitalist market societies democracy is likely to be 'captured' or 'constrained' by corporate elite interests, or why the struggle for power in capitalist democracy is really 'organized combat', which is typically won by business interests.

In Marxist theory, the role of political parties and governments in determining distributional outcomes is placed in the context of the structural dependence of capitalist societies on the profitability of capital. This constitutes the most important power resource for capital. In market economies, private decisions rather than public power govern material production. Political power, however, depends on the societal surplus produced in the private economy, which is extracted through taxation. Hence, 'those who occupy positions of power in a capitalist state are in fact powerless unless the volume of the accumulation process allows them to derive (through taxation) the material resources necessary to promote any political ends' (Offe 1984: 120). It is a paradox that redistributive social policy, which aims at reforming capitalism, depends on that very system for its resources.

As a consequence of this dependency, one can speak of an institutional self-interest of the state in the profitability of capital. 'Although the agents of accumulation are not primarily interested in "using" the power of the state, state actors must be interested – for the sake of their own power – in guaranteeing and safe-guarding a "healthy" accumulation process' (Offe 1984: 120). The market economy imposes constraints upon the state. The state has limited room to manoeuvre when it encounters the boundaries of capitalist rationality. The structurally induced dominant position of capital is a key power resource.

> The constraints that the capitalist economy imposes upon the state, thereby disorganizing its capacity to maintain 'order' by responding effectively to political demands and requirements, are based upon capital's power to obstruct [...]. The ultimate political sanction is non-investment or the threat of it (just as the ultimate source of power of the individual capitalist vis-à-vis the individual worker is non-employment or termination of employment). The foundation of capitalist power and domination is this institutionalized right of capital withdrawal, of which economic crisis is nothing but the aggregate manifestation. (Offe 1984: 244)

The neo-pluralists, for their part, argue that not all societal groups are equally well equipped to lobby politicians and bureaucrats for policy reforms, and that the state cannot be viewed as an impartial and neutral institution. Neo-pluralist theory stresses that in market society, corporate or business interests have a privileged position. Businessmen are, in a sense, public yet constitutionally unrecognized and uncontrolled officials. They make decisions in the market (where and how much to invest, how to organize work, whether to substitute labour with new technology, and so on) and perform functions that are public, in the sense that they affect the public interest in terms of, for instance, control over productivity, income and employment (Lindblom 1977). Because these functions are performed by businessmen, the economic well-being and social security of all depend on their actions. 'Consequently, government officials cannot be indifferent to how well business performs its functions. Depression, inflation, or other economic distress can bring down a government. A major function of government, therefore, is to see to it that businessmen perform their tasks' (Lindblom 1977: 173).

Both entrepreneurs and the market have to be nurtured by the state, as we saw in Chapter 7. Governments provide necessary inducements, and these comprise

> whatever businessmen need as a condition for performing tasks that fall to them in a market system: income and wealth, deference, prestige, influence, power, and authority, among others. Every government in these systems accepts a responsibility to do what is necessary to assure profits high enough to maintain as a minimum employment and growth. (Lindblom 1977: 174)

Business, then, occupies a politically privileged position in market societies. The businessmen's threat of non- or disinvestment is often enough in itself for a democratic government to succumb to their demands. But on top of that, businessmen are well organized and operate politically, using disproportionally large amounts of money (in comparison to labour organizations) with which they influence public policy, e.g. via lobbying, the financing of political campaigning, and political advertising.

The scope of the structurally dominant capital (Marxists) or the privileged position of business (neo-pluralists), however, is most likely much more limited than the theories suggest (see Becker 1986). First, the position of capital does not guarantee that all demands are met. Such a view would reduce democratic politics to only one contextual element, the economic, and could not account for conflicts of interests, for instance between firms and between employers and the state. Indeed, the very existence of redistributive policies is evidence against the proposition of an all-powerful position of business.

Second, the notion of a 'strike of investment' presupposes that businessmen are capable of using this instrument unrestrictedly. To be sure, there exists a capacity to obstruct, blackmail or positively influence government policy, but it is not absolute. The refusal to invest and to innovate, although it happens, obviously comes at a great cost to a firm. Similarly, the diminishing territorial and economic significance of national borders under globalization may provide great resources for businessmen's capacity to influence politics, but threatening to transfer productive capital abroad only makes sense as a feasible political option when investments and production elsewhere would be (more) profitable. The option exists, but may be restricted, as, for instance, in the case of high-tech industries that depend on a highly skilled labour force that may not be available in otherwise more attractive countries. Third, the profitability of a single firm is not what counts: it is, rather, the level of profits in the economy as a whole that is the constant worry of a government. Society and public policies depend on the general state of the economy and not on how every individual firm thrives.

These considerations suggest that a strong version of a theory of 'captured democracy' and 'organized combat' is probably not tenable. Yet, arguments against such a strong theory of the privileged position of business should not blind the observer to real asymmetries of power. As Streeck (1995: 393, fn 6) once argued, '[...] fashionable desires not to sound like a "vulgar Marxist" do not do away with the fact that an incoming president of the European Commission is more likely to return a phone call from the president of Philips, especially if he also happens to be president of the European Business Roundtable, than from one of the firm's assembly-line workers'. As it is, the last decade has witnessed an accumulation of empirical evidence, above all else from the United States, which all points in this direction.

One empirical investigation suggesting that there might be some truth in the pessimistic accounts is published in Martin Gilens' book *Affluence and Influence* from 2012. Gilens collected surveys of the American public's preferences for all sorts of policy proposals to get an idea of what policies Americans want. In total, 1,923 survey questions were collected, covering the years from 1981 to 2002, all of them on issues specific enough to judge whether the policy proposal was later turned into legislation. For each survey question, Gilens then calculated the income gradient in preferences, i.e. how much support different income groups gave to a proposal. In this way, it became possible to see whether policy proposals that were backed by the richer segments of society had a bigger chance of being adopted than those supported by lower-income groups. The results were clear-cut. If the rich and the poor do not agree, the rich win: policy changes in the direction that the rich prefer.

In another study of the link between income and representation, Bartels (2008: 252–82) calculated the correspondence between the preferences of American voters in 50 states in the late 1980s and early 1990s, on the one hand, and the voting behaviour of the senators, on the other. The findings align well with those of Gilens. As summed up by Bartels (ibid.: 260, emphasis in original), senators' 'votes were quite responsive to the ideological views of their middle- and high-income constituents. In contrast, the views of low-income constituents had *no* discernible impact on the voting behavior of the senators.' Hacker and Pierson (2010), as noted above, have similarly studied the influence of elite actors on policy-making in the United States from the 1970s until today. They conclude that the lack of impact of many ordinary voters is a comparatively recent phenomenon, which, to a certain extent, can be attributed to the collapse of the labour movement and other pro-poor organizations. In other words, much would indicate that the perhaps slightly old-fashioned phrases of the Marxists and neo-pluralists relate to some important real-world developments that can explain why rising inequality in a country such as the United States does not translate into more redistribution, as Meltzer and Richard would expect. The link between public preferences and policies has been cut.

Conclusion

The chapter started out by asking a straightforward question: who decides in the politics of inequality? The answer was much more complicated than the simple question. The famous Meltzer–Richard model predicts that the more unequal a society is, the more redistribution there will be, because this is what the median-income voter wants. And the median voter gets it her way, because parties seeking office need her support to get a majority of votes. This prediction fails to pass empirical tests, however, because in reality redistribution is higher in more equal than in unequal countries, a phenomenon labelled the 'Robin Hood paradox'.

There are several ways to solve the paradox. One is by introducing social insurance as another preference that voters may have. This changes the picture radically. How much redistribution or insurance people seek depends on how likely it is that they will lose their income and how much this will hurt. If the structure of risks is relatively equal in a society, i.e. when middle-class voters and lower-income groups have an approximately equal risk of losing their job, then income maintenance will enjoy the most support. This perspective on the politics of inequality is important, because it reminds us that the economic context matters for voters' preferences, and that a changing context can alter the potential for coalitions between different segments of the public.

The power resources approach focuses on the strength of left parties and unions. Here, attention is less on the preferences of the median voter, but more on the preferences of workers and other core constituencies of social democratic and socialist parties. There is a lot of evidence to suggest that where the labour movement has been strong historically, redistribution has been most encompassing. Yet, it is also clear that the traditional power resources of the labour movement have declined substantially since around 1980. In big welfare states, other factors have emerged to substitute for the pro-redistributive effect of the labour movement. These include, above all else, the vested interests of recipients and public employees directly benefitting from the continuing existence of generous policies. In contrast, where redistribution never got very far in the first place, it has been easier for those wanting less redistribution to get their way. It is probably no coincidence that we have the most compelling evidence on so-called captured democracy from the United States, a country where not only the labour movement has been weak traditionally, but also the power decline has been particularly dramatic.

It is important to stress that the various explanations presented here need not preclude each other. Politics is unlikely to be mono-causal. We believe it is proven beyond doubt that citizens react to changing socio-economic circumstances such as rising unemployment, just as the work of Rehm (2011), Margalit (2013) and Owens and Pedulla (2014), among others, has shown. Dire economic straits change the terms of the debate in politics, forcing all mainstream parties to provide solutions to the problem faced by a substantial part of the electorate. However, although crises make both right-leaning voters and parties more concerned about the consequences of joblessness, this does not wash away all partisan differences. This is partly because right-leaning voters tend to return to their old beliefs quickly, and partly because the policy solutions proposed by right parties to solve unemployment and poverty remain distinct from the solutions of the left.

This is why partisanship historically has mattered greatly for the politics of inequality. We believe it has been documented thoroughly that parties cater to their core constituencies – at least as far as these make their voices heard in elections and, in the case of leftist voters, via union membership. Left parties will generally be more pro-redistribution than right parties, and over time this has manifested itself in lower inequality in countries where the left has dominated. Where the left governed for long periods of time and the unions were strong, powerful feedback effects came about, creating renewed support for redistributive policies. Established and encompassing redistributive policies are politically and institutionally well entrenched and tend to reinforce their own public support base, even in the face of weakening power of the left and declining electoral turnout of lower-income groups.

Chapter 11

What future for the politics of inequality?

This book started out by highlighting a great puzzle: why do modern-day capitalist democracies host such wildly different levels of inequality? Given that we are dealing with countries that share the same basic economic and political features – they are capitalist market economies and representative democracies – the first expectation should be that inequality is roughly similar everywhere. But it is not. Because economic inequality negatively affects health, reduces social mobility, and is bad for political participation in democratic processes, understanding the source of this cross-country variation in inequality is important.

The core solution to the puzzle lies in appreciating that both the market economy and democracy come in different forms. Market economies can be liberal, statist or social – or some combination of these – but all are capitalist. Companies compete against each other on the market to maximize the individual company's profit. The decision to hire and (more conditionally) fire workers rests with the employer. The physical and structural capital used in production is overwhelmingly owned by private actors such as companies, banks and stockholders. Employees depend on the labour market because they need to sell their human capital (labour power, skills) to employers. These key characteristics produce the power asymmetries between employers and employees characteristic of capitalism in all its varieties. Moreover, they create substantial market inequalities, because physical and structural capital owners earn rent from their assets, and some wage earners receive higher pay than other wage earners. This holds true for all capitalist market societies, and yet there are big differences between the liberal, statist and social market economies in the extent to which they reinforce or moderate power asymmetry and market inequality.

Whereas the liberal market economies in many ways live up to the ideal of a classic capitalist economy with limited government intervention, large power disparities and high inequality, the statist and social market economies both promote a much more hands-on approach, but with diverging effects on the distribution of power and income. The statist market economies are characterized by a great extent of government intervention. Wage-setting is centralized, employment protection is encompassing, and business operations are in general reined in by a lot

155

of bureaucracy. This reduces overall inequality, but also creates a labour market with many well-protected insiders pitched against a large group of jobless or temporarily employed and low-paid outsiders. Social market economies invest heavily in human capital and are better at staying out of the way of business, but still have centralized wage bargaining and reasonable employment protection. This creates low inequality, in part because there are so few outsiders in these economies.

The three types of market economy are matched by the three types of welfare state. Often, the market economy and the welfare state are so intertwined that it is difficult to see where one ends and the other begins. The complementarities between seemingly disconnected features, such as the generosity of unemployment benefits, public childcare and how easy it is to start a business, make countries stick to the path they began on decades ago. Adding to the path dependence of the market economy–welfare state nexus are the derived effects on preference articulation. Poorer citizens tend to be less interested in politics, feel that they are less likely to make a dent in politics, and consequently abstain from voting much more than better-off people. This means that politicians have fewer incentives to advocate policies that could benefit the marginalized, which increases the risk of even more political apathy further down the road.

All of this suggests that countries will stay on their chosen path virtually forever. Yet, at the same time, the social and economic context of these models has been changing dramatically, and arguably in more profound ways, than ever since the Industrial Revolution. For one thing, the fiscal sustainability of the welfare state is under mounting pressure, as a result of which governments are forced to prioritize between different social policy areas even more than previously. Second, a whole new set of social needs has emerged in the past few decades, including those stemming from new and less stable family structures, large-scale migration and globalization (Van Kersbergen and Vis 2014). With new demands on an already shrinking pool of resources, the political task of prioritizing social policy objectives and resources is getting even harder. We therefore close the book by discussing how these changes already appear to be altering the politics of inequality, as well as what the future might bring.

The Fiscal Sustainability of the Welfare State

The sustainability of existing welfare state arrangements is challenged by several developments at once, including an ageing population, rising public debt and a slowdown of long-term growth rates. Whereas some countries are more exposed than others to some of these hazards, no country escapes them all. And what is more, the pressure these challenges exert has become much higher in recent years, seriously threatening to undercut the capability to uphold the same levels of generosity that people have become used to. As pointed out in Chapter 8, all rich and well-established democracies in the world have large welfare states. They are frequently set up not so much to fight inequality as, rather, to protect and advance the interests of the middle class and the affluent, yet they still cost a lot of money, and hence – given the key importance of the middle class – potentially produce a huge political problem.

Let us look at the challenges in some more detail. For starters, the solid line in Figure 11.1 summarizes the increase in the proportion of people 65 or older since 1960 in the 23 countries for which we have data that far back. The percentage of elderly is shown on the vertical axis. In 1960, 9.3 per cent of the populace was 65 or older, which then steadily and dramatically increased to a little more than 17 per cent five decades later. The only exception to the secular rise of the elderly segment in societies occurs in the first part of the 1980s, when the massive death toll among young men in their twenties during World War II is visible. The cause of the rising proportion of older people is a combination of reduced fertility and better health care, both of which are, in fact,

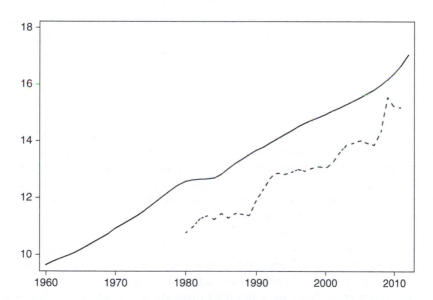

Figure 11.1 *Proportion of elderly and public spending on pensions and health care*

Note: Proportion of elderly is the solid line and is measured as the share of the population 65 or older. Spending is measured as all public and mandatory private spending going to old age pensions and health care.

Source: Armingeon et al. (2014) and OECD (2013a).

partly accomplishments of the welfare state. People have fewer children and live longer. That people live longer is, of course, happy news, and low fertility rates, to a certain extent, reflect the freedom of women to decide when and with whom they want to have babies. Yet, the rising share of the elderly and the declining number of children also form a financial burden. When old people leave the labour market, they stop paying contributions and start claiming pensions instead, effectively creating a double loss to society, while at the same time the number of people of working age who can pay for these expenses is declining. Old people, moreover, are also heavy users of hospitals, driving health care spending up.

The dashed line in Figure 11.1 shows average public and private mandatory spending on old age pensions and health care since 1980, the first year with data available. Spending has gone up from 10.8 per cent of GDP in 1980 to 15.2 per cent by the end of the period, a 40.7 per cent increase, and it is clear how the share of the elderly and pension and health care spending track each other. Because of the low fertility rates, it is possible to foresee that this state of affairs is unlikely to improve any time soon. Across the OECD, average fertility rates today stand at 1.7, which is below the circa 2.1 that allows a population to reproduce itself over time (Adema et al. 2014b: 42–3). The fiscal burden of paying for all the elderly people will, in all likelihood, continue to grow during the next decades, unless, obviously, entitlements are cut or taxes are raised. We will return to the chance of this happening later.

Another fundamental shift is the decline of long-term growth rates. Figure 11.2 displays real GDP growth since 1960 for the same countries as in Figure 11.1. Several things are visible. First, we observe that there are large swings from boom to bust and back again, something we also found in the comparison between Sweden and the United States in Chapter 6. Good economic times typically last around 5 years, after which a shorter downturn sets in. Second, and more important for our current purpose, we see from the dashed trend line that average growth rates have gradually become lower. In the 1960s and early 1970s, growth was normally around 5 per cent of GDP every year. For most of the countries for which we have data, this high-growth era began in the aftermath of World War II and lasted roughly 25 years. From the early 1970s until the Great Recession that started in 2008, average growth was in the 2–3 per cent range, after which it dropped even further (see Antolin-Diaz et al. 2014 for a detailed discussion of decline in long-term growth).

Declining growth is a vital phenomenon, because it systematically constrains governments' ability to finance social protection and redistribution. However, as is apparent from the spending figures in Figure 11.1, this has not meant that public spending has declined. Rather, the opposite has occurred. But with revenue declining and spending rising, public debt

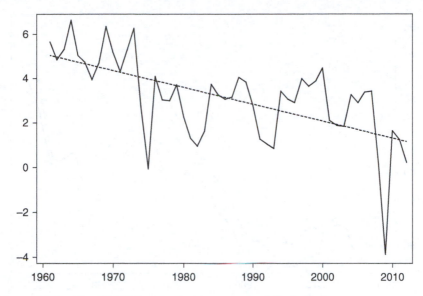

Figure 11.2   *Yearly GDP growth rates corrected for inflation*

Source: Armingeon et al. (2014).

has naturally shot through the roof. Figure 11.3 displays public debt as a percentage of GDP for all countries on average (the solid line) and the United States (the dashed line). Despite some pushbacks during upturns, public debt has been rising fairly consistently since 1960. The United States' debt is included in the figure to illustrate that rising debt is found almost everywhere, even in an economy that some right-leaning observers view as particularly admirable. Some of the countries with lowest public debt are actually the Nordic countries. Whereas public debt in the United States by 2014 stands at 122.6 per cent of the GDP, it is only 62.4 per cent in Sweden, 57.3 per cent in Denmark (in 2013, the latest year with data) and 32.2 per cent in Norway (OECD 2015c). One reason for such a relatively good performance is that the Nordic countries tax a lot more than the United States, so there is simply less need to accumulate debt, because citizens are made to pay today rather than tomorrow (Norway is also helped by its oil industry). In the United States, in contrast, it is politically extremely difficult to raise taxes, making it necessary to take on more debt.

All of these problems together – ageing, slower growth and rising debt – have been around for a long time. Yet, because the challenges are rapidly intensifying, their impact on the politics of inequality is likely to increase too. Countries such as Japan, Italy, France and the United States, just to mention some of the prominent culprits, have been running budget deficits for decades, with a few short exceptional surplus

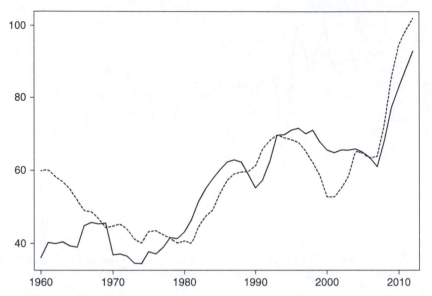

Figure 11.3   *Public debt as a percentage of GDP across the OECD and in the United States*

Source: Armingeon et al. (2014).

periods only. This implies that the ability to deal with inequality and the major problems it causes is itself severely constrained. This is particularly unfortunate because of the emergence of new social risks that also require government action if rising inequality is to be stopped or avoided.

New Problems

Like ageing, a changing family structure has slowly emerged as an important social problem in the past couple of decades. Crucially, while the risks of old age and sickness are reasonably well covered in most countries via old age pensions and generous health care, new and more unstable family forms create risks that are not properly being dealt with. Old age pensions and health care are some of the oldest and most elaborate welfare state programmes in existence. Before World War II, almost all countries introduced some pension provision for the old and treatment for the sick, which they then massively expanded after the war when the economic boom allowed it (Korpi 1989; Huber and Stephens 2001; Lindert 2004). As evident in Figure 11.1, the amount spent on these two risks has increased substantially, effectively reducing the room for spending on other risks.

The traditional family structure consists of a male breadwinner, a female housewife and their children. The husband is expected to bring home the entire income of the household, whereas the wife is expected to stay at home taking care of the house, rearing the children and – in many countries – looking after family members in need of help. Although the wife's earnings from her own job in reality were often needed too, certainly in poorer households, the ideal was clearly that the wife stayed at home. With the post-war economic boom, it became possible for millions of families to live out this vision of the good family life. From the 1970s onwards, however, this slowly started to change. Divorce rates went up, and many women decided not to marry at all. From 1970 to 2010, divorce rates doubled in the OECD, whereas the proportion of children born outside marriage tripled from 11 to almost 33 per cent. Across the OECD, 10 per cent of all children now live in so-called reconstituted families, i.e. in households where the biological parent lives together with a new partner and their respective children, while 15 per cent of children live in single-parent households (Adema et al. 2014b: 27–9).

In many countries, social policies are not geared to deal with this new lifestyle at all. Not least in continental and southern Europe, the male breadwinner–female carer model has inspired much social legislation. Here, the male breadwinner earns not only the income, but also the social rights that are attached to his job. The generosity of benefits is determined by his occupational history, e.g. how long he worked before needing the benefit, how highly paid he was, and how long he contributed to insurance. Benefits tend to be comparatively generous for employees with a long work history and extended contribution record, and are meant to cover the needs of the entire family. The virtually non-existent childcare, and this applies to several, but not all, Anglo-Saxon countries as well, means that if a couple have a child, the only viable solution often is for the wife to take care of it herself, even if this means leaving her job or education. In principle, the system functions well by its own logic (although not always in practice), but only as long as people actually stick to the traditional family model. Divorcees, single parents and people who never enjoyed a steady job can be highly exposed. Under these conditions, inequalities are almost certain to increase as the group of marginalized people grows in size (Esping-Andersen 1999; 2009; Bonoli 2005; Häusermann and Schwander 2012).

Another major new development concerns increasing economic globalization. One aspect of this is cross-border trade. Figure 11.4 shows the combined volume of imports and exports as a percentage of GDP since 1960. From the modest levels of the 1960s, cross-border trade gradually climbed in the 1970s and 1980s. Cross-border trade exploded in the 1990s with the EU's single market, the free trade agreement of 1994 that established the World Trade Organization, the fall in

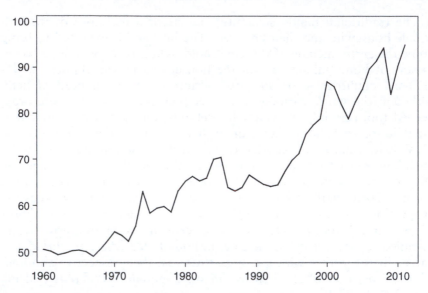

Figure 11.4   *Import and export as a percentage of GDP*

Source: Armingeon et al. (2014).

transportation costs, and the IT revolution. Many countries – Germany, Austria, the Netherlands, Ireland, Sweden, Switzerland and Denmark, among others – have cross-border trade worth the same as or more than their entire economy as measured by GDP. Luxembourg, amazingly, sees cross-border trade totalling 300 per cent of GDP. Being able to compete on the world markets is obviously essential in such a situation, but is made extra demanding by the relatively high wages earned by ordinary workers in these countries.

Increasing cross-border trade is supplemented by an increasing movement of capital. Frequently, the companies trading across borders are not owned by investors living in the country of the company. The German carmaker Opel is owned by the American General Motors, whereas American Chrysler is owned by Italian Fiat, just to give an example from the world of cars. Such foreign direct investment is vital for the operation of today's market economies and is supported by a web of huge multinational banks. However, foreign direct investment not only facilitates growth, it also – all else being equal – makes companies less dependent on workers in any particular country. In the words of Scheve and Slaughter (2004: 662), foreign direct investment 'increases firms' elasticity of demand for labor. More-elastic labor demands, in turn, raise the volatility of wages and employment, all of which tends to make workers feel less secure.' This is akin to the mechanism we saw in Chapter 10, namely, that an increasing risk of unemployment makes people more supportive of redistribution and unemployment protection.

Economic globalization, in sum, creates two opposing pressures. On the one hand, it involves a pressure for wage restraint and generally lower production costs. On the other hand, it generates calls for more security for ordinary workers, who feel exposed to a greater risk of unemployment when firms can easily ship jobs abroad. In many countries in North America and north-western Europe, this insecurity is enhanced by an inflow of immigrants from less affluent places. In the United Kingdom, for instance, the immigrant population of Poles grew from a little over 60,000 in 2001 to 688,000 in 2013. In the United States, millions of illegal immigrants from Latin America are willing to accept jobs with very low wages and poor working conditions. Labour migration has become one of the hottest political issues in many countries, because it potentially fuses together many manual workers' fears of losing their jobs with xenophobia and, in Europe, anti-EU sentiments.

Future Politics

In the heyday of the post-war boom, popular demands for more redistribution and better social protection could be met if the politicians in charge had the ideological predisposition to do so, or if strong societal organizations such as the unions pushed them hard enough to take action. Even after the slump of the second half of the 1970s, social policy expansion was still an option, especially during upturns, as in the late 1990s and mid-2000s before the Great Recession, and with the aid of public borrowing. Over the course of decades, cross-country differences in the composition of governments and the strength of the labour movement created the distinct market economies and welfare state models that characterize the most advanced democracies today (Korpi 1989; 2006; Esping-Andersen 1990; 1999; van Kersbergen 1995; Huber and Stephens 2001; 2014).

The political freedom to appease popular demands has been declining for some time now, but was accelerated by the Great Recession, which caused exploding debt and even lower growth than previously. This is occurring at the same time as many wage earners are experiencing unprecedented exposure to (new and old) social risks from economic globalization that threaten their livelihood and from new, more vulnerable groups entering the labour market. With less money to go around and more risks from which protection is needed, the scene is set for an even more intense battle over who should get what, when, how.

When speculating about the direction of the future politics of inequality, it is relevant to ask how the power resources of different social groups and social and political actors have fared in recent years. Looking first at business, we hold that increasing international competition – all else being equal – means that the threat of downsizing and massive lay-offs, or moving production abroad altogether, is becoming ever more credible. The Marxists and neo-pluralists may, as we discussed in Chapter 10, have oversold their argument that business is the most powerful actor in society, but much suggests that policies preferred by business will find an increasingly positive reception among political decision-makers. Although employers do hold different preferences across different types of market economies, we are generally likely to witness a continuous drive for less strict employment protection, lower corporate taxation and more individualized wage-setting, all of which can be expected to have inegalitarian consequences and hence will contribute to political inequality.

Another group that remains politically strong is the middle class, if only for the simple reason that political parties need its support to win office. As Pierson (1996: 147) observes, the welfare state creates its own constituency. Once social programmes are up and running, they become entrenched, and the bigger the number of beneficiaries, the more entrenched they become. The really popular programmes in all advanced democracies are health care and old age pensions, i.e. those that most people believe (or fear) they will need some time in the future. In countries with generous provisions for the jobless and the poor, notably in the Nordic countries, public support for these parts of the welfare state still tends to be high, but even here pensions and health care enjoy the biggest backing. Programmes that benefit relatively small segments of the populace are typically not supported by many.

For re-election-oriented politicians, the lesson is clear enough. In a situation where cuts in social provisions have to be made, attention should be, if at all possible, on anything but health care and old age pensions. To be sure, because of the sheer size of health care and old age pensions, it is often not possible to avoid cutting entitlements here. Not least in southern and continental Europe, the pension age has been low and benefits often high, as a result of which pensions here constitute a massive drain on the public purse. Still, we expect retrenchment in these areas to be limited and phased in over many years. Much more dramatic cuts have already happened, and will presumably continue to happen, in programmes aimed at the poor, the temporarily employed and the jobless. This is where it is politically least risky to cut and the best option to reprioritize the social budget without suffering an electoral backlash. Obviously, increasing inequality is the price to pay for this politically rational strategy.

The precise effect on inequality, however, will strongly depend on existing labour market and welfare state arrangements. Unemployment benefits are being curtailed also in countries such as Denmark and Sweden, but the skill level among the least educated remains higher than in most other places, and changes in wage-setting will take a very long time to translate into more substantial wage inequalities. Much the same applies elsewhere. Even though the statist market economies of southern and continental Europe have begun to cut red tape regarding business, the process will be slow and the effects will take a long time to appear. In the liberal market economies, it is unlikely that path-diverging political choices will be made that will decrease inequality. On the contrary, in the United Kingdom, for one example, conservative politicians have seized the opportunity created by the Great Recession to launch an unparalleled austerity offensive. Cutting welfare programmes, government personnel and salaries, and state services is estimated to reduce total public spending to 35 per cent of GDP by 2020, the lowest figure since the 1930s. Over the long haul, then, the trends that we observe today mostly point in the direction of increasing inequality – with all its adverse effects on health outcomes, social mobility and democratic participation. Despite scattered mass protests in some countries, we do not catch sight of the emergence of social movements, political parties or other types of forces that are strong enough to counter the inegalitarian trends. Indeed, politics in the next decade will continue to be the politics of inequality.

References

Acemoglu, Daron, Suresh Naidu, Pascual Restrepo and James A. Robinson (2013), Democracy, Redistribution and Inequality, *National Bureau of Economic Research Working Paper 19746*, Cambridge (MA): National Bureau of Economic Research.

Adema, Willem, Pauline Fron and Maxime Ladaique (2014a), How Much Do OECD Countries Spend on Social Protection and How Redistributive Are their Tax/Benefit Systems? *International Social Security Review* 67 (1): 1–25.

Adema, Willem, Nabli Ali and Olivier Thévenon (2014b), Changes in Family Policies and Outcomes: Is there Convergence? *OECD Social, Employment and Migration Working Papers*, No. 157, Paris: OECD.

Alesina, Alberto and Dani Rodrik (1994), Distributive Politics and Economic Growth, *The Quarterly Journal of Economics*, 109 (2): 465–90.

Almond, Gabriel and Sydney Verba (1963), *The Civic Culture: Political Attitudes and Democracy in Five Nations*, Princeton: Princeton University Press.

Alvaredo, Facundo, Anthony B. Atkinson, Thomas Piketty and Emmanuel Saez (2015), *The World Top Incomes Database*, http://topincomes.g-mond. parisschoolofeconomics.eu/ (accessed 15 February 2015).

Andersen, Jørgen Goul (2011), From the Edge of the Abyss to Bonanza – and Beyond: Danish Economy and Economic Policies 1980–2011, *Comparative Social Research* 28 (11): 89–65.

Anderson, Christopher J. and Pablo Beramendi (2008), Income, Inequality, and Electoral Participation, in Pablo Beramendi and Christopher J. Anderson (eds), *Democracy, Inequality, and Representation. A Comparative Perspective*, New York: Russell Sage Foundation, pp. 278–311.

Anderson, Elizabeth S. (1999), What Is the Point of Equality? *Ethics* 109 (2): 287–337.

Antolin-Diaz, Juan, Thomas Drechsel and Ivan Petrella (2014), Following the Trend: Tracking GDP when Long-run Growth is Uncertain, *Fulcrum Research Papers*, 16 March 2015.

Armingeon, Klaus, Laura Knöpfel, David Weisstanner and Sarah Engler (2014), *Comparative Political Data Set I 1960–2012*, Bern: Institute of Political Science, University of Berne.

Arneson, Ben A. (1925), Non-Voting in a Typical Ohio Community, *American Political Science Review*, 19 (04): 816–25.

Arneson, Richard (2008), Rawls, Responsibility, and Distributive Justice, in Marc Fleurbaey and John A. Weymark (eds), *Justice, Political Liberalism, and Utilitarianism: Themes from Harsanyi and Rawls*, Cambridge: Cambridge University Press, pp. 80–107.

Atkinson, Anthony B. (1970), On the Measurement of Inequality, *Journal of Economic Theory*, 2 (3): 244–63.

Atkinson, Anthony B. (2003), Income Inequality in OECD Countries: Data and Explanations, *CESifo Economic Studies*, 49 (4): 479–513.

Atkinson, Anthony B. (2004), The Luxembourg Income Study (LIS): Past, Present and Future, *Socio-Economic Review*, 2 (2): 165–90.

Atkinson, Anthony B. (2015a), *Inequality. What Can Be Done?* Cambridge, MA: Harvard University Press.

Atkinson, Anthony B. (2015b), Interview, http://www.prospectmagazine.co.uk/blogs/jonathan-derbyshire/inequality-and-what-can-be-done-about-it-an-interview-with-anthony-atkinson (accessed 25 June 2015).

Atkinson, Anthony B., Thomas Piketty and Emanuel Saez (2011), Top Incomes in the Long Run of History, *Journal of Economic Literature*, 49 (1): 3–71.

Axelsen, David V. and Lasse Nielsen (2014), Sufficiency as Freedom from Duress, *Journal of Political Philosophy*, 23 (4): 406–26.

Babones, Salvatore J. (2008), Income Inequality and Population Health: Correlation and Causality, *Social Science & Medicine*, 66 (7): 1614–26.

Bachmann, Ronald, Peggy Bechara and Sandra Schaffner (2012), Wage Inequality and Wage Mobility in Europe, *Ruhr Economic Papers*, 386.

Bartels, Larry M. (2008), *Unequal Democracy: The Political Economy of the New Gilded Age*, Princeton: Princeton University Press.

Bassanini, Andrea, Luca Nunziata and Danielle Venn (2009), Job Protection Legislation and Productivity Growth in OECD Countries, *Economic Policy*, 24 (58): 349–402.

Becker, Gary S. and Nigel Tomes (1986), Human Capital and the Rise and Fall of Families, *Journal of Labor Economics*, 4 (3): 1–39.

Becker, Uwe (1986), *Kapitalistische Dynamik und politisches Kräftespiel: zur Kritik des klassentheoretischen Ansatzes*, Frankfurt: Campus.

Björklund, Anders and Markus Jäntti (2009), Intergenerational Income Mobility and the Role of Family Background, in Wiemer Salverda, Brian Nolan and Timothy M. Smeeding (eds), *The Oxford Handbook of Economic Inequality*, Oxford: Oxford University Press.

Blyth, Mark (2001), The Transformation of the Swedish Model: Economic Ideas, Distributional Conflict, and Institutional Change, *World Politics*, 54 (1): 1–26.

Bonoli, Giuliano (2005), The Politics of the New Social Policies: Providing Coverage against New Social Risks in Mature Welfare States, *Policy & Politics*, 33 (3): 431–49.

Bradley, David, Evelyne Huber, Stephanie Moller, François Nielsen and John D. Stephens (2003), Distribution and Redistribution in Postindustrial Democracies, *World Politics*, 55 (2): 193–228.

Bradley, David H. and John D. Stephens (2007), Employment Performance in OECD Countries. A Test of Neoliberal and Institutionalist Hypotheses, *Comparative Political Studies*, 40 (12): 1486–510.

Brady, David (2009), *Rich Democracies, Poor People: How Politics Explain Poverty*, Oxford: Oxford University Press.

Brooks, Clem and Jeff Manza (2007), *Why Welfare States Persist: The Importance of Public Opinion in Democracies*, Chicago: University of Chicago Press.

Busemeyer, Marius (2014), *Skills and Inequality*, Cambridge: Cambridge University Press.

Campbell, Angus, Philip E. Converse, Warren E. Miller and Donald E. Stokes (1960), *The American Voter*, Chicago: University of Chicago Press.

Campbell, John L. and Ove K. Pedersen (eds) (2001), *The Rise of Neoliberalism and Institutional Analysis*, Princeton: Princeton University Press.

Castles, Francis G. (1978), *The Social Democratic Image of Society: A Study of the Achievements and Origins of Scandinavian Social Democracy in Comparative Perspective*, London: Routledge & Kegan Paul.

Chetty, Raj, Nathaniel Hendren, Patrick Kline, Emmanuel Saez and Nicholas Turner (2014), Is the United States Still a Land of Opportunity? Recent Trends in Intergenerational Mobility, *NBER Working Paper* 19844.

Cingano, Federico (2014), Trends in Income Inequality and its Impact on Economic Growth, *OECD Social, Employment and Migration Working Papers*, 163, Paris: OECD.

Clarke, George R. G. (1995), More Evidence on Income Distribution and Growth, *Journal of Development Economics*, 47 (2): 403–27.

Clasen, Jochen and Daniel Clegg (2011), *Regulating the Risk of Unemployment: National Adaptations to Post-Industrial Labour Markets in Europe*, Oxford: Oxford University Press.

Coase, Ronald (1937), The Nature of the Firm, *Economica*, 16 (4): 386–405.

Congressional Budget Office (2013), *The Distribution of Major Tax Expenditures in the Individual Income Tax System*, Congress of the United States/Congressional Budget Office.

Corak, Miles (2013), Income Inequality, Equality of Opportunity, and Intergenerational Mobility, *The Journal of Economic Perspectives*, 27 (3): 79–102.

Cowell, Frank (2011), *Measuring Inequality*, Oxford: Oxford University Press.

Coyle, Diane (2014), *GDP. A Brief but Affectionate History*, 2nd Edition, Princeton: Princeton University Press.

Crisp, Roger (2003), Equality, Priority, and Compassion, *Ethics*, 113 (4): 745–63.

Crouch, Colin (2011), *The Strange Non-Death of Neoliberalism*, Cambridge: Polity.

Cunha, Flavio, James J. Heckman, Lance Lochner and Dimitri V. Masterov (2006), Interpreting the Evidence on Life Cycle Skill Formation, *Handbook of the Economics of Education*, 1: 697–812.

Currie, Janet and Douglas Almond (2011), Human Capital Development before Age Five, in Orley Ashenfelter and David Card (eds), *Handbook of Labor Economics*, Vol. 4B, Amsterdam: Elsevier, pp. 1315–486.

Cusack, Thomas, Torben Iversen and Philipp Rehm (2006), Risks at Work: The Demand and Supply Sides of Government Redistribution, *Oxford Review of Economic Policy*, 22 (3): 365–89.

Dahl, Robert A. (1971), *Polyarchy: Participation and Opposition*, New Haven: Yale University Press.

Dahl, Robert A. (1989), *Democracy and Critics*, New Haven: Yale University Press.

Daniels, Norman, Bruce P. Kennedy and Ichiro Kawachi (1999), Why Justice Is Good for Our Health: The Social Determinants of Health Inequalities, *Daedalus*, 128 (4): 215–51.

Danish Ministry of Taxation (Skatteministeriet) (2014), BoligJobordningen benyttes mest af de velhavende, http://www.skm.dk/aktuelt/nyheder/2014/august/boligjo bordningen-benyttes-mest-af-de-velhavende/ (accessed 1 July 2015).

David, Paul A. (1985), Clio and the Economics of QWERTY, *The American Economic Review*, 75 (2): 332–7.

Davies, James B. (2009), Wealth and Economic Inequality, in Wiemer Salverda, Brian Nolan and Timothy M. Smeeding (eds), *The Oxford Handbook of Economic Inequality*, Oxford: Oxford University Press.

De Beer, Paul (2014), Groeiende beloningsverschillen in Nederland, in Monique Kremer, Mark Bovens, Erik Schrijvers and Robert Went (eds), *Hoe ongelijk is Nederland? Een verkenning van de ontwikkeling en gevolgen van economische ongelijkheid*, Amsterdam: Amsterdam University Press, pp. 59–77.

Deininger, Klaus and Lyn Squire (1998), New Ways of Looking at Old Issues: Inequality and Growth, *Journal of Development Economics*, 57 (2): 259–87.

Delhey, Jan and Georgi Dragolov (2014), Why Inequality Makes Europeans Less Happy: The Role of Distrust, Status Anxiety, and Perceived Conflict, *European Sociological Review*, 30 (2): 151–65.

Djankov, Simeon, Caralee McLiesh and Rita Maria Ramalho (2006), Regulation and Growth, *Economics Letters*, 92 (3): 395–401.

Dworkin, Ronald (1981), What Is Equality? Part II: Equality of Resources, *Philosophy and Public Affairs*, 10 (4): 283–345.

Easton, David Jack Dennis (1967), The Child's Acquisition of Regime Norms: Political Efficacy, *American Political Science Review*, 61 (01): 25–38.

Eichengreen, Barry (2008), *The European Economy since 1945: Coordinated Capitalism and Beyond*, Princeton: Princeton University Press.

Eichengreen, Barry and Torben Iversen (1999), Institutions and Economic Performance: Evidence from the Labour Market, *Oxford Review of Economic Policy*, 15 (4): 121–38.

Esping-Andersen, Gøsta (1985), *Politics against Markets: The Social Democratic Road to Power*, Princeton: Princeton University Press.

Esping-Andersen, Gøsta (1990), *The Three Worlds of Welfare Capitalism*, Cambridge: Polity.

Esping-Andersen, Gøsta (1999), *Social Foundations of Postindustrial Economies*, Oxford: Oxford University Press.

Esping-Andersen, Gøsta (2009), *Incomplete Revolution: Adapting Welfare States to Women's New Roles*, Cambridge: Polity.

Esping-Andersen, Gøsta (2015), Welfare Regimes and Social Stratification, *Journal of European Social Policy*, 25 (1): 124–34.

Esping-Andersen, Gøsta and Kees van Kersbergen (1992), Contemporary Research on Social Democracy, *Annual Review of Sociology*, 18: 187–208.

Estevez-Abe, Margarita M., Torben Iversen and David Soskice (2001), Social Protection and the Formation of Skills: A Reinterpretation of the Welfare State, in Peter A. Hall and David Soskice (eds), *Varieties of Capitalism. The Institutional Foundations of Comparative Advantage*, Oxford: Oxford University Press, pp. 145–83.

European Commission (2015), AMECO Database. http://ec.europa.eu/economy_finance/db_indicators/ameco/index_en.htm (accessed 13 December 2015).

European Social Survey Round 4 Data (2008), Data file edition 4.3, Norwegian Social Science Data Services, Norway – Data Archive and distributor of ESS data.

European Social Survey Round 6 Data (2012), Data file edition 2.1, Norwegian Social Science Data Services, Norway – Data Archive and distributor of ESS data.

Eurostat (2015), Total Expenditure on Social Protection per Head of Population, http://ec.europa.eu/eurostat/tgm/table.do?tab=table&plugin=1&language =en&pcode=tps00099 (accessed 30 June 2015).

Finkel, Steven E. (1985), Reciprocal Effects of Participation and Political Efficacy: A Panel Analysis, *American Journal of Political Science*, 29 (4): 891–913.

Fishkin, Joseph (2014), *Bottlenecks: A New Theory of Equal Opportunity*, Oxford and New York: Oxford University Press.

Frankfurt, Harry G. (1988), Equality as Moral Ideal, in Harry G. Frankfurt, *The Importance of What We Care About. Philosophical Essays*, Cambridge: Cambridge University Press, pp. 134–58.

Frankfurt, Harry G. (2015), *On Inequality*, Princeton: Princeton University Press.

Galbraith, John Kenneth (1982), Reagan Economic Policy: Another Confession, *Nieman Reports*, 36 (1): 10–11.

Garfinkel, Irwin, Lee Rainwater and Timothy Smeeding (2010), *Wealth and Welfare States: Is America a Laggard or Leader?* Oxford: Oxford University Press.

Garrett, Geoffrey (1998), *Partisan Politics in the Global Economy*, Cambridge: Cambridge University Press.

Gilens, Martin (2012), *Affluence and Influence: Economic Inequality and Political Power in America*, Princeton: Princeton University Press.

Goodin, Robert and John Dryzek (1980), Rational Participation: The Politics of Relative Power, *British Journal of Political Science*, 10 (03): 273–92.

Gosepath, Stefan (2011), Equality, *The Stanford Encyclopedia of Philosophy* (Spring 2011 Edition), http://plato.stanford.edu/archives/spr2011/entries/equality/.

Green-Pedersen, Christoffer and Michael Baggesen-Klitgaard (2009), Between Economic Constraints and Popular Entrenchment : The Development of the Danish Welfare State 1982–2005, in Ursula Bazant, Simon Hegelich and Klaus Schubert (eds), *The Handbook of European Welfare Systems*, London: Taylor & Francis, pp. 139–54.

Guillaud, Elvire (2013), Preferences for Redistribution: An Empirical Analysis over 33 Countries, *The Journal of Economic Inequality*, 11 (1): 57–78.

Hacker, Jacob S. and Paul Pierson (2010), Winner-Take-All Politics: Public Policy, Political Organization, and the Precipitous Rise of Top Incomes in the United States, *Politics & Society*, 38 (2): 152–204.

Hall, Peter A. (1993), Policy Paradigms, Social Learning, and the State: The Case of Economic Policymaking in Britain, *Comparative Politics*, 25 (3): 275–96.

Hall, Peter A. and David Soskice (2001), An Introduction to Varieties of Capitalism, in Peter A. Hall and David Soskice (eds), *Varieties of Capitalism: The Institutional Foundations of Comparative Advantage*, Oxford: Oxford University Press, pp. 1–51.

Harrison, Bennett and Barry Bluestone (1988), *The Great U-Turn: Corporate Restructuring and the Polarizing of America*, New York: Basic Books.

Harvey, David (2005), *A Brief History of Neoliberalism*, Oxford: Oxford University Press.

Hausman, Daniel M. and Matt Sensat Waldren (2011), Egalitarianism Reconsidered, *Journal of Moral Philosophy*, 8 (4): 567–86.

Häusermann, Silja and Hanna Schwander (2012), Varieties of Dualization? Labor Market Segmentation and Insider-Outsider Divides across Regimes, in Patrick Emmenegger, Silja Häusermann, Brunu Palier and Martin Seeleib-Kaiser (eds), *The Age of Dualization: The Changing Face of Inequality in Deindustrializing Societies*, Oxford: Oxford University Press, pp. 27–51.

Heckman, James J. (2011), The Economics of Inequality, *American Educator* (Spring Edition): 31–47.

Heckman, James J. and Stefano Mosso (2014), The Economics of Human Development and Social Mobility, *Annual Review of Economics*, 6: 689–733.

Hopkin, Jonathan and Mark Blyth (2012), What Can Okun Teach Polanyi? Efficiency, Regulation and Equality in the OECD, *Review of International Political Economy*, 19 (1): 1–33.

Hout, Michael and Emily Beller (2006), Intergenerational Social Mobility: The United States in Comparative Perspective, *The Future of Children*, 16 (2): 19–36.

Howard, Christopher (2007), *The Welfare State Nobody Knows: Debunking Myths about US Social Policy*, Princeton: Princeton University Press.

Huber, Evelyne and John D. Stephens (2001), *Development and Crisis of the Welfare State: Parties and Policies in Global Markets*, Chicago: University of Chicago Press.

Huber, Evelyne and John D. Stephens (2014), Income Inequality and Redistribution in Post-Industrial Democracies: Demographic, Economic and Political Determinants, *Socio-Economic Review*, 12 (2): 245–67.

Huffington Post (2014), http://www.huffingtonpost.ca/2014/01/21/kevin-oleary-inequality_n_4637887.html (accessed 5 February 2015).

IMF (2014), Redistribution, Inequality, and Growth, *IMF Staff Discussion Note* 14/02.

IMF (2015), Causes and Consequences of Income Inequality: A Global Perspective, *IMF Staff Discussion Note* 15/13.

Inequality Watch (2012), *Poverty in Europe: The Current Situation*, http://inequalitywatch.eu/spip.php?article99&lang=en (accessed 6 February 2015).

Institute on Taxation and Economic Policy (2015), *Who Pays? A Distributional Analysis of the Tax Systems in All 50 States*, 5th Edition, Washington, DC: Institute on Taxation and Economic Policy.

Iversen, Torben and David Soskice (2006), Electoral Institutions and the Politics of Coalitions: Why Some Democracies Redistribute More than Others, *American Political Science Review*, 100 (2): 165–81.

Iversen, Torben and David Soskice (2009), Distribution and Redistribution: The Shadow of the Nineteenth Century, *World Politics*, 61 (3): 438–86.

Jenkins, Stephen P. and Philippe van Kerm (2009), The Measurement of Economic Inequality, in Wiemer Salverda, Brian Nolan and Timothy M. Smeeding (eds), *The Oxford Handbook of Economic Inequality*, Oxford: Oxford University Press, pp. 40–67.

Jennings, M. Kent, Laura Stoker and Jake Bowers (2009), Politics across Generations: Family Transmission Reexamined, *The Journal of Politics*, 71 (3): 782–99.

Jensen, Carsten (2008), Worlds of Welfare Services and Transfers, *Journal of European Social Policy*, 18 (2), 151–62.

Jensen, Carsten (2010), Issue Compensation and Right-Wing Government Social Spending, *European Journal of Political Research*, 49 (2): 282–99.

Jensen, Carsten (2014), *The Right and the Welfare State*, Oxford: Oxford University Press.

Jensen, Carsten and Michael Bang Petersen (2016), The Deservingness Heuristic and the Politics of Health Care, *American Journal of Political Science*. Early view.

Jerrim, John and Lindsey Macmillan (2015), Income Inequality, Intergenerational Mobility, and the Great Gatsby Curve: Is Education the Key? *Social Forces* (first online, accessed 18 March 2016).

Jones, Bryan D. and Walter Williams (2008), *The Politics of Bad Ideas: The Great Tax Cut Delusion and the Decline of Good Government in America*, New York: Longman.

Justesen, Mogens K. (2008), The Effect of Economic Freedom on Growth Revisited: New Evidence on Causality from a Panel of Countries 1970–1999, *European Journal of Political Economy*, 24 (3): 642–60.

Kauppinen, Antti (2012), What Is Wrong with Economic Inequality? http://www.academia.edu/1307269/What_Is_Wrong_With_Economic_Inequality (accessed 6 February 2015).

Kenworthy, Lane (2008), *Jobs with Equality*, Oxford: Oxford University Press.

Kenworthy, Lane and Jonas Pontusson (2005), Rising Inequality and the Politics of Redistribution in Affluent Countries, *Perspectives on Politics*, 3 (3): 449–71.

Kondo, Naoki, Grace Sembajwe, Ichiro Kawachi, Rob M. van Dam, S. V. Subramanian and Zentaro Yamagata (2009), Income Inequality, Mortality, and Self Rated Health: Meta-analysis of Multilevel Studies, *BMJ*, 339: b4471.

Korpi, Walter (1978), *The Working Class in Welfare Capitalism: Work, Unions, and Politics in Sweden*, London: Taylor & Francis.

Korpi, Walter (1983), *The Democratic Class Struggle*, London: Routledge.

Korpi, Walter (1989), Power, Politics, and State Autonomy in the Development of Social Citizenship: Social Rights during Sickness in Eighteen OECD Countries since 1930, *American Sociological Review*, 54 (3): 309–28.

Korpi, Walter (2002), The Great Trough in Unemployment: A Long-Term View of Unemployment, Inflation, Strikes, and the Profit/Wage Ratio, *Politics & Society*, 30 (3): 365–426.

Korpi, Walter (2006), Power Resources and Employer-Centered Approaches in Explanations of Welfare States and Varieties of Capitalism: Protagonists, Consenters, and Antagonists, *World Politics*, 58 (02): 167–206.

Korpi, Walter and Joakim Palme (1998), The Paradox of Redistribution and Strategies of Equality: Welfare State Institutions, Inequality, and Poverty in the Western Countries, *American Sociological Review*, 63 (5): 661–87.

Korpi, Walter and Joakim Palme (2003), New Politics and Class Politics in the Context of Austerity and Globalization: Welfare State Regress in 18 Countries, 1975–95, *American Political Science Review*, 97 (03): 425–46.

Korpi, Walter and Joakim Palme (2007), *The Social Citizenship Indicator Program (SCIP)*, Swedish Institute for Social Research, Stockholm University.

Kotz, David M. (2015), *The Rise and Fall of Neoliberal Capitalism*, Cambridge, MA: Harvard University Press.

Kuznets, Simon (1955), Economic Growth and Income Inequality, *The American Economic Review*, XLV (1): 1–28.

Kwon, Hyeok Yong and Jonas Pontusson (2010), Globalization, Labour Power and Partisan Politics Revisited, *Socio-Economic Review*, 8(2): 251–81.

Lane, Robert E. (1959), *Political Life: Why People Get Involved in Politics*, Glencoe: The Free Press.

Larsen, Christian Albrekt (2008), The Institutional Logic of Welfare Attitudes: How Welfare Regimes Influence Public Support, *Comparative Political Studies*, 41 (2): 145–68.

Larsen, Christian Albrekt and Thomas Engel Dejgaard (2013), The Institutional Logic of Images of the Poor and Welfare Recipients: A Comparative Study of British, Swedish and Danish Newspapers, *Journal of European Social Policy*, 23(3): 287–99.

Lasswell, Harold D. (1936), *Politics: Who Gets What, When, How*, New York: Meridian.

Lavoie, Marc and Engelbert Stockhammer (2013), Wage-Led Growth: Concepts, Theories, and Policies, in Marc Lavoie and Engelbert Stockhammer, *Wage-Led Growth: An Equitable Strategy for Economic Recovery*, Houndsmills: Palgrave Macmillan, pp. 13–39.

Lazear, Edward P. and Sherwin Rosen (1981), Rank-Order Tournaments as Optimum Labor Contracts, *The Journal of Political Economy*, 89(5): 841–64.

Lewis, Jane (1992), Gender and the Development of Welfare Regimes, *Journal of European Social Policy*, 2 (3): 159–73.

Lewis, Michael (1993), *The Culture of Inequality*, Amherst: University of Massachusetts.

Lindblom, Charles E. (1977), *Politics and Markets: The World's Political-Economic Systems*, New York: Basic.

Lindert, Peter H. (2004), *Growing Public: Volume 1, The Story: Social Spending and Economic Growth since the Eighteenth Century* (Vol. 1), Cambridge: Cambridge University Press.

Lippert-Rasmussen, Kasper (2012), Democratic Egalitarianism versus Luck Egalitarianism: What Is at Stake? *Philosophical Topics*, 40 (1): 117–34.

Lippert-Rasmussen, Kasper (2015), *Luck Egalitarianism*, London: Bloomsbury.

LIS (2015). Key Figures, http://www.lisdatacenter.org/data-access/key-figures/download-key-figures/ (accessed 18 March 2016).

Luebker, Malte (2014), Income Inequality, Redistribution, and Poverty: Contrasting Rational Choice and Behavioral Perspectives, *Review of Income and Wealth*, 60 (1): 133–54.

Margalit, Yotam (2013), Explaining Social Policy Preferences: Evidence from the Great Recession, *American Political Science Review*, 107 (1): 80–103.

Marglin, Stephen and Amit Bhaduri (1990), Profit Squeeze and Keynesian Theory, in Stephen Marglin and Juliet Schor, *The Golden Age of Capitalism. Reinterpreting the Postwar Experience*, Oxford: Oxford University Press, pp. 153–86.

Marmot, Michael (2005), *The Status Syndrome: How Social Standing Affects Our Health and Longevity*, New York: Owl Books.

Maslow, Abraham H. (1966 [2002]), *The Psychology of Science: A Reconnaissance*, Chapel Hill: Maurice Basset.

McCarthy, Nolan and Jonas Pontusson (2009), The Political Economy of Inequality and Redistribution, in Wiemer Salverda, Brian Nolan and Timothy Smeeding (eds), *Oxford Handbook of Economic Inequality*, Oxford: Oxford University Press, pp. 665–92.

McKnight, Abigail and Frank Cowell (2014), Social Impacts: Health, Housing, Intergenerational Mobility, in Wiemer Salverda, Brian Nolan, Daniele Checchi, Ive Marx, Abigail McKnight, István György Tóth and Herman van de Werfhorst, *Changing Inequalities in Rich Countries: Analytical and Comparative Perspectives*, Oxford: Oxford University Press, pp. 169–95.

Meltzer, Allan H. and Scott F. Richard (1981), A Rational Theory of the Size of Government, *The Journal of Political Economy*, 89 (5): 914–27.

Milanovic, Branko (2016), *Global Inequality. A New Approach for the Age of Globalization*, Cambridge, MA: Harvard University Press.

Ministry for Economic Affairs and the Interior (2013), *Storomfordeling via offentlig service*, Copenhagen: The Ministry for Economic Affairs and the Interior.

Myles, John and Paul Pierson (2001), The Comparative Political Economy of Pension Reform, in Paul Pierson (ed.), *The New Politics of The Welfare State*, Oxford: Oxford University Press, pp. 305–33.

Nijhuis, D. O. (2009), Revisiting the Role of Labor: Worker Solidarity, Employer Opposition, and the Development of Old-Age Pensions in the Netherlands and the United Kingdom, *World Politics*, 61 (2): 296–329.

North, Douglass (1990), *Institutions, Institutional Change and Economic Performance*, Cambridge: Cambridge University Press.

Nozick, Robert (1974), *Anarchy, State, and Utopia*, Oxford: Blackwell.

Nussbaum, Martha C. (1993), Non-Relative Virtues: An Aristotelian Approach, in Martha Nussbaum and Amartya Sen (eds), *The Quality of Life*, Oxford: Oxford University Press, pp. 242–70.

Nussbaum, Martha C. (2001), *Women and Human Development: The Capabilities Approach*, Cambridge: Cambridge University Press.

Nussbaum, Martha C. (2006), *Frontiers of Justice: Disability, Nationality, Species Membership*, Cambridge, MA: Harvard University Press.

Nussbaum, Martha C. (2011), *Creating Capabilities: The Human Development Approach*, Cambridge, MA: Harvard University Press.

O'Neill, Marin (2008), What Should Egalitarians Believe? *Philosophy & Public Affairs*, 36 (2): 119–56.

Obama, Barack (2013), Remarks by the President on Economic Mobility, The White House Office of the Press Secretary, https://www.whitehouse.gov/the-press-office/2013/12/04/remarks-president-economic-mobility (accessed 23 February 2016).

OECD (2010), *Economic Policy Reforms: Going for Growth*, Paris: OECD.

OECD (2011), *Divided We Stand: Why Inequality Keeps Rising*, Paris: OECD.

OECD (2013a), Social Expenditure (SOCX), www.oecd.org/social/expenditure.htm (accessed 2 May 2015).

OECD (2013b), Income Distribution, OECD Social and Welfare Stati-stics (data-base), http://www.oecd.org/social/income-distribution-database.htm (accessed 2 February 2015).

OECD (2013c), *The Survey of Adult Skills. Reader's Companion*, Paris: OECD.

OECD (2014a), *Education at a Glance 2014*, Paris: OECD.

OECD (2014b), *Social Expenditure Update. Social Spending is Falling in Some Countries, but in Many Others it Remains at Historically High Levels*, www .oecd.org/social/expenditure.htm.

OECD (2015a), GDP per hour worked (indicator), doi: 10.1787/1439e590-en (accessed 28 July 2015).

OECD (2015b), Income Distribution Database, http://www.oecd.org/social/income-distribution-database.htm (accessed 17 July 2015).

OECD (2015c), General Government Debt (indicator), https://data.oecd.org/gga/general-government-debt.htm (accessed 25 July 2015).

Offe, Claus (1984), *Contradictions of the Welfare State*, London: Hutchinson.

Oishi, Shigehiro, Selin Kesebir and Ed Diener (2011), Income Inequality and Happiness, *Psychological Science*, 22 (9): 1095–100.

Okun, Arthur M. (1975), *Equality and Efficiency: The Big Tradeoff*, Washington, DC: Brookings Institution.

Onaran, Özlem and Thomas Obst (2015), Wage-led Growth in the EU15 Member States.The Effects of Income Distribution on Growth, Investment, Trade Balance, and Inflation. Greenwich University, working paper.

Owens, Lindsay A. and David S. Pedulla (2014), Material Welfare and Changing Political Preferences: The Case of Support for Redistributive Social Policies, *Social Forces*, 92 (3): 1087–113.

Oxfam (2014), *Even it Up. Time to End Extreme Inequality*, Oxford: Oxfam GB.

Palier, Bruno (ed.) (2010), *A Long Goodbye to Bismarck? The Politics of Welfare Reforms in Continental Europe*, Amsterdam: Amsterdam University Press.

Palma, José Gabriel (2011), Homogeneous Middles vs. Heterogeneous Tails, and the End of the 'Inverted-U': It's All about the Share of the Rich, *Development and Change*, 42 (1): 87–153.

Paskov, Marii, Klarita Gërxhani and Herman G. van de Werfhorst (2013), Income Inequality and Status Anxiety, *GINI Discussion Paper* 90, Amsterdam: University of Amsterdam.

Pateman, Carole (1971), Political Culture, Political Structure and Political Change, *British Journal of Political Science*, 1 (03): 291–305.

PEW (2014), Global Attitudes Survey, http://www.pewglobal.org/topics/income-inequality (accessed 18 March 2016).

Picavet, Emmanuel (2013), Consequentialist and Nonconsequentialist Dimensions in the Ethical Evaluation of Inequality, in Jean-Christophe Merle (ed.), *Spheres of Global Justice. Volume 2 Fair Distribution: Global Economic, Social and Intergenerational Justice*, Dordrecht: Springer, pp. 491–500.

Pierson, Paul (1994), *Dismantling the Welfare State?: Reagan, Thatcher and the Politics of Retrenchment*, Cambridge: Cambridge University Press.

Pierson, Paul (1996), The New Politics of the Welfare State, *World Politics*, 48 (02): 143–79.

Pierson, Paul (2004), *Politics in Time: History, Institutions, and Social Analysis*, Princeton: Princeton University Press.

Piketty, Thomas (2014), *Capital in the Twenty-First Century*, Cambridge, MA: Harvard University Press.

Pontusson, Jonas (2005), *Inequality and Prosperity: Social Europe vs. Liberal America*, Ithaca and London: Cornell University Press.

Pontusson, Jonas (2013), Unionization, Inequality and Redistribution, *British Journal of Industrial Relations*, 51 (4): 797–825.

Pontusson, Jonas and David Rueda (2007), Income Inequality and Partisan Politics in Industrialized Democracies, unpublished manuscript, http://www.princeton.edu/csdp/events/Pontusson020807/Pontusson020807.pdf.

Pontusson, Jonas and David Rueda (2010), The Politics of Inequality: Voter Mobilization and Left Parties in Advanced Industrial States, *Comparative Political Studies*, 43 (6): 675–705.

Prillaman, Soledad A. and Kenneth J. Meier (2014), Taxes, Incentives, and Economic Growth: Assessing the Impact of Pro-Business Taxes on US State Economies, *The Journal of Politics*, 76 (2): 364–79.

Prior, Markus (2010), You've Either Got It or You Don't? The Stability of Political Interest over the Life Cycle, *The Journal of Politics*, 72 (3): 747–66.

Przeworski, Adam (1985), *Capitalism and Social Democracy*, Cambridge: Cambridge University Press.

Quiggin, John (2012), *Zombie Economics: How Dead Ideas Still Walk among Us*, Princeton: Princeton University Press.

Raz, Joseph (1988), *The Morality of Freedom*, Oxford: Oxford University Press.

Reagan, Ronald (1988), Remarks at the Welcoming Ceremony for British Prime Minister Margaret Thatcher 16 November 1988, http://www.presidency.ucsb.edu/ws/?pid=35167 (accessed 26 January 2016).

Rehm, Philipp (2011), Social Policy by Popular Demand, *World Politics*, 63 (2): 271–99.

Rehm, Philipp, Jacob S. Hacker and Mark Schlesinger (2012), Insecure Alliances: Risk, Inequality, and Support for the Welfare State, *American Political Science Review*, 106 (2): 386–406.

Reich, Robert (2014), Why the Economy Is Still Failing Most Americans, http://robertreich.org/post/98668011635 (accessed 28 July 2015).

Roemer, John E. (2011), The Ideological and Political Roots of American Inequality, *GINI Discussion Paper 8*, Amsterdam: AIAS.

Rosanvallon, Pierre (2013), *The Society of Equals*, Cambridge, MA: Harvard University Press.

Rothstein, Bo (1998), *Just Institutions Matter: The Moral and Political Logic of the Universal Welfare State*, Cambridge: Cambridge University Press.

Rueda, David and Jonas Pontusson (2000), Wage Inequality and Varieties of Capitalism, *World Politics*, 52 (3): 350–83.

Saez, Emmanuel and Gabriel Zucman (2014), Wealth Inequality in the United States since 1913: Evidence from Capitalized Income Tax Data (No. w20625), National Bureau of Economic Research.

Sapolsky, Robert (2005), Sick of Poverty, *Scientific American*, 293 (6): 92–9.

Scheffler, Samuel (2003), What Is Egalitarianism? *Philosophy and Public Affairs*, 31 (1): 5–39.

Scheve, Kenneth and Matthew J. Slaughter (2004), Economic Insecurity and the Globalization of Production, *American Journal of Political Science*, 48 (4): 662–74.

Scheve, Kenneth and David Stasavage (2009), Institutions, Partisanship, and Inequality in the Long Run, *World Politics*, 61 (02): 215–53.

Schlozman, Kay Lehman, Sidney Verba and Henry A. Brady (2012), *The Unheavenly Chorus: Unequal Political Voice and the Broken Promise of American Democracy*, Princeton: Princeton University Press.

Scruggs, Lyle (2014), Social Welfare Generosity Scores in CWED 2: A Methodological Genealogy, CWED Working Paper Series WP01, February 2014,
available at http://cwed2.org/Data/CWED2_WP_01_2014_Scruggs.pdf.

Scruggs, Lyle, Detlef Jahn and Kati Kuitto (2014), Comparative Welfare
Entitlements Dataset 2. Version 2014-03, University of Connecticut &
University of Greifswald.

Sen, Amartya (1989), Development as Capability Expansion, *Journal of Development Planning*, 19 (1): 41–58.

Sen, Amartya (1992), *Inequality Reexamined*, New York: Russell Sage Found-
ation/Oxford: Clarendon.

Sher, George (2014), *Equality for Inegalitarians*, Cambridge: Cambridge
University Press.

Skocpol, Theda (1992), *Protecting Soldiers and Mothers*, Cambridge, MA:
Harvard University Press.

Slothuus, Rune (2007), Framing Deservingness to Win Support for Welfare
State Retrenchment, *Scandinavian Political Studies*, 30 (3): 323–44.

Smeeding, Timothy M. (2013), On the Relationship between Income Inequality
and Intergenerational Mobility, *GINI Discussion Paper 89 August 2013*,
Amsterdam: AIAS.

Smith, Adam (1776 [1991]), *The Wealth of Nations*, New York: Prometheus.

Solt, Frederick (2008), Economic Inequality and Democratic Political Engage-
ment, *American Journal of Political Science*, 52 (1): 48–60.

Solt, Frederick (2010), Does Economic Inequality Depress Electoral Participation? Testing the Schattschneider Hypothesis, *Political Behavior*, 32 (2):
285–301.

Solt, Frederick (2014), The Standardized World Income Inequality Database,
Working paper, SWIID Version 5.0, October 2014.

Stephens, John D. (1979), *The Transition from Socialism to Capitalism,* Urbana,
IL: University of Illinois Press.

Stiglitz, Joseph E. (2013), *The Price of Inequality*, New York and London:
W. W. Norton & Company.

Streeck, Wolfgang (1995), From Market-Making to State-Building? Reflections
on the Political Economy of European Social Policy, in Stephan Leibfried
and Paul Pierson (eds), *European Social Policy: Between Fragmentation and
Integration*, Washington, DC: The Brookings Institution, pp. 389–431.

Streeck, Wolfgang and Kathleen Thelen (2005), Introduction: Institutional
Change in Advanced Political Economies, in Wolfgang Streeck and Kathleen
Thelen (eds), *Beyond Continuity. Institutional Change in Advanced Political
Economies*, Oxford: Oxford University Press, pp. 1–39.

Svallfors, Stefan (2012), *Contested Welfare States: Welfare Attitudes in Europe
and Beyond*, Stanford: Stanford University Press.

Temkin, Larry S. (1993), *Inequality*, Oxford: Oxford University Press.

The Equality Trust (2014), *The Cost of Inequality*, https://www.equalitytrust
.org.uk/sites/default/files/The%20Cost%20of%20Inequality%20%20-%20
full%20report.pdf (accessed 18 March 2016).

The Equality Trust (2016), The Spirit Level Data, https://www.equalitytrust.org
.uk/civicrm/contribute/transact?reset=1&id=5 (accessed 18 March 2016).

Therborn, Göran (1995), *European Modernity and Beyond: The Trajectory of
European Societies, 1945-2000*, London: Sage.

Thewissen, Stefan (2014), Is It the Income Distribution or Redistribution that Affects Growth? *Socio-Economic Review*, 12 (3): 545–71.

Tingsten, Herbert (1937), *Political Behaviour*, London: P. S. King and Son.

Tóth, István György, Dániel Horn and Márton Medgyesi (2014), Rising Inequalities: Will Electorates Go for Higher Redistribution?, in Wiemer Salverda, Brian Nolan, Daniele Checchi, Ive Marx, Abigail McKnight, István György Tóth and Herman van de Werfhorst (eds), *Changing Inequalities in Rich Countries: Analytical and Comparative Perspectives*, Oxford: Oxford University Press, pp. 195–217.

US Census Bureau (2014), Poverty Thresholds, https://www.census.gov/hhes/www/poverty/data/threshld/ (accessed 15 May 2015).

Van Kersbergen, Kees (1995), *Social Capitalism: A Study of Christian Democracy and the Welfare State*, London and New York: Routledge.

Van Kersbergen, Kees (1998), De cultuur van gelijkheid. De herverdeling van inkomen, in Jan Ramakers, Gerrit Voerman and Rutger Zwart (eds), *Illusies van Den Uyl? De spreiding van kennis, macht en inkomen*, Amsterdam: Het Spinhuis, pp. 67–88.

Van Kersbergen, Kees and Philip Manow (eds) (2009), *Religion, Class Coalitions, and Welfare States*, Cambridge: Cambridge University Press.

Van Kersbergen, Kees and Barbara Vis (2014), *Comparative Welfare State Politics. Development, Opportunities, and Reform*, Cambridge: Cambridge University Press.

Van Oorschot, Wim (2000), Who Should Get What, and Why? On Deservingness Criteria and the Conditionality of Solidarity among the Public, *Policy & Politics*, 28 (1): 33–48.

Van Oorschot, Wim (2006), Making the Difference in Social Europe: Deservingness Perceptions among Citizens of European Welfare States, *Journal of European Social Policy*, 16 (1): 23–42.

Verba, Sydney, Kay Lehman Schlozman and Henry Brady (1995), *Voice and Equality: Civic Voluntarism in American Politics*, Cambridge, MA: Harvard University Press.

Visser, Jelle (2013), Institutional Characteristics of Trade Unions, Wage Setting, State Intervention and Social Pacts database, version 4, http://www.uva-aias.net/208 (accessed 15 April 2015).

Visser, Jelle and Daniele Checchi (2009), Inequality and the Labor Market: Unions, in Wiemer Salverda, Brian Nolan and Timothy M. Smeeding (eds), *The Oxford Handbook of Economic Inequality*, Oxford: Oxford University Press, pp. 230–56.

Wallerstein, Michael (1999), Wage-Setting Institutions and Pay Inequality in Advanced Industrial Societies, *American Journal of Political Science*, 43 (3): 649–80.

Wilensky, Harold L. (1975), *The Welfare State and Equality: Structural and Ideological Roots of Public Expenditures*, Berkeley: University of California Press.

Wilkinson, Richard and Kate Pickett (2009 [2010 version]), *The Spirit Level: Why Greater Equality Makes Societies Stronger*, New York: Bloomsbury.

Williamson, Oliver E. (1975), *Markets and Hierarchies: Analysis and Antitrust Implications*, New York: Free.

Wolff, Jonathan (1991), *Robert Nozick: Property, Justice and the Minimal State*, Cambridge: Polity.

World Bank (2014), *Ease of Doing Business Index in 2014*, http://www.doingbusiness.org/rankings (accessed 1 June 2015).

World Bank (2015), World Databank, http://databank.worldbank.org/data/home.aspx (accessed 1 May 2015).

Zucman, Gabriel (2013), The Missing Wealth of Nations: Are Europe and the US Net Debtors or Net Creditors? *The Quarterly Journal of Economics*, 128 (3): 1321–64.

Index